Data Structure and Algorithm

DATA STRUCTURE AND ALGORITHM

Nikhat Raza Khan, Manmohan Singh, Piyush Kumar Shukla and Ramesh Prasad Aharwal

ARCLER PRESS

www.arclerpress.com

Data Structure and Algorithm

Nikhat Raza Khan, Manmohan Singh, Piyush Kumar Shukla and Ramesh Prasad Aharwal

Arcler Press
224 Shoreacres Road
Burlington, ON L7L 2H2
Canada
www.arclerpress.com
Email: orders@arclereducation.com

ISBN: 978-1-77469-522-7 (Hardcover)

ABOUT THE AUTHORS

Dr Nikhat Raza Khan, Associate Professor & Head, working in dept. of computer science and Engineering, IES College of Technology Bhopal. Her Experience is more than 17+ yrs and since last 10 yrs serves her work in the field of research, She is a member of CSI, IEEE, ISTE, REST, computer society and various others journals since 2009, She has published more than 35 research papers in reputed International and National journals. Her main research work focuses on Mobile ADHOC Network, Cryptography Algorithms, Network Security, Cloud Security and Privacy, Big Data Analytics, IoT and Computational Intelligence based education. Dr. Nikhat Won best women research award in feb.2019.

Dr. Manmohan Singh, Professor, Department of Computer Science and Engineering, IES College of Technology Bhopal M.P India, his Experience is more than 15+ yrs and since last 10 yrs serves work in the field of research, he is a member of various professional bodies, he has published more than 25 research papers in reputed International and National journals

Dr. Piyush Kumar Shukla, PDF (Computer Engineering) & PhD (Computer Science & Engineering), Department of Computer Science & Engineering, UIT- Rajiv Gandhi Proudyogiki Vishwavidyalaya, (Technological University of Madhya Pradesh), India.

Dr. Ramesh Prasad Aharwal, Asstt. Prof. Department of Mathematics, Govt P.G. College Damoh M.P India.

TABLE OF CONTENTS

LIST OF FIGURES

LIST OF TABLES

LIST OF ABBREVIATIONS

ADT	abstract data type
LIFO	last-in first-out
MST	minimum spanning tree
POS	position

PREFACE

This book provides a comprehensive introduction to the modern study of computer algorithms. It presents many algorithms and covers them in considerable depth, which makes their design and analysis accessible to all levels of readers. We have tried to keep explanations elementary without sacrificing depth of coverage or accuracy.

Each chapter presents an algorithm, a design technique, an application area, or a related topic. Algorithms are described in English and in a "pseudocode" designed to be readable by anyone who has done a little programming. The book contains over 200 pages with facts and figures illustrating how the algorithms work. Since we emphasize efficiency as a design criterion, we include careful analyzes of the running times of all our algorithms. Since we emphasize efficiency as a design criterion, we include careful analyzes of the running times of all our algorithms.

The text is intended primarily for use in undergraduate or graduate courses in algorithms or data structures. Because it discusses engineering issues in algorithm design, as well as mathematical aspects, it is equally well suited for self-study by technical professionals.

To the teacher We have designed this book to be both versatile and complete. You should find it useful for a variety of courses, from an undergraduate course in data structures up through a graduate course in algorithms. Because we have provided considerably more material than can fit in a typical one-term course, you can consider this book to be a "buffet" or "smorgasbord" from which you can pick and choose the material that best supports the course you wish to teach.

You should find it easy to organize your course around just the chapters you need. We have made chapters relatively self-contained, so that you need not worry about an unexpected and unnecessary dependence of one chapter on another. Each chapter presents the easier material first and the more difficult material later, with section boundaries marking natural stopping points. In an undergraduate course, you might use only the earlier sections from a chapter; in a graduate course, you might cover the entire chapter. Each section ends with exercises, The exercises are generally short questions that test basic mastery of the material. Some are simple self-check thought exercises, whereas others are more substantial and are suitable as assigned homework.

We hope that this textbook provides with an enjoyable introduction to the field of algorithms. We have attempted to make every algorithm accessible and interesting. To help you when you encounter unfamiliar or difficult algorithms, we describe each one in a step-by-step manner. We also provide careful explanations of the mathematics needed to understand the analysis of the algorithms.

We have tried, however, to make this a book that will be useful to you now as a course textbook and also later in your career as a mathematical desk reference or an engineering handbook.

CHAPTER 1

PREREQUISITE

CONTENTS

1.1. INTRODUCTION

In this chapter, concept of data, data structure, structural programming, top–down design, abstract data type, array, structure, character strings, pointers, dynamic memory allocation and pointer to structure is covered. In array one, two, and multi-dimensional arrays with their operations are discussed. The implementation of structure is covered with the help of example. The character strings with their storage structure and operations are covered in this chapter. The pointer with their dynamic allocation is also discussed. The implementation of structure with the help of pointer is also covered.

1.2. CONCEPT OF DATA REPRESENTATION

Data is simply values or sets of values. A data field refers to a single unit of values. Data items or fields that are divided into sub-items are called group items.

For example, an employee name may be divided into three parts: first name, middle name, and last name. Those that are not divided into sub-items are called elementary or single items like- social security number.

Collection of data is frequently organized into hierarchy of fields, records, and files. A field is a single elementary unit of information representing an attribute of an entity, a record is the collection of field values of a given entity and a file is the collection of records of the entities in a given set.

For example, an employee is an entity; his attributes(fields) and values are:

Attributes: Name	Age	Sex	Social_Security_Number
Values: S. Jain	27	M	100-00-222

Entities with the similar attributes like- set of the entire employee form an entity set.

1.3. DATA STRUCTURES

Data may be organized in many different ways, the logical and mathematical model of a particular organization of data is called a data structure.

The choice of a data model depends on the consideration that it must be rich enough in structure to mirror the actual relationships of the data in the real world and the structure should be simple enough so that, one can efficiently process the data, when necessary.

Data structure = Organized data + Allowed operations

The data structure is a collection of data elements that can be characterized by its organization and the operations that are defined on it, i.e., "The organized collection of data is called data structure."

The data structures are classified into the following categories:

1. **Linear Data Structures:** In this type of data structures, processing of data items is possible in linear manner, i.e., data can be processed one by one sequentially. It contains the following type of data structures:
   i. Array;
   ii. Linked list;
   iii. Stack and queue.
2. **Non Linear Data Structures:** In this type of data structures, insertion, and deletion is not possible in a linear manner. It contains the following type of data structures:
   i. Tree;
   ii. Graph.

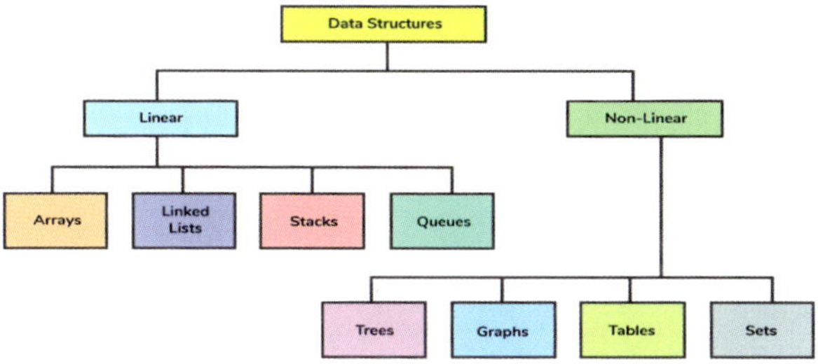

Types of data structure can be shown by flow chart.

1.3.1. Operations on Data Structures

The data appearing in data structures are processed by means of certain operations. In fact, the particular data structures that one chooses for a given situation depends largely on the frequency with which specific operations are performed. The following are the operations of data structures, which play major role in the processing of data:

- **Traversing:** Accessing each record exactly once so that certain items in the record may be processed. This accessing is also known as visiting.

- **Searching:** Finding the location of the record with a given key item or finding the location of all records which satisfy one or more conditions.
- **Inserting:** Adding a new record in the data.
- **Deleting:** Removing a record from the data.
- **Sorting:** Arranging the records in some logical order (numerical or alphabetical order).
- **Merging:** Combining the records in two different sorted files into a single sorted file.

For example, an organization contains a membership file in which each record contains the following data for a given member:

Name Address Tele_number Age Sex

- Suppose we want to find the names of all members, then we would traverse the file to obtain the data;
- Suppose we want to obtain address for a given name, then we would search the file for the record containing the name;
- Suppose a new person joins the organization, then we would insert the record into the file;
- Suppose a member dies, then we would delete the relative record from the file.

1.4. STRUCTURAL PROGRAMMING

The structural programming provide a well-defined, clear, and simple approach to program design. This method is easier to understand, evaluate, and modify. It has single entry and a single exit. So, we know that the execution starts with the first statement and terminates with the last statement in the sequence. The clarity and modularity in structural programming help in finding an error and redesigning the required section of code.

The structural programming requires the following three control constructs to implement the program design:

- **Sequence Construct:** It is simply a sequence of two or more statements, which can be executed in a sequence (Figure 1.1).

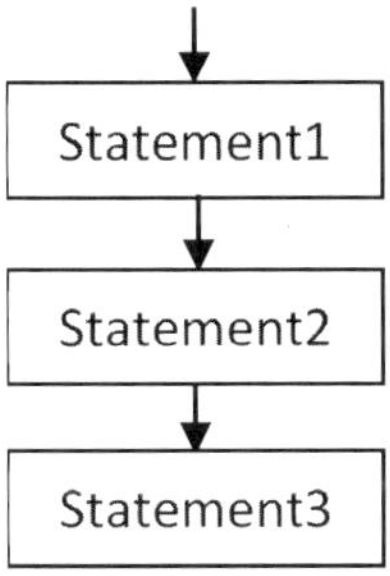

Figure 1.1. Sequence construct.

- **Conditional Construct:** In this construct, the execution of statements depends on the condition. We can alter the order of statements execution by using selection and iteration (Figure 1.2).

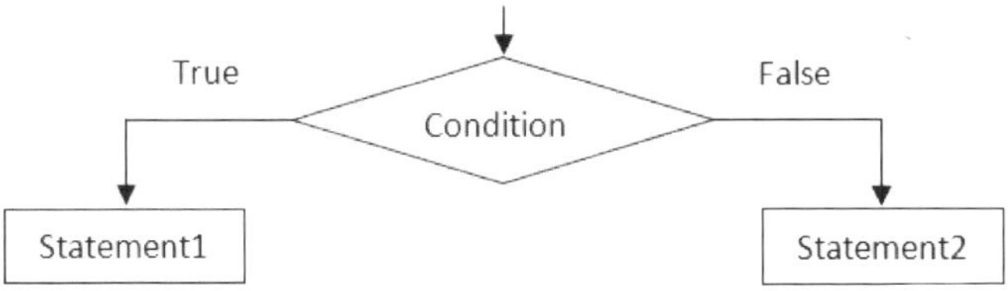

Figure 1.2. Conditional construct.

- **Looping Construct:** In this construct, the sequence of statements is executed repeatedly as long as the condition is true. It is known as looping or iteration (Figure 1.3).

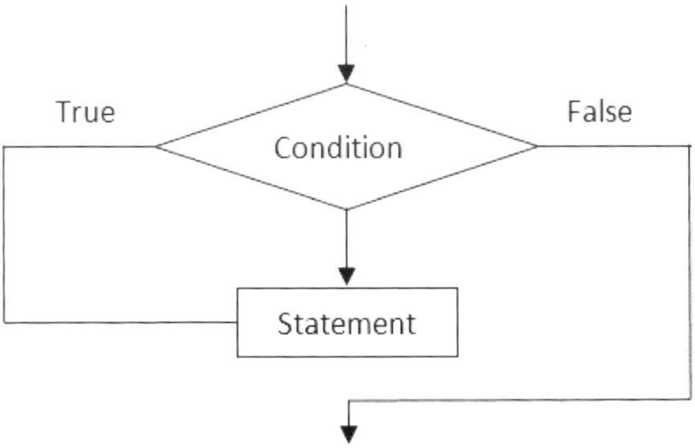

Figure 1.3. Looping construct.

1.5. TOP-DOWN DESIGN

The top–down design is a technique for stepwise refinement of algorithm design. In this technique, the whole concentration is on the major problem.

The top–down design approach represents a successive refinement of functions and the process of refinement is continued until the lowest level module can be designed without further analysis.

In this design approach, we take the general statements that we have about the solution, one at a time and break them down into a set of more precisely defined sub-problems. These sub-problems should more accurately describe how the final goal is to be reached. It is necessary that the way, in which the sub-problems need to interact with each other, be precisely defined. Only in this way it is possible to preserve the overall structure of the solution to the problem. The process of repeatedly breaking down a problem into sub-problems and then each sub-problem into still smaller sub-problems must continue until we eventually end up with sub-problems, which can be implemented as program statements.

The top–down design structure is viewed as tree structure shown in Figure 1.4. The module is divided into sub-modules and the doted boxes represent the non-leaf module.

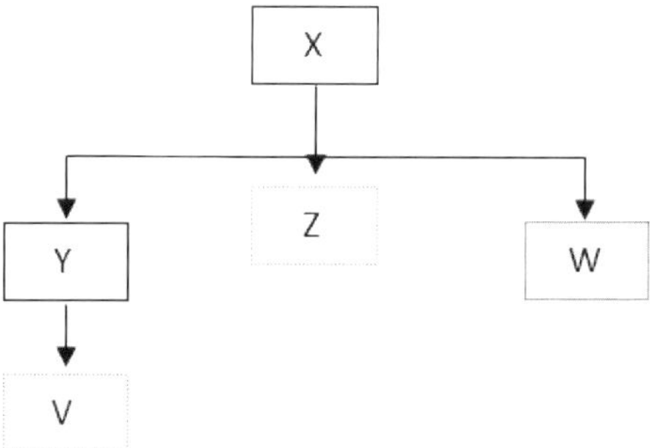

Figure 1.4. Top–down design.

1.6. ABSTRACT DATA TYPE

All programming languages use a set of predefined data types, known as base data types, which describe a set of objects with similar characteristics. Base data types are subject to a predefined set of operations. For example, the integer data type allows operations such as addition, subtraction, multiplication, and division. Like base data types, abstract data type describes a set of similar objects. However, abstract data type operations are user defined.

In defining an abstract data type as a mathematical concept, we are not concerned with its implementation issues like- time and space requirements. To understand ADT clearly, let us see, which is meant by abstraction.

An abstraction is the structuring of a nebulous problem into well-defined entities by defining their data and operations. Consequently, these entities combine data operations. They are not decoupled from each other.

The data structure can only be accessed with defined operations. This set of operations is called interface and is exported by the entity. An entity with the properties just described is called an abstract data type(ADT).

Figure 1.5 shows an ADT, which consists of abstract data structure and operations. Only the operations are viewable from the outside and define the interface.

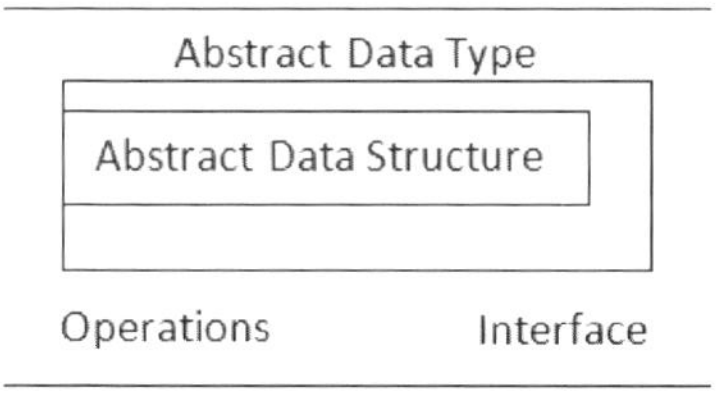

Figure 1.5. An abstract data type.

1.7. ARRAY

"An array is a structured data type made up of a finite, fixed size, collection of homogenous ordered elements."

Homogenous means, all the elements are of the same data type, ordered means all elements are arranged sequentially, finite means there is a last element and fixed size means that the size of the array must be known at compile time.

The accessing mechanism of array is direct, which means we can access any element directly without first accessing the preceding elements; accessing is done by the use of an index that allows us to specify the desired element by giving its position in the collection.

1.7.1. One Dimensional Array

The array whose items are specified by one subscript are known as one-dimensional array.

1.7.1.1. Storage of One Dimensional Array in Memory

The data represented in an array is actually stored in the memory cells in straightforward manner because computer memory is linear.

Storage for element X[I+1] will be adjacent to storage for element X[I] for I = 1, 2, …. N. To find the actual address of an element, we need to subtract lower bound from the position of the desired entry and then add the result to the address of the first cell in the sequence and multiply it by the size of each element of array.

$B + (I - L) \times S$

where; B is the address of the first cell of array called base address; and S is the size of each element of array; I is the position of the desired entry; and L is the lower bound of the subscript.

For example, let us take an array X of 20 elements and we desire to find the address of element X[6]. If the first cell in the sequence is at address 100 and suppose that the size of each element stored is one byte, what is the address of X[6]?

$B = 100$

$I = 6$

$L = 1$

$S = 1$

Address of X[6] = $100 \times (6 - 1) \times 1$

$= 100 + 5$

$= 105$

To find the total number of cells required of an array, we need to subtract lower bound from upper bound, add one to it and multiply it with the size of each element of array.

Number of cell = [(upper bound – lower bound) + 1] × size

$= [(UB - LB) + 1] \times S$

For example, let us take an array X[2.20]. If the base address is 20 and size of each element is 1 unit then to find out the address of X[4] and also the total number of cells required for storage, we shall proceed in the following manner:

B = 20

L =2

I = 6

S = 4

Address of X[6] = 20 + (6 – 2) × 4

= 20 + 4 × 4

= 20 + 16

= 36

Number of cell = [(20 – 2) + 1] × 4

= [18 + 1] × 4

= 19 × 4

= 76

1.7.1.2. Declaration of One Dimensional Array

There are three things that need to be specified to declare a one dimensional array in most of the programming languages:

- the type of data to be stored in data elements;
- the array name;
- the subscript or index range.

In C language, the array can be declared as follows:

storage_class type_specifier   Array_name[index]

For example,

```
int       list[20];
char      color[40];
```

In first declaration list is the array's name; the elements of list can hold integer data and the number of elements is 20, i.e., subscripts range from 1 to 20. Similarly, In second declaration color is the array's name; the elements of color can hold character data and the number of elements is 40, i.e., subscripts range from 1 to 40.

An array declaration tells the computer two major pieces of information:

- The range of subscript allows the computer to determine how many memory locations must be allocated; and
- The array type tells the computer how much space is required to hold each value.

1.7.1.3. Initialization of One Dimensional Array

An array can be initialized just like other variable. By default the array elements are set to 0. The following are the ways of initializing an array:

storage_class type_specifier Array_name[index] = {__,__,__}

We can use a comma as a separator between two values. In another way, we can also initialize the array in which we can omit the size of the array at the time of initialization.

storage_class type_specifier Array_name[] = {__,__,__}

For example,

int price[4] = {25,30,40,50};

After the initialization, the array price will take the initial values as follows:

price[0] = 25

price[1] = 30

price[2] = 40

price[3] = 50

The memory representation of the array price is shown in Table 1.1.

Table 1.1. Array Price in Memory

Index	Info
0	25
1	30
2	40
3	50

double salary[] = {1000,2000,3000,4000,5000};

In this case, the computer is able to calculate the size of the array.

The number of initializers can be equal to or less than the size of the array. It cannot be more than the size of the array. The following initialization generates an error message at the time of compilation.

int list [4] = {12,23,34,45,56};

Let us take an example in which we show the initialization of array of character.

char city[8] = “Gwalior”;

In this case, the array city is initialized by the string “Gwalior.” The last element is the terminator ‘\0’ character. We can also initialize the character array with less than the size of the array defined.

char book[20] = “Data Structure”;

In this case, the remaining elements in the array are initialized with ‘\0’ characters. If the string is equal to or greater than the array size, the compiler will give the error message.

char book[12] = “Data Structure”;

It is possible to omit the size of the array at the time of initialization. For example, an array can be initialized as follows:

char name[] = “Prof. Sanjay Jain”;

In this case, the computer is able to calculate the size of the array.

1.7.1.4. Various Operations of One Dimensional Array

Let us suppose that LIST is a one-dimensional linear array of integers. The following are the operations, which are performed on the one dimensional array:

- **Traversal Operation:** Traversing is the process by which we can visit or access and process each element of array exactly once. For example, suppose we have an array LIST of integers in the computer memory, as shown in Table 1.2. If we want to visit each element of array LIST then this visiting process is called traversing.

Table 1.2. LIST of Integers

Index	**Info**
0	4
1	8
2	12
3	16

4	20
5	24
6	28
7	32
8	36
9	40

i. **Algorithm:** Following are the steps for traversal operation:

a. [Initialize the counter]

Set (counter) i = 0

b. [Traverse each element of the array]

Repeat Step (c) and (d) while i <= n

c. [Visit element and performs the operation]

Apply operation to list[i]

d. [Increment counter]

Set i:= i +1

e. End.

ii. Equivalent C Function:

```
void traversal(int list[], int n)
{
int i;
i=0;
while(i<n)
{
printf("Element at position %d is:,"i);
printf("%d\n,"list[i]);
i++;
}
}
```

iii. **Implementation of Traversal Function:** The following program array_traversal.c shows the array implementation of the traversal function for integers stored in the computer memory:

```
/*array_traversal.c*/
```

```
#include<stdio.h>
#include<stdlib.h>
void traversal(int[],int);
void main()
{
int i=0,list[100],n;
printf(“This program performs the one dimensional array traversal operation
on numbers!\n”);
printf(“How many numbers in the array:”);
scanf(“%d,”&n);
printf(“!!Please enter the number!!\n”);
while(i<n)
{
printf(“Input value for the %d:,”i);
scanf(“%d,”&list[i]);
i++;
}
traversal(list,n);
}
void traversal(int list[], int n)
{
int i=0;
printf(“!!Entered element in the array after traversing the array are!!\n”);
while(i<n)
{
printf(“Element at position %d is:,”i);
printf(“%d\n,”list[i]);
i++;
}
printf(“\n”);
}
```

iv. **Output of the Program:** This program performs the one dimensional array traversal operation on numbers!

How many numbers in the array:8

!!Please enter the number!!

Input value for the 0: 12

Input value for the 1: 23

Input value for the 2: 34

Input value for the 3: 45

Input value for the 4: 56

Input value for the 5: 67

Input value for the 6: 78

Input value for the 7: 89

!!Entered element in the array after traversing the array are!!

Element at position 0 is: 12

Element at position 1 is: 23

Element at position 2 is: 34

Element at position 3 is: 45

Element at position 4 is: 56

Element at position 5 is: 67

Element at position 6 is: 78

Element at position 7 is: 89

2. **Insertion Operation:** Insertion is the operation by which we can add an element in the array at the desired position.

For example, suppose we have an array of multiple of 4, named as TABLE, as shown in table 1.3. But by mistake we forget one of the table entry 24. Now, we want to insert 24 in the proper place so that we get the desired table of 4. By inspecting the array, we find that 24 is missing at position 6. Before inserting 24 in the array, we have to move each element of the array from position 6 to 9, one position down. For this the following steps are performed (Tables 1.3(a) and 1.3(b)):

Table 1.3(a). Table of Multiple of 4

Index	Info
0	4
1	8
2	12
3	16
4	20
5	28
6	32
7	36
8	40
9	

Table 1.3(b). After Insertion 24

Index	Info
0	4
1	8
2	12
3	16
4	20
5	24
6	28
7	32
8	36
9	40

I=9 [Represents number of elements in the array]

TABLE[9]=TABLE[8]=40

I = I –1 = 9–1

TABLE[8]=TABLE[7]=36

I = I –1 = 8–1

TABLE[7]=TABLE[6]=32

I = I –1 = 7–1

TABLE[6]=TABLE[5]=28

I = I –1 = 6–1

TABLE[5]=24[Newly inserted element]

The result after insertion of 24 is shown in Table 1.3(b).

i. **Algorithm:** Following are the steps for insertion operation:

a. [Initialize the counter with the size of the array]

Set (counter) i:= n

b. [Traverse each element of the array until we find the desired position]

Repeat step (c) and (d) while i >= position(desired position)

c. [Move element downward]

Set list[i+1]:= list[i]

d. [Decrease counter]

Set i:= i –1

e. [Insert element at the desired position]

Set list[position]:= item

f. [Reset the array size]

Set n = n+1

g. [Return the new array size]

return(n)

h. End.

ii. **Equivalent C Function**

```
int insertion(int list[], int n, int position, int item)
{
int i;
i=n;
while(i>=position)
{
list[i+1] = list[i];
i– –;
}
list[position] = item;
```

```
n= n+1;
return n;
}
```

iii. **Implementation of Insertion Function:** The following program array_insertion.c shows the array implementation of the insertion function for integers stored in the computer memory:

```
/*array_insertion.c*/
#include<stdio.h>
#include<stdlib.h>
int insertion(int[],int,int,int);
void display(int[],int);
void main()
{
int i=0,list[100],n,position,item;
printf("This program performs the one dimensional array insertion operation on numbers!\n");
printf("How many numbers are there in the array:");
scanf("%d,"&n);
printf("!!Please enter the number!!\n");
while(i<n)
{
printf("Input value for the %d:,"i);
scanf("%d,"&list[i]);
i++;
}
display(list,n);
printf("Enter the position where we want to add a new number:");
scanf("%d,"&position);
printf("Please enter the number for the position:");
scanf("%d,"&item);
n = insertion(list,n,position,item);
```

```
display(list,n);
}
void display(int list[], int n)
{
int i=0;
printf("!!Entered elements in the array are!!\n");
while(i<n)
{
printf("Element at position %d is:,"i);
printf("%d\n,"list[i]);
i++;
}
printf("\n");
}
int insertion(int list[], int n, int position, int item)
{
int i;
i=n;
while(i>=position)
{
list[i+1] = list[i];
i– –;
}
list[position] = item;
n= n+1;
return n;
}
```

iv. **Output of the Program:** This program performs the one dimensional array insertion operation on numbers!

How many numbers are there in the array: 5

!!Please enter the number!!

Input value for the 0: 12

Input value for the 1: 23

Input value for the 2: 34

Input value for the 3: 56

Input value for the 4: 67

!!Entered elements in the array are!!

Element at position 0 is: 12

Element at position 1 is: 23

Element at position 2 is: 34

Element at position 3 is: 56

Element at position 4 is: 67

Enter the position where we want to add a new number: 3

Please enter the number for the position: 45

!!Entered elements in the array are!!

Element at position 0 is: 12

Element at position 1 is: 23

Element at position 2 is: 34

Element at position 3 is: 45

Element at position 4 is: 56

Element at position 5 is: 67

3. **Deletion Operation:** Deleting an element from the end of an array is simple but deleting an element from the desired position is difficult and requires moving all the elements up-word to fill up the gap into the array (Tables 1.4(a) and 1.4(b)).

i. **Algorithm:** Following are the steps for deletion operation:

a. [Initialize the counter with the size of the array and assign the desired position data value to item]

Set (counter) i:= n & item:= list[position]

b. [Update the list]

Repeat step (c) and (d) while (position <= n)

c. [Move element upward]

Set list[position]:= list[position+1]

d. [Increase counter]

Set position:= position +1

e. [Reset the array size]

Set n = n–1

f. [Return the new array size]

return(n)

g. End.

ii. Equivalent C Function

```
int deletion(int list[], int n, int position)
{
int i,item;
i=n;
item = list[position];
printf("Deleted item from the position %d is: %d\n," position,item);
while(position<=n)
{
list[position] = list[position+1];
position++;
}
n= n–1;
return n;
}
```

Table 1.4(a). List of Number

Index	**Info**
0	12
1	23
2	34
3	45
4	56
5	67
6	78
7	89

Table 1.4(b). After Deleting 45

Index	Info
0	12
1	23
2	34
3	56
4	67
5	78
6	89
7	

For example, suppose we have a list of 7 number LIST, as shown in Table 1.4. If we want to delete the number 45, it is required to update list of numbers. After deleting 45 at the position 4, it is necessary to move each element of the array from position 5 to 8 one position up. For this the following steps are performed:

Position of the number 45 in the list is 4.

LIST[3]=LIST[4]=56

LIST[4]=LIST[5]=67

LIST[5]=LIST[6]=78

LIST[6]=LIST[7]=89

LIST[7]=NULL

The resulting list after deletion is shown in Table 1.4(b).

iii. **Implementation of Deletion Function:** The following program array_deletion.c shows the array implementation of the deletion function for integers stored in the computer memory:

```
/*array_deletion.c*/
#include<stdio.h>
#include<stdlib.h>
int deletion(int[],int,int);
void display(int[],int);
void main()
{
int i=0,list[100],n,position;
```

```
printf("This program performs the one dimensional array deletion operation on numbers!\n");
printf("How many numbers are there in the array:");
scanf("%d,"&n);
printf("!!Please enter the number!!\n");
while(i<n)
{
printf("Input value for the %d:,"i);
scanf("%d,"&list[i]);
i++;
}
display(list,n);
printf("Enter the position from where we want to delete a number:");
scanf("%d,"&position);
n = deletion(list,n,position);
display(list,n);
}
void display(int list[], int n)
{
int i=0;
printf("!!Entered elements in the array are!!\n");
while(i<n)
{
printf("Element at position %d is:,"i);
printf("%d\n,"list[i]);
i++;
}
printf("\n");
}
int deletion(int list[], int n, int position)
{
```

```
int i,item;
i=n;
item = list[position];
printf("Deleted item from the position %d is:%d\n,"position,item);
while(position<=n)
{
list[position] = list[position+1];
position++;
}
n= n–1;
return n;
}
```

iv. **Output of the Program:** This program performs the one dimensional array deletion operation on numbers!

```
How many numbers are there in the array: 5
!!Please enter the number!!
Input value for the 0: 12
Input value for the 1: 23
Input value for the 2: 34
Input value for the 3: 45
Input value for the 4: 56
!!Entered elements in the array are!!
Element at position 0 is: 12
Element at position 1 is: 23
Element at position 2 is: 34
Element at position 3 is: 45
Element at position 4 is: 56
Enter the position from where we want to delete a number: 3
Deleted item from the position 3 is: 45
!!Entered elements in the array are!!
Element at position 0 is: 12
Element at position 1 is: 23
```

Element at position 2 is: 34

Element at position 3 is: 56

1.7.2. Multi-Dimensional Array

If There are two or more subscripts for referencing array elements then it is called multi dimensional array.

A two dimensional array is a structured data made up of a finite collection of homogenous elements. Each element is ordered in two dimensions.

The accessing is done with the help of a pair of subscripts, which allows us to specify which element in the collection we want to access. The first subscript represents the elements position(rows) and other represents the elements(columns).

1.7.2.1. Storage of Two-Dimensional Array in Memory

The two-dimensional array will be represented in memory by a block of mxn sequential memory locations.

To find the actual address of an element in two dimensional array we use the following formula:

- **For Column:** LOC(LIST[j,k]) = B + W × [m × (k – 1) + (j – 1)]
- **For Row:** LOC(LIST[j,k]) = B + W × [n × (j – 1) + (k – 1)]

where; 'B' is the address of the first cell of array and is called base address; and 'W' is the size of each element of array; 'm' represents the first index of the array; and 'n' represents the second index of the array; 'j' and 'k' represent the desired element first and second subscript, respectively.

For example, let us take an array LIST[20,5]. Suppose B(LIST) = 100 and there are W=5 words per memory cell. Calculate the address of LIST[5,2].

For row:

LOC(LIST[j,k]) = B + W × [n × (j – 1) + (k – 1)]

j = 5

k = 2

W = 5

B = 100

m = 20

n = 5

LOC(LIST[5,2]) = 100 + 5 × [5 × (5 – 1) + (2 – 1)]

= 100 + 5 × [5 × 4 + 1]

= 100 + 5 × [20 + 1]

= 100 + 5 × 21

= 100 + 105

= 205

To find the total number of cells required for a two dimensional array, we use the following formula:

Number of elements = [(UB of I'st Dim. – LB of I'st Dim)+1] × [(UB of II'nd Dim. – LB of II'nd Dim)+1]

Number of Cell = No. of elements x size

For example, let us take an array LIST[20,5]. Suppose the size of each element is 2 unit, find out the total number of cells required for storage.

UB of I'st Dim. = 20

LB of I'st Dim = 1

UB of II'nd Dim. = 5

LB of II'nd Dim = 1

No. of elements = [(UB of I'st Dim. – LB of I'st Dim)+1] × [(UB of II'nd Dim. – LB of II'nd Dim)+1]

No. of elements = [(20 – 1) + 1] × [(5 – 1) + 1]

= [19 + 1] × [4 + 1]

= 20 ×5

= 100

Number of Cell = No. of elements x size

= 100 ×2

= 200

1.7.2.2. Declaration of Two-Dimensional Array

The syntax for the declaration of two dimensional array is:

storage_class type_specifier array_name[index][index]

For example,

int list[3][4];

char color[30][21];

In the first declaration the list can be thought of as a table having three rows and four columns. Similarly, In the second declaration color is the array name; the array color in an array of 30 names of color, each name consists of not more than 20 characters, the last character being the string terminator '\0.'

1.7.2.3. Initialization of Two-Dimensional Array

If a two dimensional array definition includes the assignment of initial values, then care must be taken to the order in which the initial values are assigned to the array elements. The elements of the first row will be assigned first and then elements of the second rows will be assigned, and so on.

For example,

int list[3][4] = {10,20,30,40,50,60,70,80,90,100,110,120};

Here, the list can be thought of as a table having three rows and four columns. After the initialization the array list will take the initial values as follows:

list[0][0] = 10 list[0][1] = 20 list[0][2] = 30 list[0][3] = 40

list[1][0] = 50 list[1][1] = 60 list[1][2] = 70 list[1][3] = 80

list[2][0] = 90 list[2][1] = 100 list[2][2] = 110 list[2][3] = 120

For example,

int list[3][4] = {10,20,30,40,50,60,70,80,90};

Here, the list can be thought of as a table having three rows and four columns. After the initialization the array list will take the initial values as follows:

list[0][0] = 10 list[0][1] = 20 list[0][2] = 30 list[0][3] = 40

list[1][0] = 50 list[1][1] = 60 list[1][2] = 70 list[1][3] = 80

list[2][0] = 90 list[2][1] = 0 list[2][2] = 0 list[2][3] = 0

The last three array elements of the third row will be zero.

Forming groups of initial values enclosed within braces can alter the natural order in which the initial values are assigned. The values within an inner pair of braces will be assigned to the elements of a row, since the second subscript increases most rapidly. If there are too few values within a pair of braces, the remaining elements of that row will be assigned zeros. The number of values within each pair of braces cannot exceed the defined row size.

For example,

```
int list[3][4] = {
{1,2,3,4},
{5,6,7,8},
{9,10,11,12}
};
```

Here, the four values in the first inner pair of braces are assigned to the array elements in the first row, the values in the second inner pair of braces are assigned to the array elements in the second row and so on. After the initialization the array list will take the initial values as follows:

list[0][0] = 1 list[0][1] = 2 list[0][2] = 3 list[0][3] = 4
list[1][0] = 5 list[1][1] = 6 list[1][2] = 7 list[1][3] = 8
list[2][0] = 9 list[2][1] = 10 list[2][2] = 11 list[2][3] = 12

Let us take another example in which we assign values only to the first three elements in each row.

```
int list[3][4] = {
{1,2,3},
{5,6,7},
{9,10,11}
};
```

After the initialization the array list will take the initial values as follows:

list[0][0] = 1 list[0][1] = 2 list[0][2] = 3 list[0][3] = 0
list[1][0] = 5 list[1][1] = 6 list[1][2] = 7 list[1][3] = 0
list[2][0] = 9 list[2][1] = 10 list[2][2] = 11 list[2][3] = 0

The last element in each row is assigned a value of zero.

For example,

```
int list[3][4] = {
{1,2,3,4,5},
{6,7,8,9,10},
```

{11,12,13,14,15}

};

In this case the compiler will generate the error message, since the number of values in each pair of braces exceeds the defined array size.

Let us take an example in which we take the two dimensional array of character.

char book[5][21] =

{

"Data,"

"Structure,"

"By,"

"Sanjay,"

"Jain"

};

The first index indicates strings, "Data," "Structure" etc. and the second index specifies the characters in the string. Each string in the array consists of 21 characters including the string terminator.

The number of characters may be less than the specified number in the array, the unfilled places will be filled in by '\0'; however, the number cannot exceed the maximum value of second index.

1.7.2.4. Various Operations of Two-Dimensional Array

Let us suppose that book is a two-dimensional linear array of strings. The following are the operations, which are performed on the two-dimensional array:

1. **Traversal Operation:** Traversing is the process by which we can visit or access and process each element of array exactly once. For example, suppose we have a two-dimensional array of books in the computer memory and we want to visit each book of array book.

i. **Algorithm:** Following are the steps for traversal operation:

a. [Initialize the counter]

Set (counter) i = 1

b. [Traverse each element of the array]

Repeat step (c) and (d) while i <= n

c. [Visit element and performs the operation]

Apply operation on book[i]

d. [Increment counter]

Set i:= i +1

e. End.

ii. Equivalent C Function:

```
void traversal(char book[][30], int n)
{
int i=1;
while(i<=n)
{
printf("Books name at %d place is:,"i);
printf("%s\n,"book[i]);
i++;
}
}
```

iii. **Implementation of Traversal Function:** The following program array_two-dim_traversal.c shows the array implementation of the traversal function for the strings of books stored in two-dimensional array of the computer memory:

```
/*array_two-dim_traversal.c*/
#include<stdio.h>
#include<stdlib.h>
void traversal(char[][30],int);
void main()
{
int i=1,m;
char book[10][30];
printf("This program performs the two dimensional array traversal operation on strings of books name!\n");
printf("How many books in the list:");
scanf("%d,"&m);
```

```
printf("!!Please enter the books!!\n");
while(i<=m)
{
printf("Input book name (%d) in a single string:,"i);
scanf("%s,"&book[i]);
i++;
}
traversal(book,m);
}
void traversal(char book[][30], int n)
{
int i=1;
printf("!!Entered books in the list after traversing the array are!!\n");
while(i<=n)
{
printf("Books name at %d place is:,"i);
printf("%s\n,"book[i]);
i++;
}
printf("\n");
}
```

iv. **Output of the Program:** This program performs the two dimensional array traversal operation on strings of books name!

```
How many books in the list: 5
!!Please enter the books!!
Input book name (1) in a single string: A.I.
Input book name (2) in a single string: C.G.
Input book name (3) in a single string: Networking
Input book name (4) in a single string: T.O.C.
Input book name (5) in a single string: S.E.
!!Entered books in the list after traversing the array are!!
Books name at 1 place is: A.I.
```

Books name at 2 place is: C.G.

Books name at 3 place is: Networking

Books name at 4 place is: T.O.C.

Books name at 5 place is: S.E.

2. **Insertion Operation:** Insertion is the operation by which we can add books in the strings of books at the desired position. Following is the algorithm, which shows the insertion operation.

i. **Algorithm:** Following are the steps for insertion operation:

a. [Initialize the counter with the size of the array]

Set (counter) i:= n

b. [Traverse each element of the array until we find the desired position]

Repeat step (c) and (d) while i >= position

c. [Move element downward]

Set book[i+1]:= book[i]

d. [Decrease counter]

Set i:= i – 1

e. [Insert element at the desired position]

Set book[position]:= item

f. [Reset the array size]

Set n = n+1

g. [Return the new array size]

return(n)

h. End.

ii. **Equivalent C Function:**

```
int insertion(char book[][20], int n, int position, char item[])
{
int i;
i=n;
while(i>=position)
{
strcpy(book[i+1],book[i]);
```

```
i– –;
}
strcpy(book[position],item);
n= n+1;
return n;
}
```

iii. **Implementation of Insertion Function:** The following program array_two-dim_insertion.c shows the array implementation of the insertion function for strings of books stored in the computer memory:

```
/*array_two-dim_insertion.c*/
#include<stdio.h>
#include<stdlib.h>
#include<string.h>
int insertion(char[][20],int,int,char[]);
void display(char[][20],int);
void main()
{
int i=1,n,position;
char book[10][20],item[20];
printf("This program performs the two dimensional array insertion operation on strings of books!\n");
printf("How many books in the array:");
scanf("%d,"&n);
printf("!!Please enter the books as a whole string!!\n");
while(i<=n)
{
printf("Input book name (%d) in a single string:,"i);
scanf("%s,"&book[i]);
i++;
}
display(book,n);
```

```
printf("Enter the posititon where we want to add a new book:");
scanf("%d,"&position);
printf("Please enter the book name for the position:");
scanf("%s,"&item);
n = insertion(book,n,position,item);
display(book,n);
}
void display(char book[][20], int n)
{
int i=1;
printf("!!Entered Books in the list are!!\n");
while(i<=n)
{
printf("Book name at %d place is:,"i);
printf("%s\n,"book[i]);
i++;
}
printf("\n");
}
int insertion(char book[][20], int n, int position, char item[])
{
int i;
i=n;
while(i>=position)
{
strcpy(book[i+1],book[i]);
i– –;
}
strcpy(book[position],item);
n= n+1;
return n;
}
```

iv. **Output of the Program:** This program performs the two dimensional array insertion operation on strings of books!

How many books in the array: 4

!!Please enter the books as a whole string!!

Input book name (1) in a single string: D.S.

Input book name (2) in a single string: A.I.

Input book name (3) in a single string: Networking

Input book name (4) in a single string: Compiler

!!Entered Books in the list are!!

Book name at 1 place is: D.S.

Book name at 2 place is: A.I.

Book name at 3 place is: Networking

Book name at 4 place is: Compiler

Enter the posititon where we want to add a new book: 2

Please enter the book name for the position: T.O.C.

!!Entered Books in the list are!!

Book name at 1 place is: D.S.

Book name at 2 place is: T.O.C.

Book name at 3 place is: A.I.

Book name at 4 place is: Networking

Book name at 5 place is: Compiler

3. **Deletion Operation:** The following is the algorithm, which shows the deletion operation in the two-dimensional array book of strings of books stored in memory.

i. **Algorithm:** Following are the steps for deletion operation:

a. [Initialize the counter with the size of the array and assign the desired position data value to item]

Set (counter) i:= n & item:= book[position]

b. [Update the list]

Repeat step (c) and (d) while (position <= n)

c. [Move element upward]

Set book[position]:= book[position+1]

d. [Increase counter]

Set position:= position +1

e. [Reset the array size]

Set n = n–1

f. [Return the new array size]

return(n)

g. End.

ii. Equivalent C Function

```
int deletion(char book[][20], int n, int position)
{
int i;
char item[20];
i=n;
strcpy(item,book[position]);
printf("Deleted book from the position %d is: %s\n," position,item);
while(position<=n)
{
strcpy(book[position],book[position+1]);
position++;
}
n= n–1;
return n;
}
```

iii. Implementation of Deletion Function: The following program array_two-dim_deletion.c shows the array implementation of the deletion function for strings of books stored in the computer memory:

```
/*array_two-dim_deletion.c*/
#include<stdio.h>
#include<stdlib.h>
#include<string.h>
int deletion(char[][20],int,int);
```

```
void display(char[][20],int);
void main()
{
int i=1,n,position;
char book[10][20];
printf("This program performs the two dimensional array deletion operation on strings of books!\n");
printf("How many books in the array:");
scanf("%d,"&n);
printf("!!Please enter the books as a whole string!!\n");
while(i<=n)
{
printf("Input book name (%d) in a single string:,"i);
scanf("%s,"&book[i]);
i++;
}
display(book,n);
printf("Enter the position from where we want to delete a book name:");
scanf("%d,"&position);
n = deletion(book,n,position);
display(book,n);
}
void display(char book[][20], int n)
{
int i=1;
printf("!!Entered Books in the list are!!\n");
while(i<=n)
{
printf("Book name at %d place is:,"i);
printf("%s\n,"book[i]);
i++;
```

```
}
printf("\n");
}
int deletion(char book[][20], int n, int position)
{
int i;
char item[20];
i=n;
strcpy(item,book[position]);
printf("Deleted book from the position %d is:%s\n,"position,item);
while(position<=n)
{
strcpy(book[position],book[position+1]);
position++;
}
n= n–1;
return n;
}
```

iv. **Output of the Program:** This program performs the two dimensional array deletion operation on strings of books!

```
How many books in the array: 5
!!Please enter the books as a whole string!!
Input book name (1) in a single string: D.S.
Input book name (2) in a single string: A.I.
Input book name (3) in a single string: C.G.
Input book name (4) in a single string: Networking
Input book name (5) in a single string: T.O.C
!!Entered Books in the list are!!
Book name at 1 place is: D.S.
Book name at 2 place is: A.I.
```

Book name at 3 place is: C.G.

Book name at 4 place is: Networking

Book name at 5 place is: T.O.C

Enter the position from where we want to delete a book name: 4

Deleted book from the position 4 is: Networking

!!Entered Books in the list are!!

Book name at 1 place is: D.S.

Book name at 2 place is: A.I.

Book name at 3 place is: C.G.

Book name at 4 place is: T.O.C

1.7.3. Triangular Array

A triangular or three-dimensional array can be compared with a book. In three-dimensional array, three dimensions can be termed as row, column, and page.

Number of rows = x (number of elements in a column)

Number of columns = y (number of elements in a row)

Number of pages = z

Assume that a_{ijk} is an element in i-th row, j-th column and k-th page.

1.7.3.1. Storage of Three-Dimensional Array in Memory

Storing a three-dimensional array means, storing the pages one by one. Storing of pages is same as storing a two-dimensional array.

To find the actual address of an element a_{ijk} in three-dimensional array we use the following formula:

Address(a_{ijk}) = Number of elements in first(k – 1) pages

+Number of elements in k-th page up to(i – 1) rows

+Number of elements in k-th page,

(in i-th row up to j-th column)

$= xy(k-1) + (i-1)y + j$

1.8. STRUCTURE

In previous topic we studied about the array, which is a data structure whose elements are all of the same type. We now turn our attention to the structure, which is a data structure whose individual elements can differ in data types. These individual elements of a structure are called structure members. So, the structure may contain different types of members like integer, character, and float. All the members of the structure are logically related.

Let us take an example of telephone list of all the users of BSNL in Gwalior City. The list contains the following information about the users:

- Name;
- Telephone_Number;
- Profession;
- Address.

This telephone list of users can be represented with the help of the structure.

1.8.1. Declaration of Structure

The composition of a structure may be defined as follows:

30 Data Structures

```
struct tag_name
{
data_type member1;
data_type member2;
....
data_type memberN;
}
```

where struct is keyword, tag_name is a name that identifies structures of this type and member1, member2, ...memberN, are individual member declarations. The individual members can be ordinary variables, pointers, arrays or other structures. Once the composition of the structure has been defined, individual structure-type variables can be declared as follows:

storage-class struct tag_name var1, var2, ...varN;

where storage-class is an optional storage class specifier, struct is required keyword, tag_name is the name that appear in the structures type declaration, and var1, var2, …varN are structure variables of type tag_name.

For example, the list of users of BSNL in Gwalior can be declared as:

```
struct Telephone_List
{
char    Name[30];
int     Telephone_Number[6];
char    Profession[30];
char    Address[80];
}
struct Telephone_List Telephone;
```

Where Telephone is a variable of type Telephone_List.

It is possible to combine the declaration of the structure composition with that of the structure variables as follows:

```
storage-class struct tag_name
{
data_type member1;
data_type member2;
….
data_type memberN;
} var1,var2,…varN;
```

For example, the list of users of BSNL in Gwalior can be declared as:

```
struct Telephone_List
{
char    Name[30];
int     Telephone_Number[6];
char    Profession[30];
char    Address[100];
}Telephone;
```

Where Telephone is a variable of type Telephone_List.

It is possible to assign initial values to the members of the structure variable, in much the same manner as the elements of the array. The initial values must appear in the order in which they will be assigned to their corresponding structure members, enclosed in braces and separated by commas. The syntax of this is:

stroage-class struct tag_name var1 = {value1,value2, ..., valueN};

where; value1, value2, ..., valueN refer to the values of the first member, second member and so on, respectively.

1.8.2. Processing a Structure

The members of a structure are usually processed individually, as separate entities. Therefore, we must be able to access the individual structure members. A structure member can be accessed by writing:

stru_var.member

where; stru_var refers to the name of a structure-type variable, and member refers to the name of a member within the structure. The period (.) is the separator between the structure-type variable and member.

For example, in the list of users of BSNL in Gwalior the individual members can be accessed as:

```
Telephone_List.Name;
Telephone_List.Telephone_Number;
Telephone_List.Profession;
Telephone_List.Address;
```

1.8.3. Implementation of Structure

The following program structure.c shows the structure implementation of the telephone list of the users of the BSNL in Gwalior City:

```
/*structure.c*/
#include<stdio.h>
/*Structure declaration for telephone list of the users*/
struct Telephone_list
{
char    Name[30];
int     Telephone_No[6];
```

```
char    Profession[30];
char    Address[80];
}Tele[100];
void main()
{
int i,n;
printf("This program maintains the telephone list of the users of the BSNL
in Gwalior city!!!\n");
printf("Please enter how many records we want in the list:\n");
scanf("%d,"&n);
printf("Please enter the information of the users\n");
for(i=0;i<n;i++)
{
printf("Name:");
fflush(stdin);
gets(Tele[i].Name);
printf("\nTelephone Number:");
scanf("%d,"Tele[i].Telephone_No);
printf("\nProfession:");
fflush(stdin);
gets(Tele[i].Profession);
printf("\nAddress:");
fflush(stdin);
gets(Tele[i].Address);
fflush(stdin);
}
printf("\n List of the users");
printf("\n ####################\n");
for(i=0;i<n;i++)
{
printf("Name:%s,"Tele[i].Name);
```

```
printf("\nTelephone Number:%d,"Telephone[i].Tele_No);
printf("\nProfession:%s,"Tele[i].Profession);
printf("\nAddress:%s,"Tele[i].Address);
}
printf("\n\n");
}
```

- **Output of the Program:** This program maintains the telephone list of the users of the BSNL in Gwalior city!!!

Please enter how many records we want in the list:

2

Please enter the information of the users

Name: Nikhat Khan

Telephone Number: 421403

Profession: Lecturer

Address: C/o. Rajendra Jain, Shinde Ki Chhawni, Lashker, Gwl.

Name: Alok Jain

Telephone Number: 230091

Profession: Student

Address: Hanuman Ghati, Lashker, Gwalior

!!! List of the users !!!

####################

Name: Nikhat Khan

Telephone Number: 421403

Profession: Lecturer

Address: C/o. Rajendra Jain, Shinde Ki Chhawni, Lashker, Gwl.

Name: Alok Jain

Telephone Number: 230091

Profession: Student

Address: Hanuman Ghati, Lashker, Gwalior

1.9. CHARACTER STRINGS

A character string is simply a number of literal characters that are combined under concatenation to form a data structure, which is more complex than a simple character element. The number of characters in a string is called its length. The string with zero characters is called the empty string or the null string. Enclosing their characters in single quotation marks will denote strings.

For example, 'RAJ KAMAL' 'LESS THAN'

1.9.1. Storing Strings

Strings can be stored in three types of structure:

1. **Fixed Length Structures:** In this structure, each line is viewed as a record, where all records have the same length, i.e., where each record accommodates the same number of characters. We will assume that our records have length 80 unless otherwise stated or implied.
2. **Variable Length with Fixed Maximum:** Although strings may be stored in fixed length memory locations, there are advantages in knowing the actual length of each string. The storage of variable length strings in memory cells with fixed lengths can be done in two ways:
   i. One can use a marker, such as two-dollar sign($$), to signal the end of the string; and
   ii. One can list the length of the string, as an additional item in the pointer array.
3. **Linked Structure:** By a linked list, we mean a linearly ordered sequence of memory cells, called nodes, where each node contains an item, called a link, which points to the next node in the list.

Strings may be stored in linked list as follows. Each memory cell is assigned one character or a fixed number of characters, and a link contained in the cell gives the address of the cell containing the next character or group of characters in the string.

1.9.2. String Operations

The following are the operations which can be used for string processing:

1. **Substring:** A string X is called a sub string of a string S if there exist strings Y and Z such that:

S = Y // X // Z

SUBSTRING(string, initial, length)

2. **Indexing:** Also called pattern matching, refers to finding the position where a string pattern P first appears in a given string text T.

INDEX(text, pattern)

If the pattern P does not appear in the text T, then INDEX is assigned the value 0. The argument "text" and "pattern" can be either string constants or string variables.

3. **Concatenation:** Let S1 and S2 be strings. The string consisting of the characters of S1, followed by the characters of S1 is called the concatenation of S1 and S2. It will denoted by S1//S2.
4. **Length:** The number of characters in a string is called its length.

LENGTH(string)

1.10. POINTERS

A pointer is a variable, which may contain the address of another variable. All variables in C except variables of type register, have an address. The address is the location where the variable exists in memory.

Pointers are used to access elements of array, pass arguments to a function by reference in order to modify the original values of the arguments, transmit arrays and strings to functions, pass functions as arguments to functions, simplify representation of multi-dimensional arrays, allocate memory spaces and create data structures. It is also applicable to all basic types of data and derived data types like: structures, unions, functions, and files.

1.10.1. Declaration of Pointers

We must use an asterisk(*) in front of a variable to declare the variable to be a pointer. This identifies the fact that the variable is a pointer. The data type that appears in the declaration refers to the object of the pointer, i.e., the data item that is stored in the address represented by the pointer, rather than the pointer itself. Thus, a pointer declaration may be written as:

type_specifier *pointer_name;

where; pointer_name is the name of the pointer variable and type_specifier refers to the data type of the pointer object.

For example,
char *p;
where; p is a pointer of type char. So, p may contain the address of a variable of type char.

1.10.2. Assignment of Valid Address to Pointers

Declaration of a pointer variable is not enough unless a specific address is placed in it. Because without that, pointer will be pointing to some memory location which may contain garbage or part of a compiler. Declaration reserves memory spaces for the pointer not for the object it points. For a valid and operational pointer variable, it must be assigned address of a variable. We can obtain the address of a simple variable by using the unary operator &.

For example,

char c;

char *p;

p = &c;

Now p contains the address of the variable c. It is important that the type of the variable and the type of the pointer be the same.

1.10.3. Accessing the Pointers Object

Once the pointer is assigned the address of the variable to which it points, the pointer and the variable are accessible. The indirection operator(*) returns the value of the variable to which the pointer points. The value of the variable is indirectly accessed through*. If the pointer value is invalid, the indirection operator will return invalid value. The indirection operator specifies the contents of a variable, which has a distinct address like A or A[20]; it cannot be applied to any expression.

Let us take an example for showing the declaration of pointer, assignment of valid address to a pointer and accessing the pointer object. The following program pointer_processing.c shows the concepts in processing of pointer variables:

/*pointer_processing.c*/

```
#include<stdio.h>
void main()
{
int A = 20;
char B = 'P';
double C = 12.24;
int *P1;
char *P2;
double *P3;
printf("The following program shows the processing concepts of pointer variables!!!!\n");
printf("Value of pointer(P1) without assigning address and without indirection operator P1=%x\n,"P1);
printf("Value of pointer(P1) without assigning address P1=%x\n,"*P1);
P1 = &A;
printf("Value of pointer(P1) without indirection operator=%x\n,"P1);
printf("Value of pointer(P1) P1=%d\n,"*P1);
printf("Value of pointer(P2) without assigning address and without indirection operatorP2=%x\n,"P2);
printf("Value of pointer(P2) without assigning address P2=%x\n,"*P2);
P2 = &B;
printf("Value of pointer(P2) without indirection operator P2=%x\n,"P2);
printf("Value of pointer(P2) P2=%c\n,"*P2);
printf("Value of pointer(P3) without assigning address and without indirection operator P3=%x\n,"P3);
printf("Value of pointer(P3) without assigning address P3=%x\n,"*P3);
P3 = &C;
printf("Value of pointer(P3) without indirection operator P3=%x\n,"P3);
printf("Value of pointer(P3) P3=%f\n,"*P3);
}
```

- **Output of the Program:** The following program shows the processing concepts of pointer variables!!!!

Value of pointer(P1) without assigning address and without indirection operator P1=cccccccc

Value of pointer(P1) without assigning address P1=c5b6c5b0

Value of pointer(P1) without indirection operator=65fdf4

Value of pointer(P1) P1=20

Value of pointer(P2) without assigning address and without indirection operatorP2=cccccccc

Value of pointer(P2) without assigning address P2=ffffffb0

Value of pointer(P2) without indirection operator P2=65fdf0

Value of pointer(P2) P2=P

Value of pointer(P3) without assigning address and without indirection operatorP3=cccccccc

Value of pointer(P3) without assigning address P3=c5b6c5b0

Value of pointer(P3) without indirection operator P3=65fde8

Value of pointer(P3) P3=12.240000

1.11. DYNAMIC MEMORY MANAGEMENT

Language C provides a powerful facility for processing pointers and standard functions for requesting additional memory and for releasing memory during program execution. For dynamic allocation of memory, we can use dynamic variables, which are created during program execution. Since dynamic variables do not exist while the program is compiled, they can not be assigned names while it is being written.

The only way to access dynamic variables is by using pointers. Once it is created, however, a dynamic variable does contain data and must have a type like any other variable.

The creation and destruction of dynamic variables is done with standard functions in C. If p has been declared as a pointer to type data_type, then the statement:

```
p = (data_type*)malloc(sizeof(data_type));
```

creates a new dynamic variable of type data_type and assigns its location to the pointer p. Where data_type denotes the types of items. The function malloc allocates a block of memory and returns a pointer to that block of memory. The number of bytes occupied by a variable of data_type is calculated by the size of operator. If there is insufficient memory to create the new dynamic variable, malloc will fail and will return NULL.

When a dynamic variable is no longer needed, the function call:

free(p);

Returns the space used by the dynamic variable to which p points to the system. After the function free(p) is called, the pointer variable p is undefined and so cannot be used until it is assigned a new value.

Let us take an example for showing the allocation and deallo-cation of memory. The program pointer_allocation.c shows this process:

```
/*pointer_allocation.c*/
#include<stdio.h>
#include<malloc.h>
#include<stdlib.h>
void main()
{
int *p,i;
printf("The following program shows the dynamic allocation of pointer variables!!!!\n");
p = (int*)malloc(10*(sizeof(int)));
printf("ADDRESS\t INFORMATION\n");
for (i =0; i <10; i++)
{
*(p+i) = 20;
printf("%x,"(p+i));
printf("\t\t%d,"*(p+i));
printf("\n");
}
free(p);
}
```

- **Output of the Program:** The following program shows the dynamic allocation of pointer variables!!!!

ADDRESS INFORMATION

780e90 20

780e94 20

780e98 20

780e9c 20

780ea0 20

780ea4 20

780ea8 20

780eac 20

780eb0 20

780eb4 20

1.12. POINTER TO STRUCTURE

A pointer can hold the address of an aggregate data type such as structure. Similar to pointers to basic data types, pointer to aggregate type can be initialized with address of statically or dynamically created information items.

We can declare a pointer variable for a structure by writing:

type_specifier *pointer_name;

where; type_specifier is a data type, which identifies the composition of the structure and pointer_name represents the name of the pointer variable.

The beginning address of a structure can be accessed in the same manner as any other address, through the use of the address(&) operator. Thus if **var** represents a structure type variable, then **&var** represents the starting address of that variable.

We can assign the beginning address of a structure variable to the pointer variable by writing:

poniter_name = &var

The structure variable and pointer declaration can be combined with the structure declaration by writing:

```
struct {
data_type member1;
data_type member2;
....
data_type memberN;
```

```
}var *pointer_name;
pointer_name = &var;
```

Let us again discuss the same example as discussed in the case of structure. The list of users of BSNL in Gwalior can be declared as:

```
struct {
char    Name[30];
int     Telephone_Number[6];
char    Profession[30];
char    Address[100];
}
    Telephone_list, *Telephone;
    Telephone = &Telephone_list;
```

An individual structure member can be accessed in terms of its corresponding pointer variable by writing:

```
pointer_name->member
```

where; pointer_name refers to a structure type pointer variable and the operator(->) is comparable to the period(.) operator as discussed in structure.

For example, in the list of users of BSNL in Gwalior the individual members can be accessed as:

```
Telephone->Name;
Telephone->Telephone_Number;
Telephone->Profession;
Telephone->Address;
```

1.12.1. Implementation of Pointer to Structure

The following program pointer_to_structure.c shows the pointer to structure implementation of the telephone list of the users of the BSNL in Gwalior City:

```
/*pointer_to_structure.c*/
#include<stdio.h>
/*Pointer to structure declaration for telephone list of the users*/
struct
{
```

```
char    Name[30];
int     Telephone_No[6];
char    Profession[30];
char    Address[80];
}
Telephone, *Tele = &Telephone;
void main()
{
int i,n;
printf("This program maintains the telephone list of the users of the BSNL
in Gwalior city!!!\n");
printf("Please enter how many records we want in the list:\n");
scanf("%d,"&n);
printf("Please enter the information of the users\n");
for(i=0;i<n;i++)
{
printf("Name:");
fflush(stdin);
gets(Tele->Name);
printf("\nTelephone Number:");
scanf("%d,"&Tele->Telephone_No);
printf("\nProfession:");
fflush(stdin);
gets(Tele->Profession);
printf("\nAddress:");
fflush(stdin);
gets(Tele->Address);
fflush(stdin);
}
printf("\n List of the users");
printf("\n ####################\n");
```

```
for(i=0;i<n;i++)
{
printf("Name:%s,"Tele->Name);
printf("\nTelephone Number:%d,"Tele->Telephone_No);
printf("\nProfession:%s,"Tele->Profession);
printf("\nAddress:%s,"Tele->Address);
}
printf("\n\n");
}
```

- **Output of the Program:** This program maintains the telephone list of the users of the BSNL in Gwalior City!!!

Please enter how many records we want in the list:

2

Please enter the information of the users:

Name: Nikhat Khan

Telephone Number: 462003

Profession: Lecturer

Address: C/o. Rajendra Jain, Shinde Ki Chhawni, Lashker, Gwl.

Name: Alok Jain

Telephone Number: 230091

Profession: Student

Address: Hanuman Ghati, Lashker, Gwalior

List of the Users

####################

Name: Nikhat Khan

Telephone Number: 462003

Profession: Lecturer

Address: C/o. Rajendra Jain, Shinde Ki Chhawni, Lashker, Gwl.

Name: Alok Jain

Telephone Number: 230091

Profession: Student

Address: Hanuman Ghati, Lashker, Gwalior

Exercise

Q.1. Write a function that counts number of vowels in a given text.

Q.2. Write a function that counts number of words in a text and also counts the words of different types.

Q.3. Write a function that inserts a sub-string in a string somewhere in the middle.

Q.4. Write a program to access number of students in a class using pointers to structure.

Q.5. Write a program to implement a structure for the following fields:

- Employee's Name
- Designation
- Department
- Address
- City
- Telephone Number

Q.6. Write a function that reads a string and transfers its reverse to another pointer variable.

CHAPTER 2

STACK, QUEUES, AND LIST

CONTENTS

2.1. INTRODUCTION

This chapter covers data structures stack, queues, and list along with their operations. These data structure are discussed in detailed with their applications. An exercise at the end of chapter is given.

2.2. A MAZING PROBLEM

A maze is a 2D matrix in which some cells are blocked. One of the cells is the source cell, from where we have to start. And another one of them is the destination, where we have to reach. We have to find a path from the source to the destination without moving into any of the blocked cells. A picture of an unsolved maze is shown in Figure 2.1.

Figure 2.1. A picture of an unsolved maze.

The solution for the above maze problem is given in Figure 2.2.

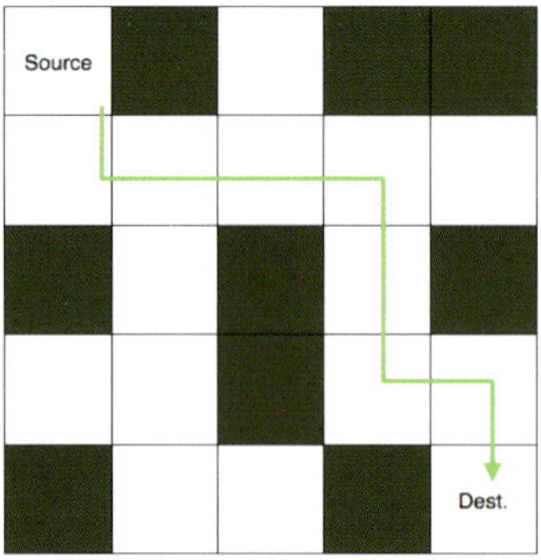

Figure 2.2. A solution for the above maze problem.

To solve this puzzle, we first start with the source cell and move in a direction where the path is not blocked. If taken path makes us reach to the destination then the puzzle is solved else, we come back and change our direction of the path taken. We are going to implement the same logic in our code also:

2.2.1. Algorithm to Solve a Rat in a Maze

Now we know about the problem, so let's see how we are going to solve it. Firstly, we will make a matrix to represent the maze, and the elements of the matrix will be either 0 or 1. 1 will represent the blocked cell and 0 will represent the cells in which we can move. The matrix for the maze shown above is:

```
0 1 0 1 1

0 0 0 0 0

1 0 1 0 1

0 0 1 0 0

1 0 0 1 0
```

Now, we will make one more matrix of the same dimension to store the solution. Its elements will also be either 0 or 1. 1 will represent the cells in our path and rest of the cells will be 0. The matrix representing the solution is:

```
1 0 0 0 0

1 1 1 1 0

0 0 0 1 0

0 0 0 1 1

0 0 0 0 1
```

Thus, we now have our matrices. Next, we will find a path from the source cell to the destination cell and the steps we will take are:

- Check for the current cell, if it is the destination cell, then the puzzle is solved.
- If not, then we will try to move downward and see if we can move in the downward cell or not (to move in a cell it must be vacant and not already present in the path).
- If we can move there, then we will continue with the path taken to the next downward cell.
- If not, we will try to move to the rightward cell. And if it is blocked or taken, we will move upward.
- Similarly, if we can't move up as well, we will simply move to the left cell.
- If none of the four moves (down, right, up, or left) are possible, we will simply move back and change our current path (backtracking).

Thus, the summary is that we try to move to the other cell (down, right, up, and left) from the current cell and if no movement is possible, then just come back and change the direction of the path to another cell.

2.3. STATIC AND DYNAMIC

In Static data structure the size of the structure is fixed. The content of the data structure can be modified but without changing the memory space allocated to it. Example of static data structure is Array.

In Dynamic data structure the size of the structure in not fixed and can be modified during the operations performed on it. Dynamic data structures are designed to facilitate change of data structures in the run time. Example of dynamic data structure is linked list.

- **Static Data Structure vs. Dynamic Data Structure:** Static Data structure has fixed memory size whereas in Dynamic Data Structure, the size can be randomly updated during run time which may be considered efficient with respect to memory complexity of the code. Static Data Structure provides more easier access to elements with respect to dynamic data structure. Unlike static data structures, dynamic data structures are flexible.
- **Use of Dynamic Data Structure in Competitive Programming:** In competitive programming the constraints on memory limit is not much high and we cannot exceed the memory limit. Given higher value of the constraints we cannot allocate a static data structure of that size so Dynamic Data Structures can be useful.

2.3.1. Static and Dynamic

- **Stack:**
- Stack is a data structure used to stare the data elements with restriction of last in first out or first in last out.
- Elements are inserted and deleted from same end called "top."
- The new element will be inserted at the top and always top most element will be deleted.

Elements: a, b, c, d, e

Insertion: a, b, c, d, e

Deletion: e, d, c, b, a

Application of stack:

- Recursive function calls;
- Balancing parenthesis;
- HTML or XML type matching;
- Redo, Undo questions;
- Page visited on browse (back button, forward button);
- Infix to postfix conversion;
- Post fix evaluation;
- Fibonicci series;
- Towers of Hanoi.
- **Stack (A.D.T.):**
- **Declaration of Data:**
- Space required to store the data elements.
- A variable top pointing to topmost element in the stack.
- **Declaration of Operation:**
- Push Operation (x): element to be insert

Insert the elements into the stack will the help of top.

- Pop ( ): Delete the element from the stack with the help of top.
- Isfull ( ): Return true if the stack is full.
- Is empty ( ): Returns true if the stack is end.
- **Implementation of Stack Using Array:**

PUSH: int 5(5), N = 5

Initially

Top = – 1

Overflow condition

Top = = N – 1

- **Implementing Multiple Stack in a Single Array:** In order to implement one recursive program we require one stack. Then if you want to implement multiple recursive programs then we need multiple stack in the memory then the concept is similar to implementing multi stack in a single array.

int S [9], N = 9, No. of stack (m) = 3

Size of each stack (n/m) = 9/3 = 3

Initially top of ith sla = I × N/m – 1.

Initially To = –1 Initially T1 = 2 Initially T 2 =5

$$Top_0 = 0 \times \frac{9}{3} - 1 = -1$$

$$Top_1 = 1 \times \frac{9}{3} - 1 = 2$$

$$Top_2 = 2 \times \frac{9}{3} - 1 = 5$$

$$Top_{300} = 300 \times \frac{9}{3} - 1 = 8$$

- **Note:** i^{th} stack overflow condition arises of 'Ti' is reaching to initial top of the $(i+1)^{th}$ stack.
- Note:
- The limitation of above implementation is if one stack is full and all the remaining stack are empty then still if will show the overflow condition.
- To avoid this problem we implement another approach.

0 1 2 3 4 5 6 7 8

stack overflow

Implementing multiple stack in a single array efficient way:

int S[9], N = 9, No. of stack = 2

Left side stack Right side stack

0 1 2 3 4 5 6 7 8

Initially TR = 9

Initially TL = – 1

Overflow condition TR – TL = 1

In the above implementation, we are implementing two stack in a single array growing in opposite direction.

- **Finding the Average Life Time of an Element in the Stack:**
- The time taken for insert or delete is 'x' & here is a delay of 'y' in every search operation.
- The life time of an element is considered as time elapsed from end of push to start of a operation that removes an element from start.

element: a, b, c, d, e

- Infix, Prefix, and Postfix:

Infix: Binary operations b/w operands

Like a + b

Operand1 operator operand 2

Prefix: Binary operation before the operand

Like + ab

Operator operand1 operand 2

Postfix: Binary operations after the operands.

Like ab +

Operand 1 operand 2 operator

E.g., Infix: A + B × (C + D)/ F + D × E

Prefix: A + B * + CD/ F + D × E

A + B × B + CD/F + D × E

A + / * B + CD F + D × E

+A / * B + CDF + * DE

+ + A/ * B + CDF × DE

Infix: A + B × (C + D)/ F + D × E

Postfix: A + B × CD + / F + D × E

A + B C D + * / F + D × E

A + B C D + * F / + D E *

A B C D + * F / + D E * +

Infix: a + b * c – d/e↑ f * g + h

Prefix a + b * c – d / ↑ ef * g +h

= a + *bc – d/ ↑ ef * g + h

= +a * bc – / d ↑ ef * + gh

= – + a * bc / d↑ ef * + g h

= – + a * bv * /

= + – + a * bc * / d ↑ e + gh

Post fix: a b c * + de + ↑ / g * – h +

- Prefix to Postfix Conversion:

In order to convert from prefix to post fix we need:

- Operator followed by
- Two operands

Then convert into postfix.

E.g.: Prefix: * + cd – ba

* cd + – ba

* cd + b a –

cd + ba – *

- Postfix to infix Conversion:

Postfix: ab * cd / – (Two operand followed immediate operator).

Note:

- In order to evaluate infix expression the need to scan in fixes expression multiple time and we need to jump from the one place to other place according to the procedure of the operator.
- The procedure must be sequential for the computer and it required good algorithm.
- The best approach converting infix express to postfix expression in a single scan and evaluating the post fix expression in a single scan.

- **Infix to Postfix Conversion (Using Operator Stack):**

1. In order to convert from infix to post fix operator stack is used, it means only operator will be push onto the stack.

Top of Stack	Next Operator	Operation
Low	High	Push
High	Low	Pop
Same	Same (L-R)	Pop
Same	Same (R-L)	Push

(If any braces comes treat it as new start with classing braces).

E.g.: **Infix:** a + b * c ↑ d – e

Postfix: a b c d ↑ * + e –

max size of stack is 3

Infix: a + b * c – d/e ↑ f * g + h

Postfix: a b c * + d e f ↑/ g * – h +

Max size of stark is 3.

- **Post Fix Evaluation (Using Operand Stack):** In order to evaluate postfix expression operand stack will be used it means only operands will be push into the stack.
- If (symbol = = Operand)

Push (symbol);

- If (symbol = = Operator)
- OP_2 = POP ( );
- OP_1 = POP ( );
- Push (OP, < operator > OP_2);
- Result will be in the stack.

E.g., Postfix: 32 * 5 + 62 /–

OP1	Operator	Op2	Result
3	*	2	6
6	+	5	11
6	/	2	3
11	–	3	8

max size: 3

- Fibonacci Series:

Time Complexity: $O(2^n)$

N	0	1	2	3	4	5	6	7	8	9	10
Fib (n)	0	1	1	2	3	5	8	13	21	34	55

Fib (n) = n, if n = 0 Or n = = 1

Fb (n–1) + Fib (n–2), otherwise.

- **Tower of Hanoi:** We need to move n discs from left side tower to right side tower.

Rule:

- Only one disc we can move at a time.
- Large size disc cannot placed on smaller size disc.

E.g.: N = 2

- L → m (1)
- L → R (2)
- M → R (1)

E.g.: n = 3

L → R (1) M → L (1)

L → M (2) M → R (2)

R → M (1) L → R (1)

L → R (3)

E.g.: n = 4

(1) L → M (1) (4) L → M (3) (7) L → M (1) (10) M → L (2)

(2) L → R (2) (5) R → L (1) (8) L → R (4) (11) R → L (1)

(3) M → R (1) (6) R → M (2) (9) M → R (1) (12) M → R (3)

(13) L → M (1) (14) L → R (2) (15) M → R (1)

Program:

Tox (N, L, M, R) T (n)

```
{
if (n = = 0)
return;
else:
```

T ox (n–1, L, R, M); – T (n–1)

Move (L → R);

Tox (n – 1, M, L, R); (n–1)

}

}

Recurrence Relation: 2 T (n – 1) +C

Time Complexity = O (2^n)

2.4. QUEUE INTRODUCTION

Queue is a data structure used to stare the data element with the restriction of first in first out or last in last out.

2.4.1. Queue Representation

Queue required two pointers (Figure 2.3):

- Front → used to delete on element
- Rare → used to insert an element.

Figure 2.3. Queue Representation.

- **Application of Queue:**
- Printer → spooler daemon
- Job scheduling
- Ticket reservation
- **Queue ADT:**
- Declaration of data:
- Space to store queue elements;
- Two pointer front and rear.
- **Declaration of Operations:**
- **Enqueue (x):** Elements to be inserted the above operation inserts

the elements in the queue with the help of rear pointer.

- **Dequeue ( ):** Delete the elements from the queue with the help of front pointer.
- **is full ( ):** Return when queue is full.
- **is empty ( ):** Returns true when queue is empty.
- **Implementation of Queue:**

Using array:

Int Q[7], N = 7

6	3	7	9	17	19	21

0 1 2 3 4 5 6

F R

Overflow condition: R = =N – 1

Initially

Front = –1;

Rear = –1;

Underflow condition F = = – 1

F = –1 0

R = –1 0 1 2 3 4 5 6

E.g., enqueue operation in the queue.

- Initially check for the overflow condition.
- If it is not overflow, if it is first insertion increment both front and rear. Otherwise increment only rear pointer and insert the element with the help of rear pointer.

Enqueue (Q, N, F, R, x) element to be inserted.

```
{if (R = = N – 1)
{pt ("Overflow condition");
Return;
}
else if (R = = –1)
{R ++;
F ++;
```

```
Q [O] = x;
}
else {
++R;
Q [R] = x;
}
}
```

E.g., dequeue operation in the queue.

```
int dequeue (Q, N, F, R)
int y
{if (F = = – 1)
{pf ("Underflow condition");
return;
}
else if (F = = R)
{y = Q[F];
F = –1;
R = –1;
}
else {
y = Q [F];
F + +;
}
return y;
}
```

- **Points to Write the Dequeue Program:**
- Initially check for the underflow condition.
- If it is not underflow then delete the element using.
- If the front and rear are same reinitialize back to –1, otherwise increment only front pointer then deleted element.

Note:

			9	17	19	21

0 1 2 3 4 5 6

F R

F = –1 0 1 2 3

R = –1 0 1 2 3 4 5 6

- In the above implementation of a linear queue when the rear pointer as reached the eight most point and front pointer is same where in the middle but still it will show overflow condition.
- Even through empty slots are available the are not efficiently utilize. To avoid the problem we will implement circular queue.

2.4.2. Static and Dynamic Queue

In implementation of the static Queue, an array will be used so all operation of queue are index based which makes it faster for all operations except deletion because deletion requires shifting of all the remaining elements to the front by one position. A static queue is a queue of fixed size implemented using array.

2.4.3. Circular Queue

Unlike the simple queues, in a circular queue each node is connected to the next node in sequence but the last node's pointer is also connected to the first node's address. Hence, the last node and the first node also gets connected making a circular link overall (Figure 2.4).

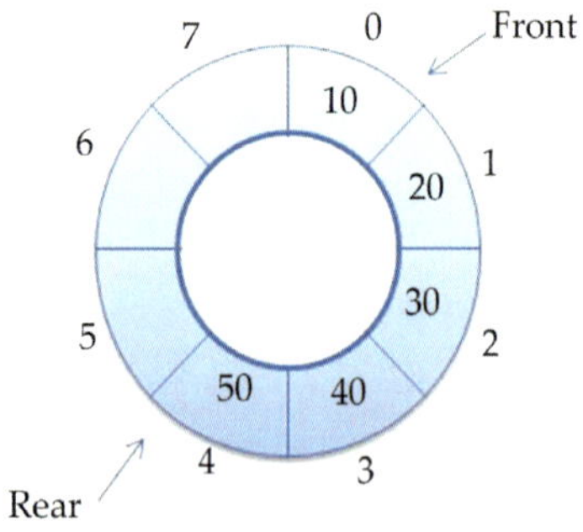

Figure 2.4. Circular Queue.

E.g.: int Q [7] N =7

0 1 2 3 4 5 6

Overflow condition (R+1)/N = = F

Underflow condition = F = = – 1

- **Input Restricted Queue:** Enqueue operation can be done only from rear but dequeue can be done both front and rear.

Q	10	20	30	40	50
0	1	2	3	4	5

Dequeue → F Enqueue → R dequeue → R

F ++ R ++ R – –

In the above implementation queue property is not satisfied because it is following FIFO and LIFO.

- Output Restricted Queue:

Q	20	30	40	50	
0	1	2	3	4	3

Dequeue → F Enqueue → R Enqueue → F

F++ R++ F – –

Dequeue operation is restricted but enqueue operation on can be done from both front rear.

2.4.4. Double Ended Queue

The doubly ended queue or dequeue allows the insert and delete operations from both ends (front and rear) of the queue (Figure 2.5).

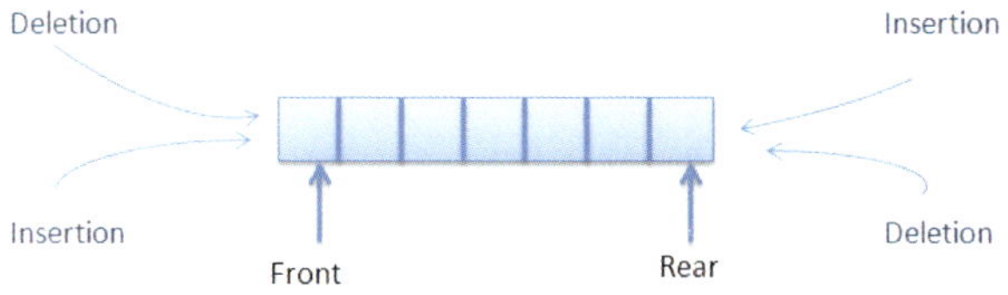

Figure 2.5. Dequeue.

E.g.:

Q 20 30 40 50

Dequeue → F Enqueue → R Enqueue → F dequeue → R

F++ R++ F – – R –

Enqueue and dequeue operations can be done from both front and rear.

2.4.5. Priority Queue

Priority queue makes data retrieval possible only through a pre determined priority number assigned to the data items.

While the deletion is performed in accordance to priority number (the data item with highest priority is removed first), insertion is performed only in the order. These are of two types:

- Ascending priority queue (delete min):

10	20	5	6	25	30

0 1 2 3 4 5

i = –1, 0

j = –1, 0, 1, 2, 3, 4, 5

Deletion: 5, 6, 10, 20, 25, 30

- Descending priority queue (delete max):

10	20	5	6	25	30

0 1 2 3 4 5

i = –1, 0

j = –1, 0, 1, 2, 3, 4, 5

Deletion: 30, 25, 20, 10, 6, 5

Implementing ascending priority queue unsorted array:

25	30	6	5	40	15

0 1 2 3 4 5

Element: 25, 30, 6, 5, 40, 15

Enqueue:

i = –1, 0

j= –1, 0, 1, 2, 3, 4, 5

j = j + 1

a[o] = x

T.C. = 0[1]

Dequeue: TC: 0(n)

Scan the entire array and find the position of the minimum element:

- y = a [min]
- a [min] = a[j];
- j = j – 1;
- **Using Sorted Array:**

Enqueue dequeue

TC = 0(n) TC = 0(1)

- Implementing Queue Using Stacks:

Q	a	b	c	d	e
0	1	2	3	4	

Elements: a, b, c, d, e

Q. Write the Psecdo Code for the Enqueue and Dequeue Operation.

Ans:

```
Enqueue (St, x)
{push (st, x);
}
int dequeue (S1, S2)
{
if (S2 is not empty)
{return pop (S2);
}
else if (S1 is empty)
{pf ("Queue is empty")
Exit ( );
}
else
while (S1 is not empty)
```

```
{x = pop (s1);
push (S2, x);
}
return pop (s2);
}
}
```

2.5. LIST

A linked list is a linear data structure, in which the elements are not stored at contiguous memory locations. The elements in a linked list are linked using pointers as shown in Figure 2.6.

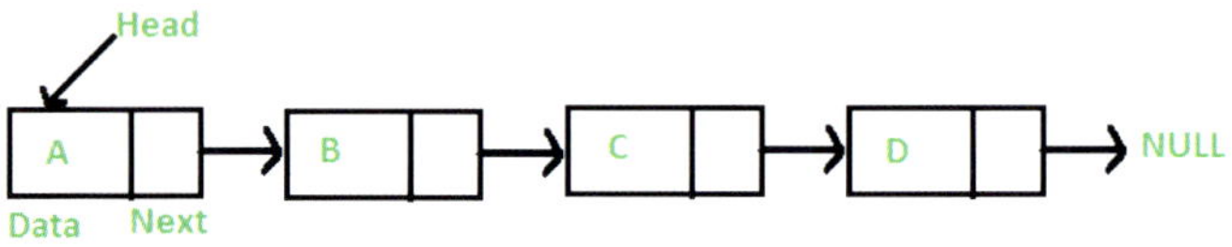

Figure 2.6. linked List.

In simple words, a linked list consists of nodes where each node contains a data field and a reference(link) to the next node in the list.

2.5.1. Implementation of Linked List

- It is a DS used to store data elements and successive elements are connected by pointers and last elements contains null.
- We can increase the size of the linked list dynamically until the memory if full.
- If the requirement is frequent insertion and deletion in various position, then the linked list is best suitable DS.
- Main drawback of linked list is, it support and sequential access.

2.5.1.1. Single Linked List

A single linked list is a collection of data objects that are linked together by certain references from one object to the next. These objects are often referred to as nodes. Each node will contain at least a single data field and a reference to the following node. Single linked lists are accessed via the first node and can be traversed until the end of the list (Figure 2.7).

Figure 2.7. Single Linked List.

Drawback of single linked list:

- In the single linked list the last node, next ptr is always NULL and not utilijed properly;
- In single linked list can traverse only in one direction;
- To eliminate this drawback we will implement circular single linked list.

2.5.2. Doubly Linked List

Doubly linked lists have two references per each node. The references point towards the next node, and the previous node. With this structure, you have two-way access to the data set, and it offers you more flexibility and speed, because you can navigate your list both directions (Figure 2.8).

Figure 2.8. Doubly Linked List.

2.5.2.1. Multilinked List

Multilinked lists are general linked lists that have multiple additional lists from a certain node. The new lists can be in any of the styles mentioned here. This style of list can be helpful for sorting a list that's broken down by the user's name and age. Or, other styles of data sets where each data point has further classifications.

2.5.3. Circular Linked List

The final type of linked list is called a circular linked list. Instead of the final node having a NULL command it will reference back to the head of the list. The structure of the list is similar to the options above (Figure 2.9).

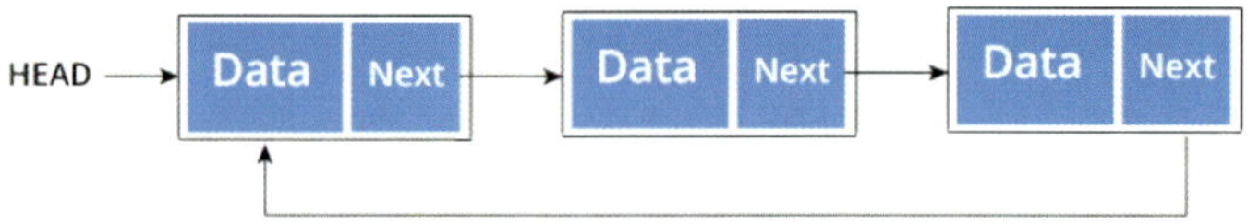

Figure 2.9. Circular Linked List.

2.5.4. Application of Linked List

Lists are one of the most popular and efficient data structures, with implementation in every programming language like C, C++, Python, Java, and C#.

Apart from that, linked lists are a great way to learn how pointers work. By practicing how to manipulate linked lists, you can prepare yourself to learn more advanced data structures like graphs and trees.

- **Linked List Operations:** Now that you have got an understanding of the basic concepts behind linked list and their types, its time to dive into the common operations that can be performed.

Two important points to remember:

- Head points to the first node of the linked list; and
- Next pointer of last node is NULL, so if next of current node is NULL, we have reached end of linked list.

In all of the examples, we will assume that the linked list has three nodes 1 → 2 → 3 with node structure as below:

```
struct node
{
int data;
struct node *next;
};
```

- **Traversing a Linked List:** Displaying the contents of a linked list is very simple. We keep moving the temp node to the next one and display its contents.

When temp is NULL, we know that we have reached the end of linked list so we get out of the while loop.

```
struct node *temp = head;
```

```
printf("\n\nList elements are – \n");
while(temp != NULL)
{
printf("%d →,"temp->data);
temp = temp->next;
}
```

The output of this program will be:

List elements are:

1 → 2 → 3 →

- **Adding Elements to Linked List:** You can add elements to either beginning, middle or end of linked list.
- **Add to Beginning:**
- Allocate memory for new node
- Store data
- Change next of new node to point to head
- Change head to point to recently created node

```
struct node *newNode;
newNode = malloc(sizeof(struct node));
newNode->data = 4;
newNode->next = head;
head = newNode;
```

- **Add to End:**
- Allocate memory for new node
- Store data
- Traverse to last node
- Change next of last node to recently created node

```
struct node *newNode;
newNode = malloc(sizeof(struct node));
newNode->data = 4;
newNode->next = NULL;
struct node *temp = head;
while(temp->next != NULL){
```

```
temp = temp->next;
}
temp->next = newNode;
```

- **Add to Middle:**
- Allocate memory and store data for new node;
- Traverse to node just before the required position of new node;
- Change next pointers to include new node in between.

```
struct node *newNode;
newNode = malloc(sizeof(struct node));
newNode->data = 4;
struct node *temp = head;
for(int i=2; i < position; i++) {
if(temp->next != NULL) {
temp = temp->next;
}
}
newNode->next = temp->next;
temp->next = newNode;
```

- **Deletion from a Linked List:** You can delete either from beginning, end or from a particular position.
- **Delete from Beginning:**
- Point head to the second node

```
head = head->next;
```

- **Delete from End:**
- Traverse to second last element
- Change its next pointer to null

```
struct node* temp = head;
while(temp->next->next!=NULL){
temp = temp->next;
}
temp->next = NULL;
```

- Delete from Middle:

- Traverse to element before the element to be deleted
- Change next pointers to exclude the node from the chain

```
for(int i=2; i< position; i++) {
if(temp->next!=NULL) {
temp = temp->next;
}
}
temp->next = temp->next->next;
```

Exercise

- Q.1. Write a program to create the linked list with ‘n’ nodes.

Ans:

```
# include < studio.h>
# include <alloch.h>
# include <conio.h>
void create node ( );
struct node:
int data;
struct node * next;
};
Type def struct node node;
Node * head = NULL;
Void main ( )}
int i, n;
pf (“Enter the no. of node:);
scount (“%d,” n);
for (i=0; i<n; i++)
create node ( );
}
create ( )
{
Node * temp
```

```
temp = (node *) malloc (Sized(node))
if (temp = =NULL) exit (0);
temp → next = NULL
print f ("Enter the value of node");
Scanf ("%d," & temp →data);
if (head = = NULL) {
head = temp;
}
else {
node * p = head;
while (p → next ! = NULL)
{p = p → next;
}
p → next = temp
p = NULL;
temp = NULL;
}
}
```

- Q.2. Write a program to count number of nodes in the given linked list.

Ans:

```
int list length (node. * head)
int count = 0;
node * p = head;
if (head = = NULL);
return count;
else
{
count = 1;
while (p → next ! = NULL)
{
```

```
p = p → next;
count ++;
}
}
return count;
}
```

- Q.3. Write a program to insert new node in the beginning of the linked list.

Ans:

```
insert at begin (node * head)
{node * temp;
temp = (node*) malloc (sized(node));
if (temp = = NULL)
exit ( );
temp → next = NULL;
print f ("Enter data element");
Scanf ("%d," & temp → data);
if (head = = NULL)
head = temp;
else {
temp → next = head;
head = temp
}
Temp = NULL;
}
```

- Q.4. Write a program to insert new node at the end of the given linked list.

Ans:

```
Insertatend (node * head)
{node * temp
Temp = (node*) malloc (size of (node))
```

```
if (temp = = NULL)
exit (O);
print f("Enter the data value");
Scanf ("%d" & temp → data);
if (head = = NULL)
head = temp;
else {
node * p = head;
while (p → next ! = NULL)
{p = p → next;
}
p → next = temp;
}
p=NULL;
temp = NULL;
}
```

- Q.5. Write a program to insert the new node at the given position.

Ans:

```
Insertatpos (node * head, int pos)
{int length, k=1;
length = list length (head);
if (pos ≤ O || POS > length +1)
printf("Invalid position");
else if (pos = = 1)
insert at begin (head);
else if (pos = = length + 1)
insert at end (head);
else {
node * p = head;
node * temp = (node *) malloc (sized of (mode));
temp → next = NULL;
```

```
pf ("Enter the data element");
Sf ("%d" & temp → data);
While (k < pos – 1)
{k ++;
p = p → next;
}
temp → next = p → next;
A → next = temp;
P= NULL;
} temp = NULL;
}
```

- Q.6. Write a program to find a middle of the given linked list.

  Ans:

```
node * middle (node * head)
{node * slow, * fast;
slow = head;
fast = head;
while (fast ! = NULL && fast → next! = NULL & & fast → next → next !
= NULL
{
slow = slow → next
fast = fast → next → next;
}
return slow;
}
```

- Q.7. Write a program to find middle of linked list using list?

  Ans:

```
node * middle (node * head)
{
int l = list length (head);
int k = 0, mid = l/2;
node * q = head;
```

```
while (k < mid)
{
q = q → next
k++;
}
return q;
}
```

- Q.8. Write a program to delete the first node of the given.

Ans:

```
delete At Begin (node * head)
{
if (head = = NULL)
return;
if (head → next = = NULL)
{
Free (head);
Head = NULL;
}
else {
node * p = head
head = head → next;
free (p);
P = NULL;
}
}
```

- Q.9. Write a program to delete the last node of the given linked list.

Ans:

```
Delete At end (node * head)
{
if (head = = NULL)
return;
```

```
if (head → next = NULL)
{
Free (head)
head = NULL;
}
else {
node * p, * q = head;
while (q → next ! = NULL)
{
P = q;
q = q → next;
}
p → next = NULL
free (q);
q = NULL;
p = NULL:
}
}
```

- Q.10. Write a program to delete the node at the given position.

Ans:

```
delete At pos (node * head, int pos)
int length = list length (head), k = 1;
if (pos ≤ 0 | | pos > length)
pf ("Invalid position");
else if (POS = = 1)
delete AT begin (head);
else if (pos = = length);
delete AT end (head);
else
{
node * p, q = head;
```

```
while (k < pos)
{
P = q;
q = q → next;
k++;
}
p → next = q → next;
Free (q);
q = NULL;
p = NULL:
}
}
```

- Q.11. Write a program to find length of circular singler linked list (CSLL).

Ans:

```
Int list length CSLL (node * head)
Int count = 0;
If (head = = NULL)
Return count;
else
{node * p = head;
Count = 1;
While (p → next ! = head)
{p = p → next;
count ++;
}
}
return count;
}
```

- Q.12. Write a program to insert the new node in the begin of the circular single linked list.

Ans:

```
Insert At Begin CSLL (node * head)
{
Node * temp;
Temp = (node *) malloc (size of (node));
temp → next = NULL;
pf ("Enter data element");
sf ("%d," & temp → data);
if (head = =NULL)
{head = temp;
head → next = head;
}
else
{node * p = head;
While (p → next ! = head)
{p = p → next;
}
P → next = temp;
head = temp;
p = NULL;
temp = NULL;
}
}
```

- Q.13. Write a program to insert the new node at the …… of CSLL.

  Ans:

```
insert A End CSLL (node * head)
node * temp;
temp = (node *) nalloc (size of (node));
if (temp = = NULL)
exit (0);
print f("Enter the data value");
Scanf ("% l," & temp → data);
```

```
if (head = = NULL)
{head = temp;
Head → next = head; temp = NULL
}
else (node * p = head;
while (p → next ! = head)
{p = p → next;
}
P → next = temp
temp → next = head;
p = NULL
temp = NULL;
}
}
```

- Q.14. Write a program to delete the last node in the CSLL.

Ans:

```
delete At end CSLL (node * head)
{if (head = = NULL)
{pf ("list is empty");
return;
}
if (head → next = = head)
{free (head);
Head = NULL;
}
else (node * p, * q = head;
while (q→ next ! = head)
{
p = q;
q = q → next;
}
```

```
P → next = head;
free (q);
q = null; p = Null;
}
}
```

- Q.15. Write a program to delete the first node of given CSL.

Ans:

```
delete At Begin CSLL (nod * head)
if (head = = NULL)
{pf ("List is empty");
Return;
}
if (head → next = = head)
{free (head);
head = NULL;
}
else
{node * p, * q = head;
p = head → next;
while (q → next ! = head)
{q = q → next;
}
q → next = p;
head = p;
Free (p);
Free (q);
P = NULL; q = NULL;
}
}
```

CHAPTER 3

TREES

CONTENTS

3.1. INTRODUCTION

This chapter covers trees with its basic terminology, formal definition of the tree and types of the tree. In case of binary tree, chapter covers its definition, representation, operations, traversal of binary tree, threaded binary trees, conversion of general tree to binary tree and binary expression tree. It also covers application of trees, searching technique like- sequential search, binary search, height balanced trees, weight balanced trees and digital search trees. Searching technique hashing with various hashing functions and collisions handling techniques are also covered in this chapter.

3.2. BASIC CONCEPTS

The concept of trees is one of the most fundamental and useful concepts in computer science. Trees have many variations, implementations, and applications. There are various applications, where tree structure is the efficient way to maintain and manipulate data, such as, compiler construction, database design, windows, operating system programs, etc. We can represent a tree as a structure consisting of nodes and edges, which represent a relationship between two nodes. Figure 3.1 shows a general tree.

Level

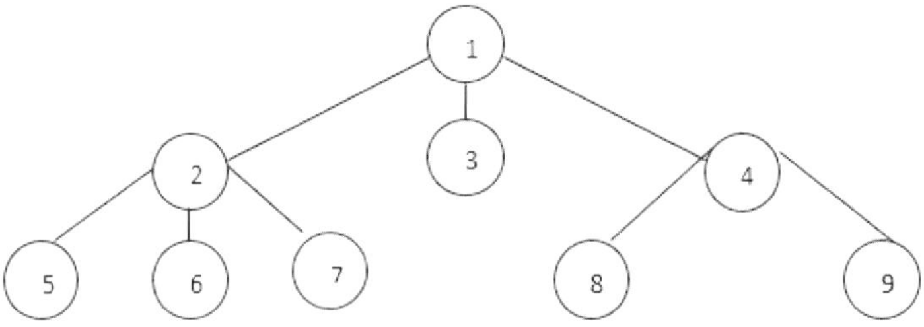

0

1

2

Figure 3.1. A general tree.

Here are some commonly used terms that apply to all trees:

- **Child:** An immediate successor node is called a child of its predecessor. The leaf node has no children.

- **Parent:** An immediate predecessor node is called the parent of its children. The root node has no parent.
- **Sibling:** The nodes which have the same parent are called siblings. In Figures 3.1, 3.5, 3.6, and 3.7 are siblings.
- **Leaf Node or Terminal Node or External Node:** A node which is at the end and does not have any child(both pointer values are NIL) is called a leaf node. In Figures 3.1, 3.5, 3.6, 3.7, 3.8, and 3.9 are the leaf nodes. It is also called terminal node. It is usually represented by the square.
- **Non Terminal Node or Internal Node:** Nodes with at least one child is sometimes called non terminal node. The circle usually represents non-terminal node.
- **Level:** The number of pointer links required to move from a given node to the root node is called the level of that node. Figure 3.1 shows the level of various nodes.
- **Depth:** The highest level number of any node in a tree is called the depth of the tree.
- **Height:** Maximum number of nodes which is possible in a path, starting from root to a leaf node is called the height of a tree. The height of a tree is obtained by:

H = (Max Level) +1

In Figure 3.1, the height of the tree is 3.

- **Ancestors and Descendents:** If there is a path from node t1 to node t2, then t1 is ancestor of t2 and t2 is a descendent of t1. The root has no ancestor, and leaves have no descendent.
- **Degree:** The maximum number of children, a node can have, is called the degree of the node. In Figure 3.1, degree of root node 1 is 1, node 2 is 3 and node 4 is 2.

3.3. TREE

Definition: Let us formally define a tree. A tree(T) is a non-empty finite collection of nodes or vertices, such that:

- There is one specially designated vertex or node called root of the tree(T),
- The remaining nodes are partitioned into a collection of sub-trees T_1, T_2,T_3,…,T_n each of which is again a tree.

Let us consider a tree T, as shown in Figure 3.2.

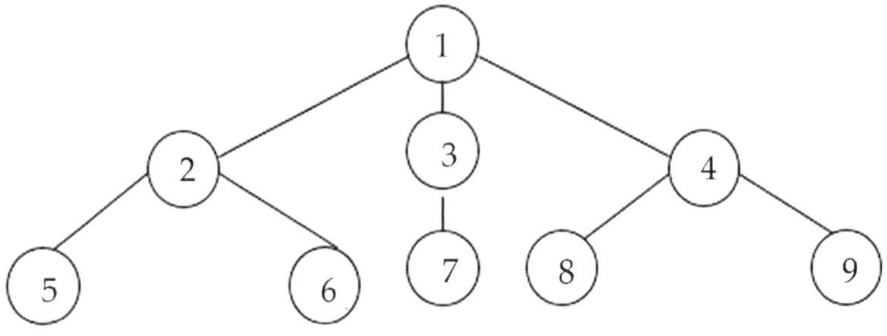

Figure 3.2. A tree T.

In this tree(T), 1 is the node called the root of the tree(T). T_1, T_2, and T_3 are sub-trees of the tree(T). T_1 (with root 2), T_2 (with root 3) and T_3 (with root 4) are again trees by the definition of the tree. The tree(T) has total 9 nodes with 8 edges.

3.4. BINARY TREE

Perhaps the most commonly used type of tree data structure is binary tree. It is the simplest type to implement and can be very efficient, if used properly. Binary tree is a specific implementation of an m-ary tree, where; m= 2, child nodes per node on the tree. In simpler terms, this means that each node on the tree contains two links to two other trees, both referred to as sub-trees. The two sub-trees are often called the left and right sub-tree. A binary tree is made of nodes that can have at most two children. The root node is the node that is not a child of any other node, and is found at the "top" of the tree structure.

Definition: Let us formally define a binary tree. A binary tree(T) is a finite set of nodes such that:

- T is empty called the null binary tree.
- T contains a distinguished node R called the root of T, and the remaining nodes of T form two ordered pairs of disjoints binary tree T_1 and T_2, which are called left sub-tree and the right sub-tree of R, respectively. Figure 3.3 shows a binary tree with 9 nodes represented by the letter B to L. B is the root of the binary tree(T). The left sub-tree of the root B consists of the nodes C, E, and F and the right sub-tree of B consist of the nodes D, H, I, K, and L.

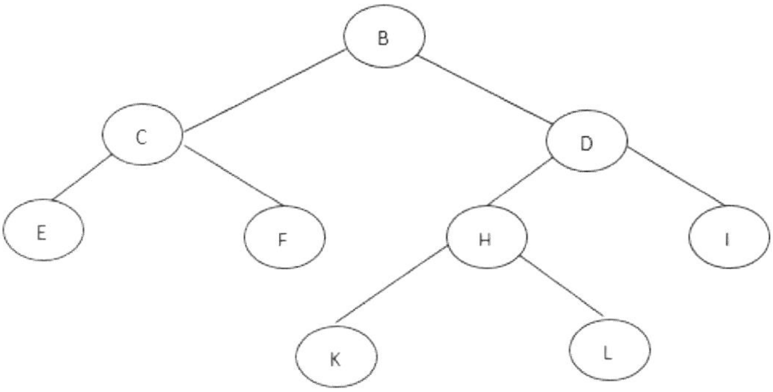

Figure 3.3. Binary tree.

3.4.1. Types of Binary Tree

There are four types of binary tree:

- Extended binary tree or 2-tree;
- Binary search tree.

1. **Complete Binary Tree:** A binary tree is a complete binary tree, if all of its level, except possibly the last, have the maximum number of possible nodes and if all the nodes at the last level appear as far left as possible. Figure 3.4 shows a complete binary tree.

Level

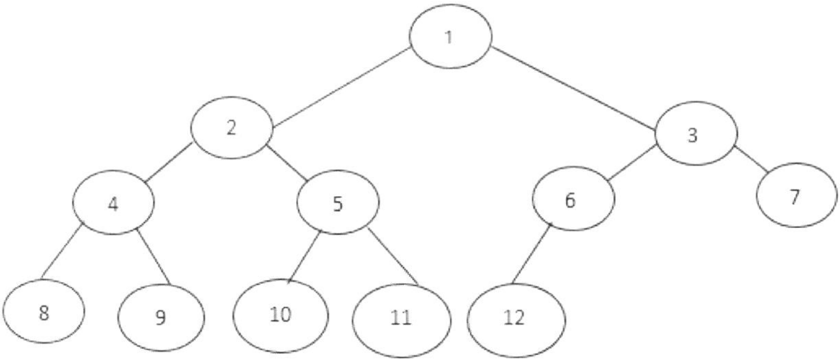

0
1
2
3

Figure 3.4. A complete binary tree.

2. **Full Binary Tree:** A binary tree is said to be a full binary tree, if all of its level have the maximum number of possible nodes. Figure 3.5 shows a full binary tree.

Level

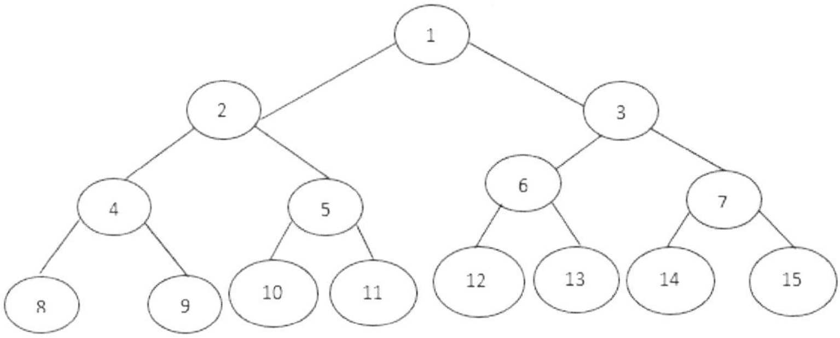

0

1

2

3

Figure 3.5. A full binary tree.

3. **Extended Binary Tree or 2-Tree:** A binary tree T is said to be extended binary tree or 2-tree if each node N has either 0 or 2 children. The nodes with 2 children are called internal nodes represented by the circle and the nodes with 0 children are called external nodes represented by the square, respectively. Figure 3.6 shows the extended binary tree.

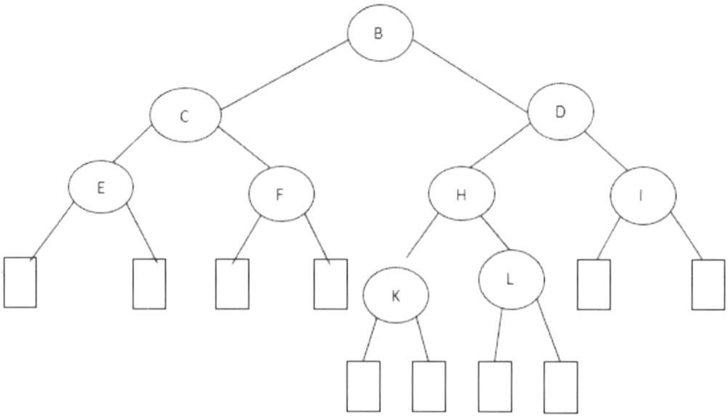

Figure 3.6. Extended binary tree or 2-tree.

4. **Binary Search Tree:** A binary search tree is a binary tree which is either empty or satisfies the following rules:

i. The info of the key in the left sub-tree is less than the info of the root;

ii. The info of the key in the right sub-tree is more than or equal to the value of the root;

iii. All the sub-trees of the left and right sub-tree observe the above two rules. Figure 3.7 shows the binary search tree.

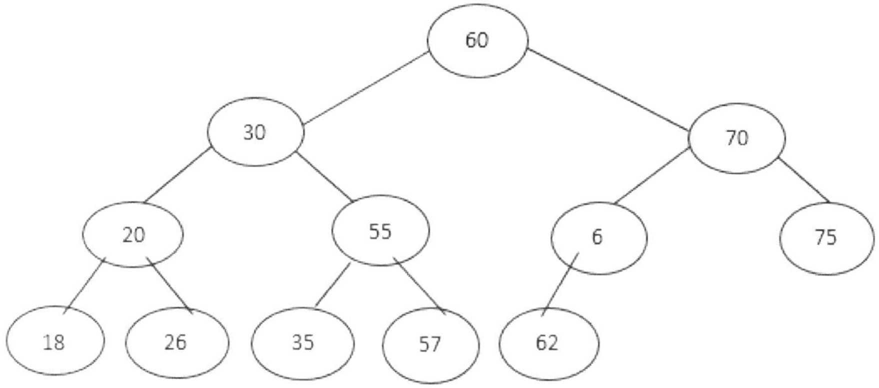

Figure 3.7. A binary search tree.

3.4.2. Representation of Binary Tree

It is often required to maintain trees in the computer memory. A binary tree must represent a hierar-chical relationship between parent node and child nodes. There are two methods for representing binary tree. First is called the linear(sequential) representation, using array and second is called linked representation, using pointers.

3.4.2.1. Linear Representation of a Binary Tree

In this representation block of memory for an array is to be allocated before going to store the actual tree in it and once the memory is allocated, the size of the tree will be restricted as the memory permits.

A sequential representation of a binary tree requires numbering of nodes, starting with nodes on level 0. The nodes are numbered from left to right.

The nodes of the binary tree are maintained in a one-dimensional array.

Following are the rules, which easily determine the locations of the root, left child and right child of any node of a binary tree in the array. Let us assume that array index starts from 1:

i. The root node is at position 1.

ii. For any node with index j, 1 < j ≤ m,(for some m):

a. PARENT(j) = [j/2]

For the node when j=1, j is the root and has no parent.

b. LEFTC(j) = 2 * j

If 2 * j > m, then j has no left child.

c. RIGHTC(j) = 2 * j +1

If 2 * j +1 > m, then j has no right child.

Let us consider the binary tree as shown in Figure 3.8.

Level 0 1
Level 1 2 3
Level 2 4 5 6 7
Level 3 8 9

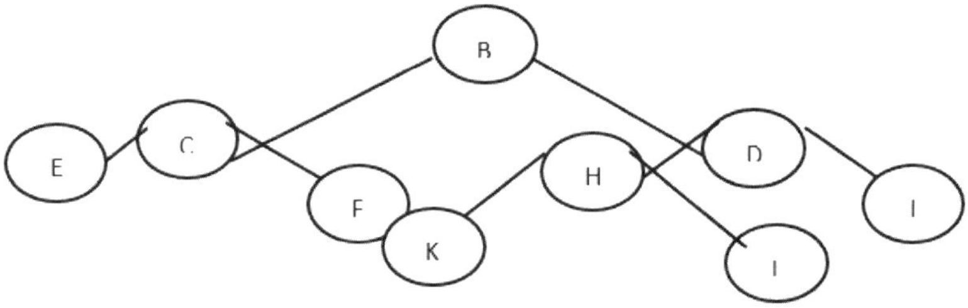

Figure 3.8. Binary tree.

The linear representation of the binary tree, using array is shown in Figure 3.9.

1	2	3	4	5	6	7	8	9	10	11	12	13	14	15
B	C	D	E	F	H	I	.	.	.	.	K	L	.	.

Figure 3.9. *Array representation of the binary tree.*

- **Drawbacks:** Except full binary tree the memory space remain unutilized in linear representation of a binary tree. It is also not possible to enhance the tree structure if the array size is fixed. Insertion and deletion of a node requires considerable data movements up and down the array, which demand excessive amount of processing time.

3.4.2.2. Linked Representation of a Binary Tree

The problem associated with the linear representation of binary tree can be overcome through the use of the linked representation. In linked representation, each node consists of three fields as shown in Figure 3.10.

Figure 3.10. Node structure.

In this structure, *left*, and *right* fields store the link of left and right child of a node, respectively. The *info* field is used for storing information associated with the node. Let us consider the binary tree as shown in Figure 3.11.

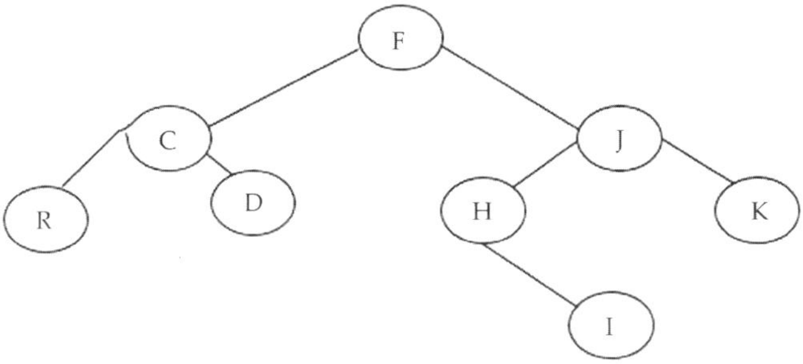

Figure 3.11. Binary tree.

Table 3.1 shows how linked representation may appear in memory of the binary tree, as shown in Figure 3.11.

Table 3.1. Linked Representation of Binary Tree

Address	info	left	right
1	F	4	7
2	–	–	–
3	B	0	0
4	C	3	6

5	–	–	–
6	D	0	0
7	J	9	11
8	–	–	–
9	H	0	10
10	I	0	0
11	K	0	0

Figure 3.12 shows the logical view of the linked representation of a binary tree shown in Figure 3.11. *ROOT* will contain the location of the parent node of binary tree. If any sub-tree is empty, then the corresponding pointer will contain the null value. If the binary tree itself is empty, then *ROOT* will contain the null value.

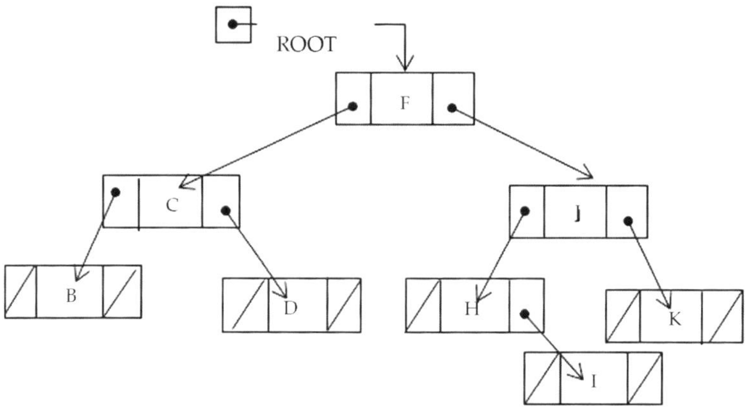

Figure 3.12. Logical view of the linked representation of a binary tree.

3.4.3. Binary Search Tree Operations

We can use the following structure to implement binary search tree operations: typedef char item;

```
typedef struct binary_tag
{
item info;
struct binary_tag *left;
struct binary_tag *right;
}BTree;
```

Following are the operations, which can be performed on a binary search tree:

- **Insertion in a Binary Search Tree:** To insert a node in a binary search tree, we must check whether the tree already contains any nodes. If tree is empty, the node is placed in the root node. If the tree is not empty, then the proper location is found and the added node becomes either a left or a right sub-tree of an existing node.

The function continues recursively until either it finds a duplicate or it hits a dead end. If it determines that the value to be added belongs to the left sub-tree and there is no left node, it creates one. If a left node exists, then it begins its search with the sub-tree beginning at this node. If the function determines, that the value to be added belongs to the right sub-tree of the current node, a similar process occurs.

Figure 3.13 shows the insertion of node 64. In this case, search start from root node as 60-70-65 then halts when it finds the dead end. So node 64 occurred in the right part of the node 65.

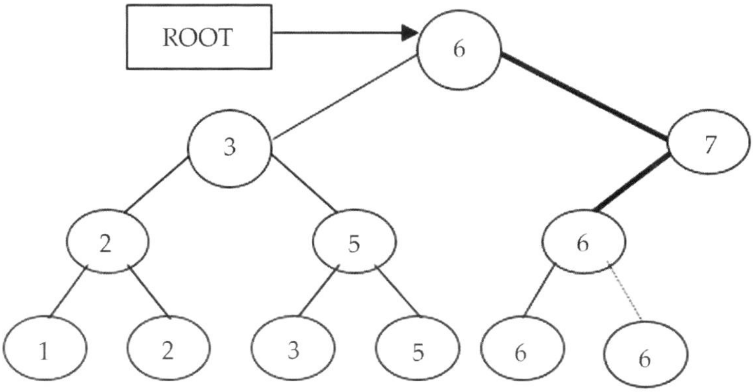

Figure 3.13. Insertion of node 64.

A. **Algorithm:** The following are the steps, which are used for insertion operation in a binary search tree:

a. [Initialize pointer to the root node]

Set pointer = root

b. [Check whether the tree is empty]

If(pointer ==NULL) then

Set pointer =(BTree *)malloc(sizeof(BTree))

pointer[left] = NULL,

pointer[right] = NULL,

pointer[info] = info

c. [Test for the left sub-tree]

If(info<pointer[info])then call recursively binary_insert function for left sub-tree

Set pointer[left] = binary_insert(pointer[left], info)

d. [Test for the right sub-tree]

If(info>pointer[info])then call recursively binary_insert function for right sub-tree

Set pointer[right] = binary_insert(pointer[right], info)

e. [Otherwise item is duplicate]

write 'item is duplicate'

f. return(pointer)

g. End.

B. Equivalent Function in C:

```
BTree *binary_insert(BTree *pointer, int info)
{
/*Check whether the tree is empty */
if(pointer==NULL)
{
pointer =(BTree)malloc(sizeof(BTree));
pointer->left = NULL;
pointer->right = NULL;
pointer->info = info;
}
else /*Test for the left child*/
if(info < pointer->info)
pointer->left = binary_insert(pointer->left,info);
else /*Test for the right child*/
if(info >pointer->info)
pointer->right = binary_insert(pointer->right,info);
else /*Duplicate entry*/
```

```
printf("Duplicate entry\n");
return(pointer);
}
```

- **Searching in a Binary Search Tree:** To search a particular node in a binary search tree. We start the search from the root node, and compare the root node with the searched node. If the values are equal the search is said to be successful and searched node is found in the tree. If the searched value is less than the value in the root node, then it must be in the left sub-tree and if there is no left sub-tree, the value is not in the tree, i.e., the search is unsuccessful. If there is a left sub-tree, then it is searched in the same way. Similarly, if the searched value is greater than the value in the root node, the right sub-tree is searched. Figure 3.14 shows the path(in shaded line) for searching of 57 in binary search tree.

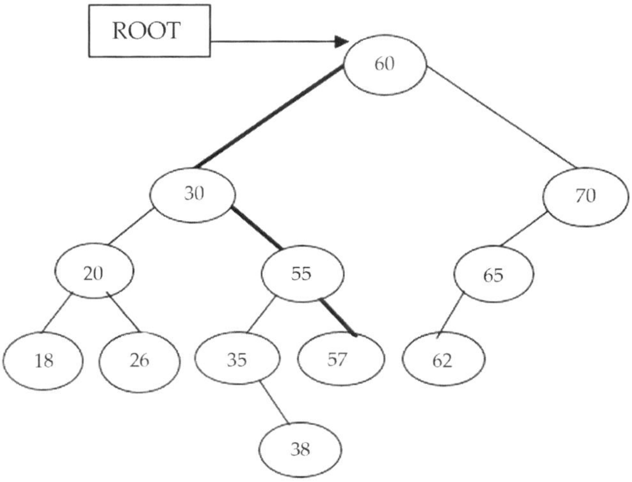

Figure 3.14. Searching of node 57.

A. **Algorithm:** The following are the steps, which are used for search operation in a binary search tree:

a. [Initialize]

Set pointer = root and flag =0

b. [Search the node in a binary search tree]

Repeat steps from (c) to (e) while(pointer !=NULL) and (flag==0)

c. [Search a node from the root]

```
if(pointer[info] ==info) then
Set flag =1,
return(flag)
d.    [Search a node in the left sub-tree]
if(info<pointer[info])then
Set pointer = pointer[left]
e.    [Search a node in the right sub-tree]
if(info>pointer[info])then
Set pointer = pointer[right]
f.    return(pointer)
g.    End.
B.    Equivalent Function in C
int binary_search(BTree *pointer, int info)
{
/*Search the node in a binary search tree*/
while(pointer!=NULL)
{
/*Search a node at the root in a binary search tree*/
if(pointer->info == info)
{
flag=1;
return(flag);
}
else /*Search a node in the left sub-tree*/
if(info <pointer->info)
pointer = pointer->left;
else /*Search a node in the right sub-tree*/
pointer = pointer->right;
}
return(flag);
}
```

- **Deletion in a Binary Search Tree:** This operation is used to delete a node(N) from non-empty binary search tree(T). The node(N) deleted from the tree depends primarily on the number of children of node(N). There are three cases to consider in deleting a node from a binary search tree.

a. If the node(N) is a leaf, just set its parent pointer to null and delete the node(N). The deleted node is now unreferenced and may be disposed-off. Figure 3.15 shows deletion of leaf node 62.

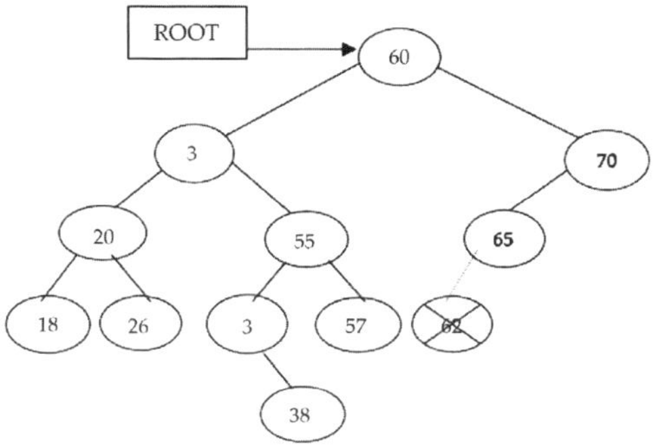

(b)

(c)

Figure 3.15. Deletion of node 62.

b. If the node(N) has just one child, point the "grandparent" to its child and delete the node(N). Figure 3.16 shows the deletion of node 70.

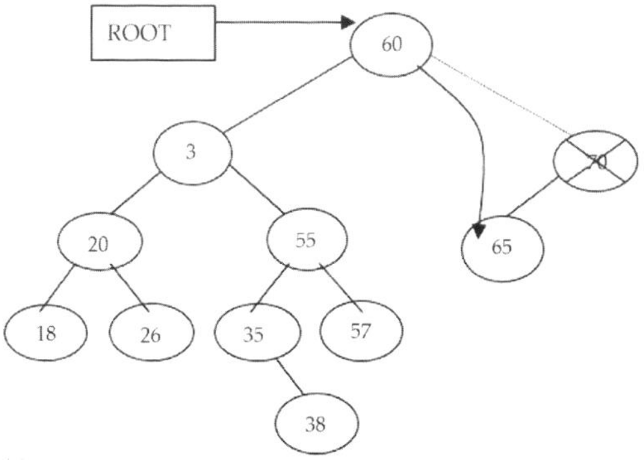

(c)

(d)

Figure 3.16. Deletion of node 70.

c. If the node(N) has two children's, then N is deleted by first deleting SUCC(N) from tree[using case1 or case2; it can be verified that SUCC(N) always occurs in the right sub-tree of node(N) and SUCC(N) never has a left child] and then replace the data content in node N by the data content in node SUCC(N). Figure 3.17 shows the deletion of 30.

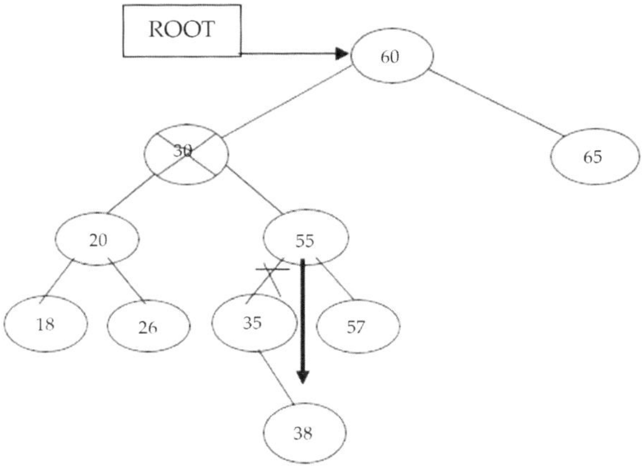

35

Figure 3.17. Deletion of node 30.

Figure 3.18 shows the binary search tree after deletion of node 30.

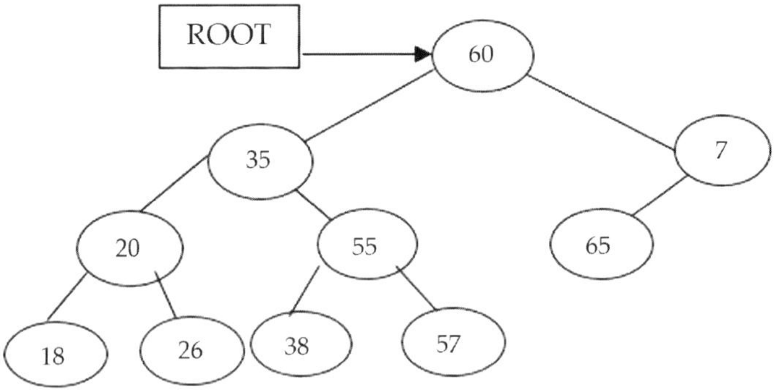

Figure 3.18. After deletion of node 30.

A. **Algorithm:** The following are the steps, which are used for deletion operation in a binary search tree:

a. [Initialize]

Set flag =0 and pointer=root

b. [Search the node in a tree]

Repeat steps from (c) to (e) while (pointer !=NULL) and (flag==0)

c. [Search a node from the root]

If(pointer[info] ==info) then

Set flag =1,

d. [Search a node in the left sub-tree]

If(info<pointer[info])then

Set parent =pointer and pointer = pointer[left]

e. [Search a node in the right sub-tree]

If(info>pointer[info])then

Set parent =pointer and pointer = pointer[right]

f. [When the node does not exist]

If(flag==0) then write 'info does not exist in the tree'

g. [Decide the case of deletion]

If(pointer[left] ==NULL) and pointer[right]==NULL) then

[Node has no child]

Set case =1

else

If(pointer[left] !=NULL) and (pointer[right]!=NULL) then

[Node contains both the childs]

Set case =3

else

[Node contains only one child]

Set case=2

h. [Deletion when node has no child]

If(case==1) then

[Node is a left child]

If(parent[left]=pointer) then

Set parent[left]=NULL

[Node is a right child]

else

Set parent[right]=NULL
return(pointer)

i. [Deletion when node contains only one child]

If(case==2) then
[Node is a left child]
If(parent[left]=pointer)then
If(pointer[left]==NULL)then
Set parent[left]=pointer[right]
else
Set parent[left]=pointer[left]
else
[Node is a right child]
If(parent[right]=pointer)then
If(pointer[left]==NULL)then
Set parent[right]=pointer[right]
else
Set parent[right]=pointer[left]
return(pointer)

j. [Deletion when node contains two childs]

If(case==3) then
[Find the in order successor of the node]
Set pointer1=pointer[right]
[Check right sub-tree is not empty]
If(pointer1!=NULL)then
Repeat while(pointer1[left]!=NULL)
[Move to the left most end]
pointer1=pointer1[left]
Set item=pointer1[info]
Call function binary_delete(pointer,item) for deletion of inorder successor
[Replace the deleted node with the inorder successor of the node]
Repeat while ((pointer !=NULL) and (flag==0))

[Search a node in the left sub-tree]
If(info<pointer[info])then
Set pointer = pointer[left]
[Otherwise search a node in the right sub-tree]
If(info>pointer[info])then
Set pointer = pointer[right]
[Otherwise search a node from the root]
If(pointer[info] ==info) then
Set flag =1 and pointer[info]=item
return(pointer)

k. End.

B. Equivalent Function in C:

```
BTree *binary_delete(BTree *pointer, int info)
{
BTree *parent,pointer1;
int flag=0,case,item1;
/*Find the location of the node*/
while(pointer!=NULL) && (flag==0)
{
if(info <pointer->info)
{
parent=pointer;
pointer = pointer->left;
}
else
if(info >pointer->info)
{
parent=pointer;
pointer = pointer->right;
}
else
```

```
flag=1;
}
/*When node does not exist*/
if(flag==0)
{
printf("Node does not exist in the tree\n");
exit(0);
}
else /*Decide the case of deletion*/
{
if(pointer->left ==NULL) && (pointer->right==NULL)
/*Node has no child*/
case =1;
else
if(pointer-> !=NULL) && (pointer->right!=NULL)
/*Node contains both the child*/
case =3;
else
/*Node contains only one child*/
case=2;
}
/* Deletion of node based on cases */
if(case==1)
{
/*Deletion when node has no child*/
if(parent->left=pointer)
parent->left=NULL;
else
parent->right=NULL;
return(pointer);
}
```

```
else
/*Deletion when node contains only one child*/
if(case==2)
{
/*Node is a left child*/
if(parent->left=pointer)
{
if(pointer->left==NULL)
parent->left=pointer->right;
else
parent->left=pointer->left;
}
else /*Node is a right child*/
if(parent->right=pointer)
{
if(pointer->left==NULL)
parent->right=pointer->right;
else
parent->right=pointer->left;
}
return(pointer);
}
else
/*Deletion when node contains two child*/
if(case==3)
{
/*Find the in order successor of the node*/
pointer1=pointer->right;
/*Check right sub-tree is not empty*/
if(pointer1!=NULL)
{
```

```
while(pointer1->left!=NULL)
/*Move to the left most end*/
pointer1=pointer1->left;
}
item=pointer1[info];
/* Delete inorder successor of the node*/
binary_delete(pointer,item);
/*Replace the deleted node with the inorder successor of the node*/
while((pointer!=NULL) && (flag==0))
{
if(info <pointer->info)
pointer = pointer->left;
else
if(info >pointer->info)
pointer = pointer->right;
else
{
flag=1;
pointer[info]= item;
}
}
return(pointer);
}
}
```

3.5. TRAVERSALS OPERATION OF A BINARY TREE

Traversing a binary tree operation is used when we like to visit each node in the tree exactly once. The traversal on a binary tree gives the listing of the nodes of a tree in a certain order. Let us consider a binary tree as shown in Figure 3.19.

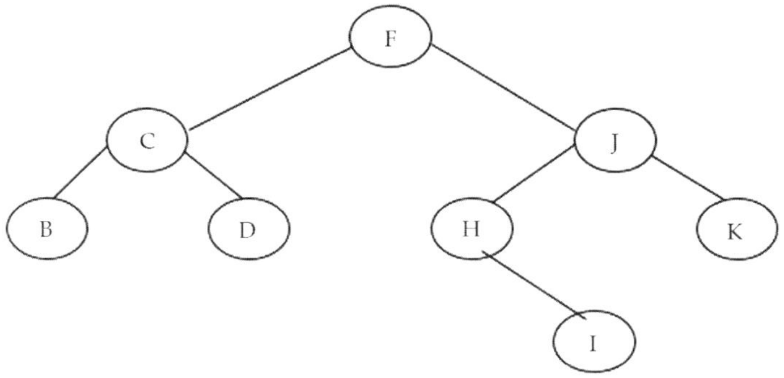

Figure 3.19. Sorted binary tree.

The tree can be traverse in four ways. These four types are as in subsections.

3.5.1. Preorder Traversal

A preorder traversal, visits each node of a sorted tree, in preorder. In other words, the root node visits first, followed by left sub-tree and finally the right sub-tree. So, in Figure 3.19, a preorder traversal would result in the following string: FCBDJHIK.

A. **Algorithm:** The following steps are used for preorder traversal operation of a binary tree:

a. [Check the node is not empty]

If(pointer != NULL) then

b. [visit the node]

Visit(pointer)

c. [Call recursively for left sub-tree]

Preorder(pointer[left])

d. [Call recursively for right sub-tree]

Preorder(pointer[right])

e. End.

B. Equivalent Function in C:

```
void Preorder(BTree * pointer)
{
if (pointer!= NULL)
{
```

```
printf("%3c,"pointer->info);
Preorder(pointer->left);
Preorder(pointer->right);
}
}
```

3.5.2. Inorder Traversal

An inorder traversal, visits each node of a sorted tree, in inorder. In other words, the left sub-tree visits first, followed by root node and finally the right sub-tree. So, in Figure 3.19, an inorder traversal would result in the following string: BCDFHIJK.

A. **Algorithm:** The following steps are used for inorder traversal operation of a binary tree:

a. [Check the node is not empty]

If(pointer != NULL) then

b. [Call recursively for left sub-tree]

Inorder(pointer[left])

c. [visit the node]

Visit(pointer)

d. [Call recursively for right sub-tree]

Inorder(pointer[right])

e. End.

B. **Equivalent Function in C:**

```
void Inorder(BTree * pointer)
{
if (pointer!= NULL)
{
Inorder(pointer->left);
printf("%3c,"pointer->info);
Inorder(pointer->right);
}
}
```

3.5.3. Postorder Traversal

A postorder traversal, visits each node of a sorted tree, in postorder. In other words, the left sub-tree visits first, followed by the right sub-tree and finally visits the root node of the tree. So, in Figure 3.19, a postorder traversal would result in the following string: ADCIHKJF.

A. Algorithm: The following steps are used for postorder traversal operation of a binary tree:

a. [Check the node is not empty]

if(pointer != NULL) then

b. [Call recursively for left sub-tree]

Postorder(pointer[left])

c. [Call recursively for rigth sub-tree]

Postorder(pointer[right])

d. [visit the node]

Visit(pointer)

e. End.

B. Equivalent Function in C:

```
void Postorder(BTree * pointer)
{
if (pointer!= NULL)
{
Postorder(pointer->left);
Postorder(pointer->right);
printf("%3c,"pointer->info);
}
}
```

3.5.4. Level by Level Traversal

In this method, we traverse level-wise, i.e., we first visit node at level '0,' i.e., root. Then we visit nodes at level '1' from left to right and so on. It is same as breadth first search. This traversal is different from other three traversals in the sense that it needs not be recursive, therefore, we may use queue kind of a data structure to implement it.

For example the level by level traversal of the binary tree given in Figure 3.19 would result in the following string: FCJBDKHI.

3.5.5. Implementation of the Traversal Operations of Binary Tree

The following program tree_traveral.c shows the implementation of traversal operations of the binary tree:

```
/*tree_traversal.c*/
#include<stdio.h>
#include<malloc.h>
typedef struct binary_tag
{
char info;
struct binary_tag *left;
struct binary_tag *right;
}BTree;
BTree *Binary_Tree(BTree *,char);
void Prerder(BTree *);
void Inorder(BTree *);
void Postorder(BTree *);
void main()
{
char ch,info;
BTree *pointer;
printf("!!!This program performs the traversal operations of a binary tree!!!\n");
printf("!!!Please enter the node infomation(a single character)of a tree in PRE ORDER!!!\n");
pointer = (BTree *)malloc(sizeof(BTree));
pointer = NULL;
do
{
```

```
printf("Enter the information of the node:");
scanf("%c,"&info);
pointer=Binary_Tree(pointer,info);
fflush(stdin);
printf("Do you want to add some other node(enter 'y' for yes):");
scanf("%c,"&ch);
fflush(stdin);
}while(ch=='y');
printf("!!!The followings are the output of the traversal operations\n!!!");
printf("\nPre order traversal of a binary tree is:");
Preorder(pointer);
printf("\nInorder traversal of a binary tree is:");
Inorder(pointer);
printf("\nPost order traversal of a binary tree is:");
Postorder(pointer);
}
BTree *Binary_Tree(BTree *pointer,char info)
{
if(pointer==NULL)
{
pointer =(BTree *)malloc(sizeof(BTree));
pointer->left = NULL;
pointer->right = NULL;
pointer->info = info;
}
else
if(info < pointer->info)
pointer->left = Binary_Tree(pointer->left,info);
else
if(info >pointer->info)
pointer->right = Binary_Tree(pointer->right,info);
```

```
else
printf("Duplicate entry\n");
return(pointer);
}
void Preorder(BTree * pointer)
{
if (pointer!=NULL)
{
printf("%3c,"pointer->info);
Preorder(pointer->left);
Preorder(pointer->right);
}
}
void Inorder(BTree * pointer)
{
if (pointer != NULL)
{
Inorder(pointer->left);
printf("%3c,"pointer->info);
Inorder(pointer->right);
}
}
void Postorder(BTree * pointer)
{
if (pointer!= NULL)
{
Postorder(pointer->left);
Postorder(pointer->right);
printf("%3c,"pointer->info);
}
}
```

3.5.5.1. Output of the Program

!!!This program performs the traversal operations on a binary tree!!!

!!!Please enter the node infomation(a single character)of a tree in PRE ORDER!!!

Enter the information of the node:f

Do you want to add some other node(enter 'y' for yes):y

Enter the information of the node:c

Do you want to add some other node(enter 'y' for yes):y

Enter the information of the node:b

Do you want to add some other node(enter 'y' for yes):y

Enter the information of the node:d

Do you want to add some other node(enter 'y' for yes):y

Enter the information of the node:j

Do you want to add some other node(enter 'y' for yes):y

Enter the information of the node:h

Do you want to add some other node(enter 'y' for yes):y

Enter the information of the node:i

Do you want to add some other node(enter 'y' for yes):y

Enter the information of the node:k

Do you want to add some other node(enter 'y' for yes):n

!!!The followings are the output of the traversal operations!!!

Pre order traversal of a binary tree is: f c b d j h i k

Inorder traversal of a binary tree is: b c d f h i j k

Post order traversal of a binary tree is: b d c i h k j f

3.6. THREADED BINARY TREE

In the linked representation of a binary tree approximately half of the entries in the link fields are with null values and thereby wasting the memory space. A. J. Perlis and C. Thornton devised a way to utilize these null value link fields. Their idea is to replace certain null entries by special pointers, which point to nodes higher in the tree. These special pointers are called threads, and binary tree with such pointers is called threaded binary tree.

3.6.1. Representation of Threaded Binary Tree

In the representation of a threaded binary tree the problem is of distinguishing a link from a thread. In computer memory, an extra 1-bit TAG field may be used to differentiate threads from ordinary pointers, or, alternatively, threads may be denoted by negative integers when ordinary pointers are denoted by positive integers.

There are three ways to thread a binary tree, these correspond to inorder, preorder, and postorder traversal. One may also select a one-way threading or a two-way threading. Unless otherwise stated, our threading will correspond to the inorder traversal of tree.

In one-way threading of tree, a thread will appear in the right field of a node and will point to the next node in the inorder traversal of tree.

Figure 3.20 shows one-way inorder threading.

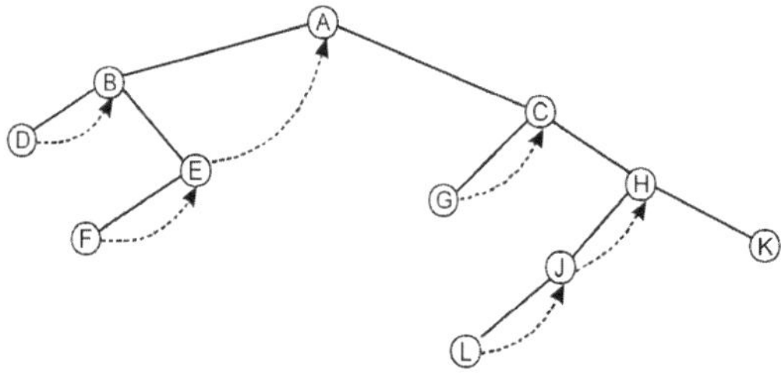

(a) One-way inorder threading

Figure 3.20. one-way inorder threading.

In two-way threading of tree, a thread will appear in the left field of a node and will point to the preceding node in the inorder traversal of tree. Figure 3.21 shows two-way inorder threading.

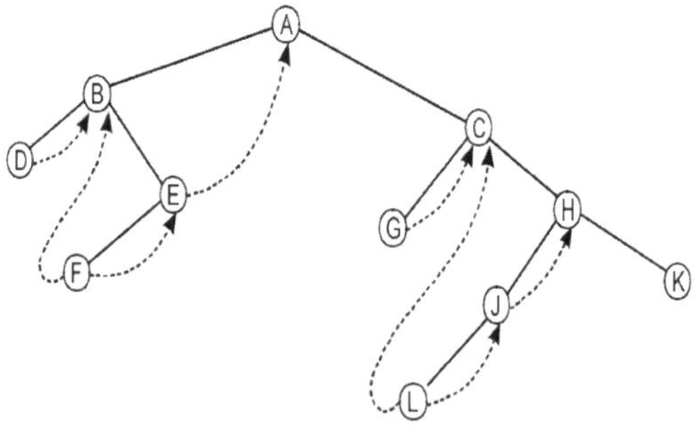

(b) Two-way inorder threading

Figure 3.21. Two-way inorder threading.

When tree does not have a header node then the left pointer of the first node and the right pointer of the last node will contain the null value. Otherwise, it will point to the header node. Figure 3.22 shows two-way inorder threading with header node.

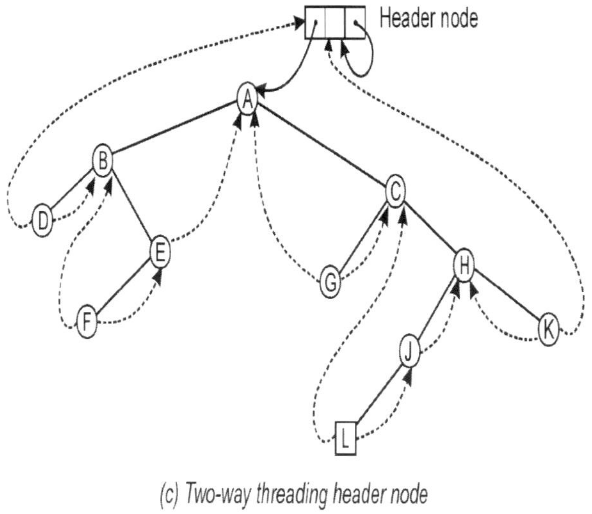

Figure 3.22. Two-way threading header node.

3.6.2. Advantages of Threaded Binary Tree

The following are the advantages of the threaded binary tree:

- The traversal operation in threaded binary tree is faster than that of its unthreaded binary tree because non-recursive implementation of threaded binary tree is possible;
- We can efficiently determine the predecessor and successor nodes starting from any node;
- Node can be easily accessible from other node;
- Implementations of insertion and deletion operations are very easy.

3.7. BINARY EXPRESSION TREE

A Binary tree is called an expression binary tree if it stores arithmetic expression. All internal nodes are operators and the leaves are operands of the binary expression tree. Figure 3.23 shows the binary expression tree of the arithmetic expression:

$E = (B–C) + (E/F) \times D$

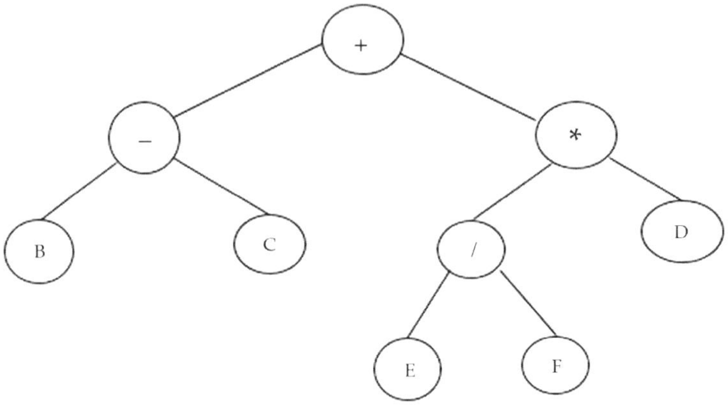

Figure 3.23. Binary expression tree.

3.8. CONVERSION OF GENERAL TREE TO BINARY TREE

Let T is a general tree. The following is the procedure for converting a general tree T to binary tree T':

i. All the nodes of the general tree(T) are also the nodes of the binary tree T.'
ii. The root of the general tree(T) is also the root of the binary tree(T').
iii. Let N be an arbitrary node of the binary tree(T') then the left child of N in T' will be the first child of the node N in the general tree(T) and the right child of N in binary tree(T') will be the next sibling of N in the general tree(T).

Let us consider the general tree, as shown in Figure 3.24. The corresponding binary tree is shown in Figure 3.25.

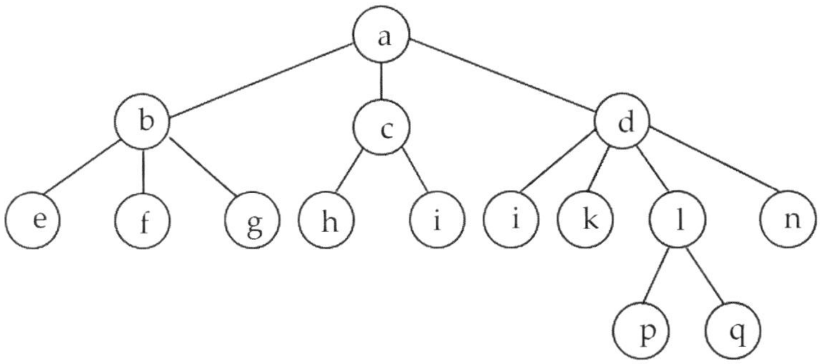

Figure 3.24. A general tree.

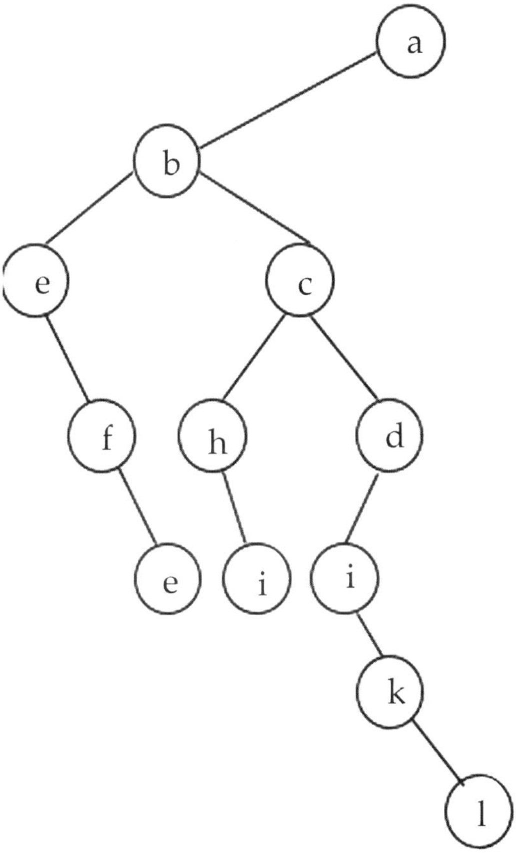

Figure 3.25. Equivalent binary tree.

3.9. APPLICATIONS OF TREE

In this topic, we cover three applications. First, describes the Huffman coding. Second, describes the decision tree and third is game tree.

3.9.1. Huffman Coding

Huffman codes belong to a family of codes with a variable length codes, i.e., individual symbols, which make a message, are represented with bit sequences of distinct length. This characteristic of the code words helps to makes data compression possible. For example, symbols A, B, C, and D are represented by following code words:

Symbol	**Code Word**
A	0
B	10
C	110
D	111

At the first look it seems that the code words are not uniquely decodable. But, the power of Huffman codes is in the fact that all code words are uniquely decodable. So the sequence of bits:

0111100110

is uniquely decodable as 'ADBAC.' Decreasing of redundancy in data by Huffman codes is based on the fact that distinct symbols have distinct frequencies of incidence. This fact helps to create such code words, which really contribute to decreasing of redundancy, i.e., to data compression.

3.9.1.1. Huffman's Algorithm

This coding system algorithm was given by Huffman in 1952. The algorithm for building Huffman code is based on the coding tree. The following are the steps:

a. Line up the symbols by falling frequencies.

b. Link two symbols with least frequencies, into one new symbol with frequency probability as a sum of frequencies of two symbols.

c. Go to Step (b) until we generate a single symbol with frequency 1.

Let us take an example how to build a set of Huffman codes. Let us consider the 10 data items, which has the following frequencies:

Data Item: A B C D E F G H I J

Frequencies:·20 03 16 12 02 08 06 05 18 10

Figure 3.26(a) to (h) shows how to construct the tree using the above algorithms. In figure 3.26(a) each data item belongs to its own sub-tree and the two sub-trees with smallest frequencies are shaded.

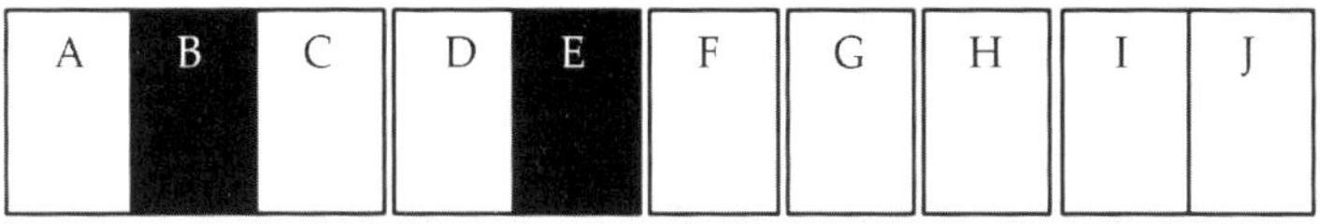

Figure 3.26(a) Two shaded sub-trees.

In Figure 3.26(b) the two shaded sub-trees with smallest frequencies are joined together to form a sub-tree with frequency ·05.

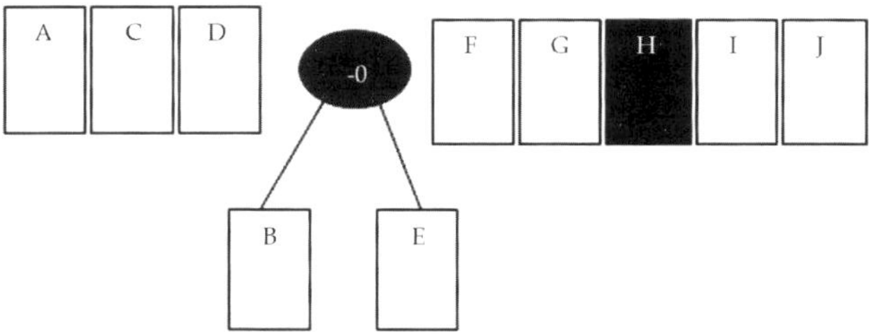

Figure 3.26(b) Two sub-trees of lowest frequencies.

Again, the current two sub-trees of lowest frequencies are joined and this process of joining of two sub-trees with lowest frequencies is continued as shown in figure 3.26(c) to (i).

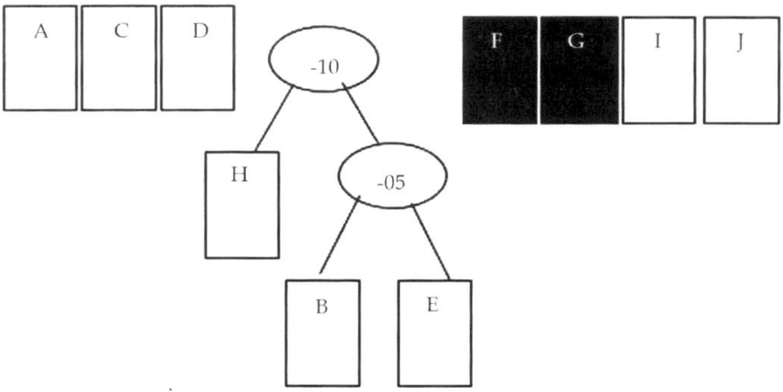

Figure 3.26(c). Two sub-trees of lowest frequencies.

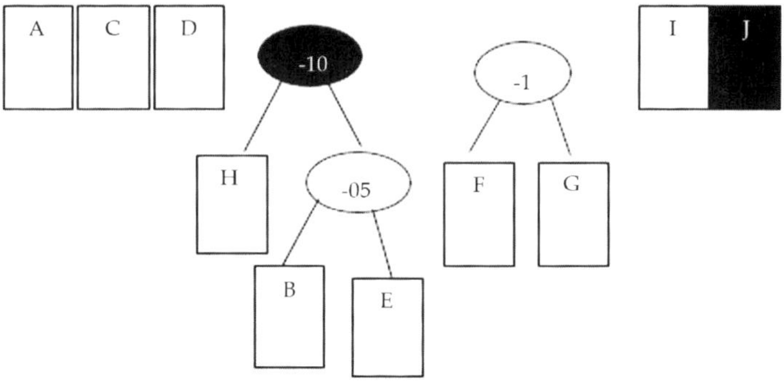

Figure 3.26(d). Two sub-trees of lowest frequencies.

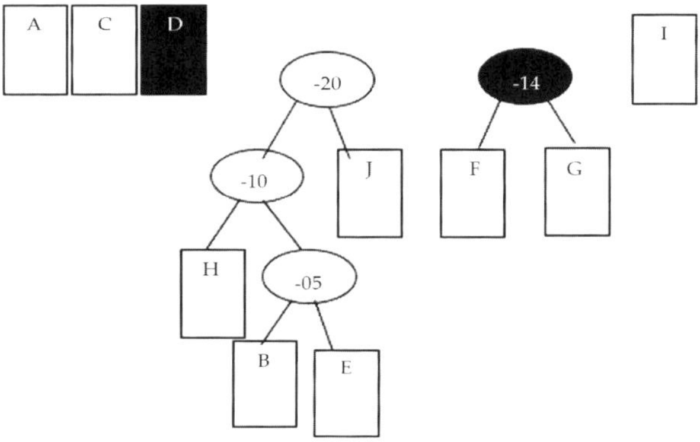

Figure 3.26(e). Two sub-trees of lowest frequencies.

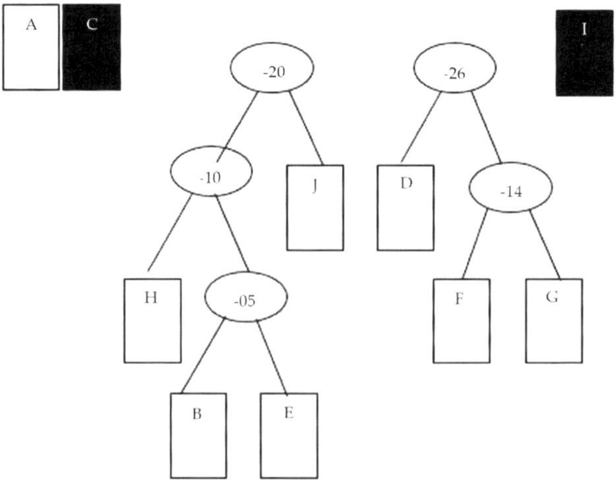

Figure 3.26(f). Two sub-trees of lowest frequencies.

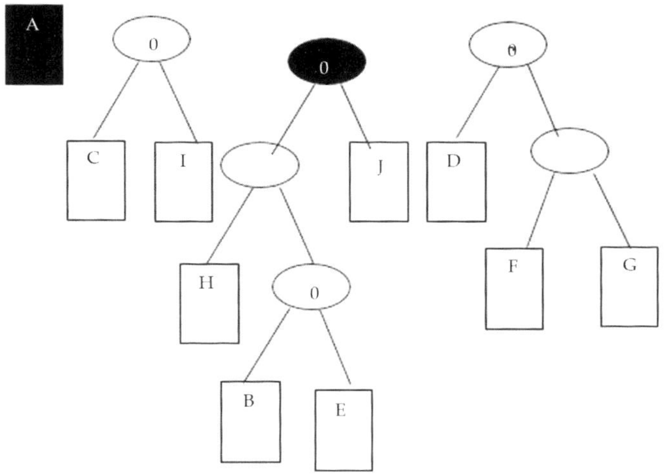

Figure 3.26(g). Two sub-trees of lowest frequencies.

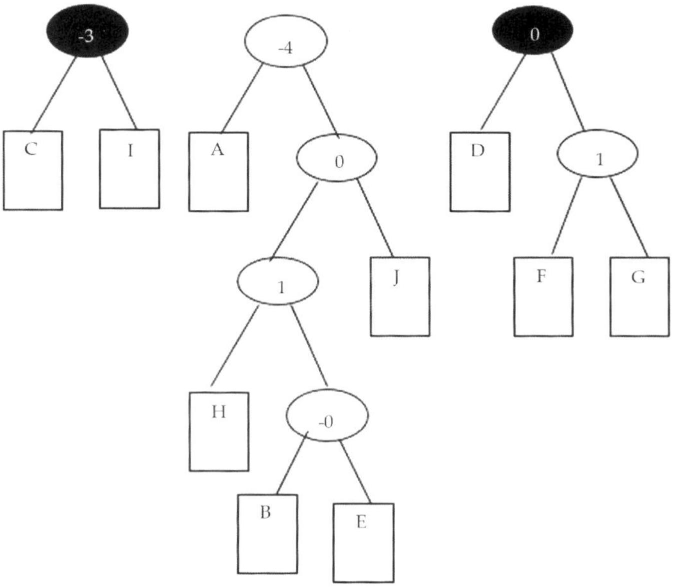

Figure 3.26(h). Two sub-trees of lowest frequencies.

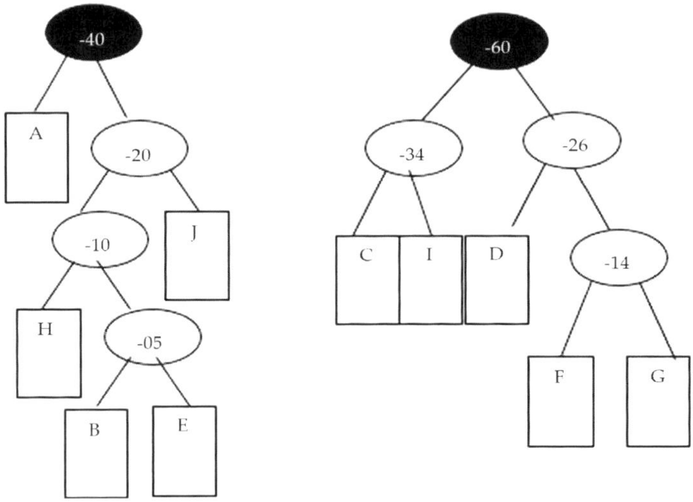

Figure 3.26(i). Two sub-trees of lowest frequencies.

Figure 3.26(j) shows the final tree formed when only two remaining sub-trees are joined together.

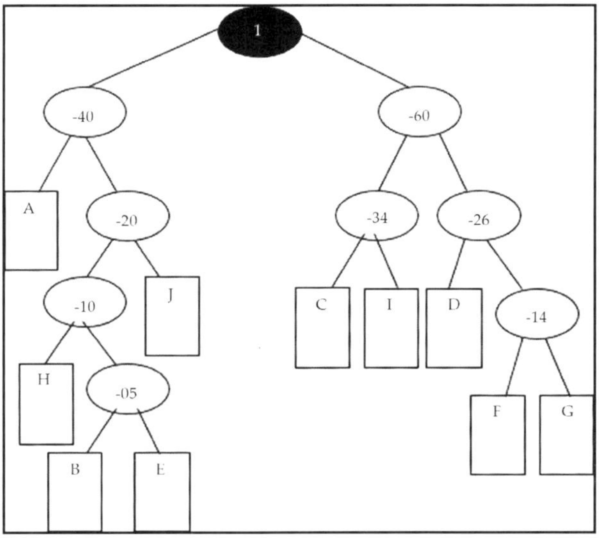

Figure 3.26(j). final tree formed (two remaining sub-trees).

3.9.2. Decision Tree

Rooted trees can be used to model problems in which a series of decisions leads to a solution. For example, a binary search tree can be used to locate items based on a series of comparisons where each comparison tells us whether we have located the item, or whether we should go down the left or right sub-tree.

More generally, we may have a rooted tree in which each internal node corresponds to a decision. At each such node, we may have a number of children (i.e., sub-trees) that correspond to each possible outcome of the decision. Such a tree is called a decision tree.

The possible solutions to a problem (i.e., set of choices that may be taken in the problem) correspond to the distinct paths from the root to the leaves of the tree.

3.9.3. Game Tree

Consider a two-player game. A solution to the game is a sequence of their alternate moves, which leads one of them to win. The solution space is the set of all possible solutions.

A rooted tree called a game tree is a useful representation of the solution space. In the game tree, a solution corresponds to a path from the root to a leaf.

On the path, edges correspond to moves of two players alternately. Suppose that you play first and the opponent plays next. Then, edges from nodes at even levels to nodes at odd levels correspond to your moves.

You may try to maximize some objective function, which is associated with likelihood of your winning. On the other hand, edges from nodes at odd levels to nodes at even levels correspond to the opponent's moves. The opponent tries to minimize the objective function so as to minimize the likelihood of your winning and hence to maximize the likelihood of his/her winning.

3.10. SEQUENTIAL OR LINEAR SEARCH

The search of a list of items in consecutive order, by examining each item in the list in turn is called a linear or, sequential search.

The most straightforward solution to this problem is to start with the lowest array index, and compare the value of the separately held item in question systematically to every item in the array to see if it is equal to one of them.

A linear search does not depend for its success on the items being searched already being in any particular order. The value being sought will either be equal to one of the ones already in the array, or it will not. If it is, the index number of the position at which it is found can be returned. Otherwise, some indication that the search has failed must be passed back. Let us consider the following list of numbers:

11 34 23 45 38 10 56 36 27 67

- **Search the Element 38:** In this technique, the searched item is compared with all the items of the array one by one, i.e., element 38 is compared to the first element 11, which is not equal to 38. Now, 38 is compared with next element, i.e., 34. It is also not equal to 38. This process continues till we reach the end of the list or the searched element is found in the list. The element 38 is found in the list at position 4. So, the search is successful and returns the position of the element within the list, i.e., 4.
- **Search the Element 40:** In this technique, the searched item is compared with all the items of the array one by one, i.e., element 40 is compared to the first element 11, which is not equal to 40. Now, 40 is compared with next element, i.e., 34. It is also not equal to 40. This process continues till we reach the end of the list or the searched element is found in the list. The element 40 is not found in the list. So, the search is unsuccessful and returns the element, which is not found in the list.

The following is the algorithm, which implements the above processing of searching:

A. Algorithm: Let LIST be a linear array with n elements and ITEM is a given element of information. This algorithm finds the position(POS) of ITEM in LIST, if the search is successful or sets POS=0. If the searched item is not found in the list, it means search is unsuccessful. Following are the steps for sequential search algorithm:

a. [Initialize counter]

Set (counter) i=1, POS=0

b. [Search element]

Repeat Step (c) and (d) while(POS==0 || i<=n)

c. [Compare searched ITEM with each element of the LIST] If ITEM == LIST[i] then the search is successful and print the

ITEM is found in the list at POS

Set POS = i, i = i + 1 and continue

d. Otherwise Set i = i+1, if(i==n) then break

e. If POS == 0 then print 'ITEM is not found in the array LIST and search is unsuccessful'

f. end.

B. Equivalent Function in C

```
void sequential_search(int LIST[], int n, int ITEM)
{
int i=1, POS;
POS = 0;
while((i<=n) || (POS==0))
{
if(ITEM == LIST[i])
{
POS = i;
printf("The search item %d is found in the LIST at position %d.\n,"ITEM,
POS);
i = i +1;
continue;
}
else
i = i +1;
if(i==n)
break;
}
if(POS == 0)
printf("The searched item %d is not found in the LIST.\n,"ITEM);
}
```

C. Implementation of Sequential Search Function: The following program search_sequential.c implements the sequential search function using the array LIST:

```
/* search_sequential.c*/
#include<stdio.h>
void sequential_search(int[],int,int);
void main()
{
int i,n,LIST[100],ITEM;
printf("This program search the specified ITEM in the LIST and return the position(POS) of the ITEM, (if found) using sequential search!!!\n");
printf("Please enter the number of elements in the LIST:\n");
scanf("%d,"&n);
printf("Enter the element of the LIST:\n");
for (i=1;i<=n;i++)
{
scanf("%d,"&LIST[i]);
}
printf("Element to be searched:\n");
scanf("%d,"&ITEM);
printf("Entered elements in the LIST are:\n");
for (i=1;i<=n;i++)
{
printf("%d\t,"LIST[i]);
}
sequential_search(LIST,n,ITEM);
}
void sequential_search(int LIST[], int n, int ITEM)
{
int i=1, POS;
POS = 0;
while((i<=n) || (POS==0))
{
if(ITEM == LIST[i])
```

```
{
POS = i;
printf("\nThe search item %d is found in the LIST at position %d.\n,"ITEM,
POS);
i = i +1;
continue;
}
else
i = i +1;
if(i==n)
break;
}
if(POS == 0)
printf("\nThe searched item %d is not found in the LIST.\n,"ITEM);
}
```

D. **Output of the Program:** This program search the specified ITEM in the LIST and return the position(POS) of the ITEM, (if found) using sequential search!!!

```
Please enter the number of elements in the LIST:
10
Enter the element of the LIST:
12
23
34
45
56
67
78
89
90
23
Element to be searched:
```

23

Entered elements in the LIST are:

12 23 34 45 56 67 78 89 90 23

The search item 23 is found in the LIST at position 2.

The search item 23 is found in the LIST at position 10.

This program search the specified ITEM in the LIST and return the position(POS) of the ITEM, (if found) using sequential search!!!

Please enter the number of elements in the LIST:

5

Enter the element of LIST:

12

23

21

34

43

Element to be searched:

29

Entered elements in the LIST are:

12 23 21 34 43

The searched item 29 is not found in the LIST.

E. **Analysis of Sequential Search Method:** Let's examine how long it will take to find an item matching a key in the LIST we have discussed so far. We are interested in:

i. the average time;

ii. the worst-case time;

iii. the best possible time.

However, we will generally be most concerned with the worst-case time as calculations based on worst-case times can lead to guaranteed performance predictions. Conveniently, the worst-case times are generally easier to calculate than average times.

If there are n items in our LIST, whether it is stored as an array or as a linked list, then it is obvious that in the worst case, when there is no item in the LIST with the desired key, then n comparisons of the key with keys of the items in the LIST will have to be made.

To simplify analysis and comparison of algorithms, we look for a dominant operation and count the number of times that dominant operation has to be performed. In the case of searching, the dominant operation is the comparison, since the search requires n comparisons in the worst case, we say this is a O(n) (pronounce this "big-Oh-n" or "Oh-n") algorithm. The best case in which the first comparison returns a match, requires a single comparison and is O(1). The average time depends on the probability that the key will be found in the LIST, this is something that we would not expect to know in the majority of cases. Thus, in this case, as in most others, estimation of the average time is of little utility. If the performance of the system is vital, i.e., it's a part of a life-critical system, then we must use the worst case in our design calculations as it represents the best guaranteed performance.

3.11. BINARY SEARCH

However, if we place our items in an array and sort them in either ascending or descending order on the key first, then we can obtain much better performance with an algorithm called binary search.

In binary search, we first compare the key with the item in the middle position of the array. If there's a match, we can return immediately. If the key is less than the middle key, then the item sought must lie in the lower half of the array; if it's greater then the item sought must lie in the upper half of the array. So we repeat the procedure on the lower (or upper) half of the array.

There are two termination conditions in binary search:

i. If low > high then the partition to be searched has no elements in it; and
ii. If there is a match with the element in the middle of the current partition, then we can return immediately.

Let us take some examples for explaining the processing of binary search method. Let us consider the following sorted list of numbers:

11, 21, 46, 52, 55, 67, 79, 81, 86, 97, 99

1. **Search for the Value 81:**
   a. The terms are numbered from 0. 10. The first search position is 5((0+10)/2=5), at which is found the number 67. The value 81 is compared to it and 81 is greater than 67(81>67).

b. Next the items from position 6 through 10 are considered. These are 79, 81, 86, 97, 99. Here, the search position is 8((6+10)/2=8) at which is the number 86, and 81 is less than 86(81<86).

c. Thus the list is reduced to items 6 through 7. The remaining list is 79, 81. The search position item is the first one holding 79, and 81 is greater than 79(81>79).

d. All that remains is the list with item 6 or 81 in it. The one wanted is equal to 81, and so has been found. So the search item 81 is found in the list.

Table 3.2 tabulates the processing steps of the searching.

Table 3.2. The Processing Steps of the Searching

Range	**List**	**Position**	**Result**	**New Range**
[0. 10]	The whole list	5 (67)	Greater	[0. 4]
[0. 4]	79, 81, 86, 97, 99	8 (86)	Less	[6. 7]
[3. 4]	79, 81	6 (79)	Greater	[7. 6] success

2. Search for 50 in the List

a. The terms are numbered from 0. 10. The first search position is 5((0+10/2=5), at which is found the number 67. The value 50 is compared to it and 50 is less than 67(50<67).

b. Next, the items from position 0 through 4 are considered. These are 11, 21, 46, 52, 55. Here, the search position is 2((0+4)/2=2) at which is the number 46, and 50 is greater than 46(50>46).

c. Thus, the list is reduced to items 3 through 4. The remaining list is 52, 55. The search position item is the first one holding 52, and 50 is less than 52(50<52).

d. All that remains is the list with item 4 or 55 in it. The one wanted is not equal to 55, and so has been not found. The bottom counter would be greater than the top counter; there would be no list left, and the search would fail and the item 50 is not found in the list.

Table 3.3 tabulates the processing steps of the searching:

Table 3.3. The Processing Steps of the Searching

Range	List	Position	Result	New Range
[0. 10]	The whole list	5 (67)	Less	[0. 4]
[0. 4]	11, 21, 46, 52, 55	2 (46)	Greater	[3. 4]
[3. 4]	52, 55	3 (52)	Less	[4. 3] fails

The following is the algorithm, which implement the above processing of searching:

A. **Algorithm:** Let LIST be a sorted linear array with n elements and ITEM is a given element of information. The variables BEG, END, and MID denotes the beginning, end, and middle position of the elements of LIST, respectively. This algorithm finds the position POS of ITEM in LIST, if the search is successful or sets POS=0. If the searched item is not found in the list, i.e., search is unsuccessful. The following are the steps for binary search algorithm:

a. [Initialize counter]

Set (counter) BEG=0, END = n, POS=0

b. [Search element]

Repeat Step (c) to (f) while(POS==0 && END>=BEG)

c. [Find the mid point of the LIST]

MID = (BEG+END)/2

d. [Compare searched ITEM with the item at mid of the LIST]

If ITEM == LIST[MID] then the search is successful

Set POS = MID and break

e. [Otherwise, check whether or not searched ITEM is less than the mid item of the LIST]

If ITEM < LIST[MID] then

Set END = MID –1

f. [Otherwise, check whether or not searched ITEM is greater than the mid item of the LIST]

Set BEG = MID +1

g. If POS==0 then

Print 'ITEM is not found in the array LIST and search is unsuccessful'

h. [Otherwise search is successful]

Print 'search is successful and item is found in the LIST at position POS'

i. End.

B. Equivalent Function in C

```
void binary_search(int LIST[], int n, int ITEM)
{
int BEG,END,POS,MID;
BEG=1;
END=n;
POS = 0;
while((BEG<=END) && (POS==0))
{
MID = (BEG+END)/2;
if(ITEM == LIST[MID])
{
POS = MID;
break;
}
else
if(ITEM < LIST[MID])
END = MID – 1;
else
BEG = MID + 1;
}
if(POS == 0)
printf("The searched item %d is not found in the LIST.\n,"ITEM);
else
printf("The searched item%d is found in the LIST at position %d.\n,"ITEM,
POS);
}
```

C. Implementation of Binary Search Function: The following program search_binary.c implements the sequential search function using the sorted array LIST:

```
/*search_binary.c*/
#include<stdio.h>
void binary_search(int[],int,int);
void main()
{
int i,n,LIST[100],ITEM;
printf("This program searches the specified ITEM in the sorted LIST and
returns the position(POS) of the ITEM, (if found) using binary search!!!\n");
printf("Please enter the number of elements in the LIST:\n");
scanf("%d,"&n);
printf("Enter the element of the LIST in ascending order:\n");
for (i=1;i<=n;i++)
{
scanf("%d,"&LIST[i]);
}
printf("Element to be searched:\n");
scanf("%d,"&ITEM);
printf("Entered elements in the LIST are:\n");
for (i=1;i<=n;i++)
{
printf("%d\t,"LIST[i]);
}
binary_search(LIST,n,ITEM);
}
void binary_search(int LIST[], int n, int ITEM)
{
int BEG,END,POS,MID;
BEG=1;
END=n;
POS = 0;
while((BEG<=END) && (POS==0))
```

```
{
MID = (BEG+END)/2;
if(ITEM == LIST[MID])
{
POS = MID;
break;
}
else
if(ITEM < LIST[MID])
END = MID – 1;
Else
BEG = MID + 1;
}
if(POS == 0)
printf("The searched item %d is not found in the LIST.\n,"ITEM);
else
printf("The searched item %d is found in the LIST at position %d.\n,"ITEM,
POS);
}
```

D. Output of the Program: This program searches the specified ITEM in the sorted LIST and returns the position(POS) of the ITEM, (if found) using binary search!!!

Please enter the number of elements in the LIST:

10

Enter the element of the LIST in ascending order:

11

12

23

34

45

56

67

78

89

90

Element to be searched:

56

Entered elements in the LIST are:

11 12 23 34 45 56 67 78 89 90

The searched item 56 is found in the LIST at position 6.

This program searches the specified ITEM in the sorted LIST and returns the position(POS) of the ITEM, (if found) using binary search!!!

Please enter the number of elements in the LIST:

5

Enter the element of the LIST in ascending order:

12

23

34

45

56

Element to be searched:

33

Entered elements in the LIST are:

12 23 34 45 56

The searched item 33 is not found in the LIST.

E. **Analysis of Binary Search Method:** Each step of the algorithm divides the block of items being searched in half. We can divide a set of n items in half at most $\log_2 n$ times. Thus the running time of a binary search is proportional to log n and we say this is a O(log n) algorithm.

F. **Comparison between Sequential and Binary Search:** Binary search requires a more complex program than our sequential search and thus for small n it may run slower than the sequential search. However, for large n,

lim log n

= 0

n->∞ n

Thus at large n, log n is much smaller than n, consequently an O(log n) algorithm is much faster than an O(n) one (Figure 3.27).

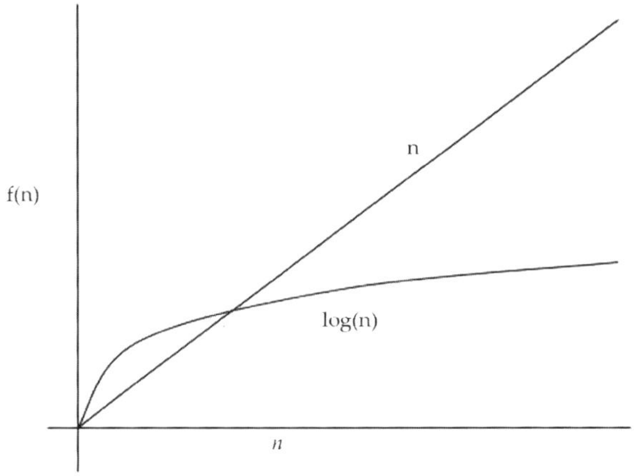

Figure 3.27. Plot of n and log n vs n.

3.12. HEIGHT BALANCED TREE

A height-balanced tree is a binary tree that has equal depth throughout the tree, +/– one level, i.e., heights do not differ from greater than one. In Figure 3.28(a), the left sub-tree of the tree has a depth of three, while the right sub-tree has a depth of two, so they are balanced, since their heights do not differ by greater than one. However, in Figure 3.28(b), the left sub-tree of the tree has a depth of three, while the right sub-tree has a depth of one, so it is not a balanced tree, since their heights differ by greater than one

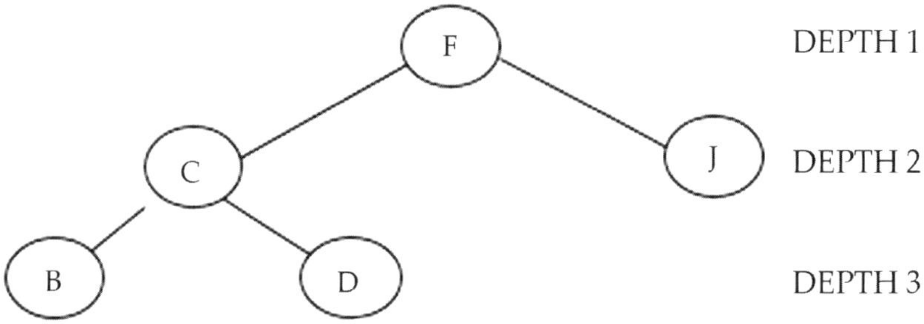

Figure 3.28(a). Height balanced tree.

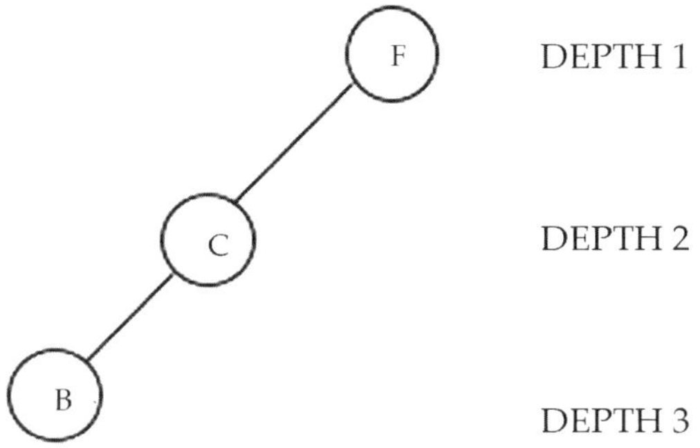

Figure 3.28(b). Height unbalanced tree.

Height balanced trees are used in order to maximize the efficiency of the operations on a tree. An unbalanced tree which, in the worst case operates like a linked list (complexity of linked list search is O(N). By balancing the tree the worst case complexity can be reduced to O(Log N).

3.13. WEIGHT BALANCED TREE

The nodes of a weight-balanced tree contain a data element, a left and right pointer, and a probability or weight field. The data element and left and right pointers are essentially the same as any other node. The probability field is a special addition for a weight-balanced tree. This field holds the probability of the node being accessed again. There are many different ways of coming up with this number. A good example of such a metric is the computing the probability according to the number of times the node has been previously searched for (Figure 3.29).

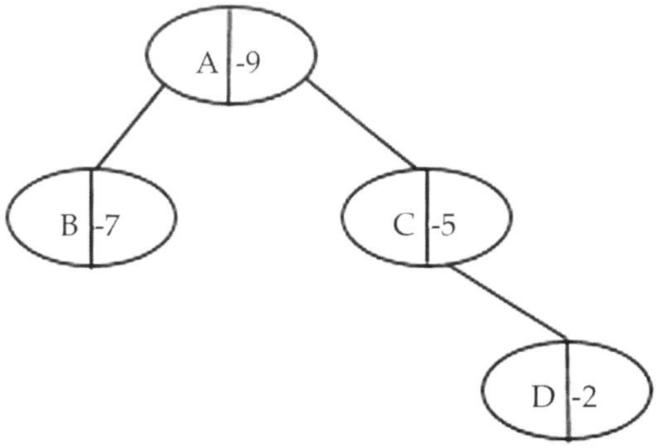

Figure 3.29. A weight balanced tree.

When the tree is set up, the nodes with the highest probability of access are placed at the top. That way the nodes that are most likely to be accessed have the lowest search time. The tree is balanced, if the weights in the right and left sub trees are as equal as possible.

The average length of a search in a weighted tree is equal to the sum of: probability × depth for every node in the tree

The tree is set up with the highest weighted node at the top of the tree or sub-tree. The left sub-tree contains nodes whose data values are less than the current node, and the right sub-tree contains nodes that have data values greater than the current data value.

3.14. MULTIWAY SEARCH TREES

Each internal node v of a multi-way search tree T has at least two children, contains d–1 items, where; d is the number of children of v. An item is of the form (k_i,x_i) for $1 \leq i \leq d-1$, where; k_i is a key such that $k_i \leq k_{i+1}$ for $1 \leq i < d-1$, x_i is an element that contains two pseudo-items $k_0 = -\infty$ and $k_d = +\infty$ (Figure 3.30(a)).

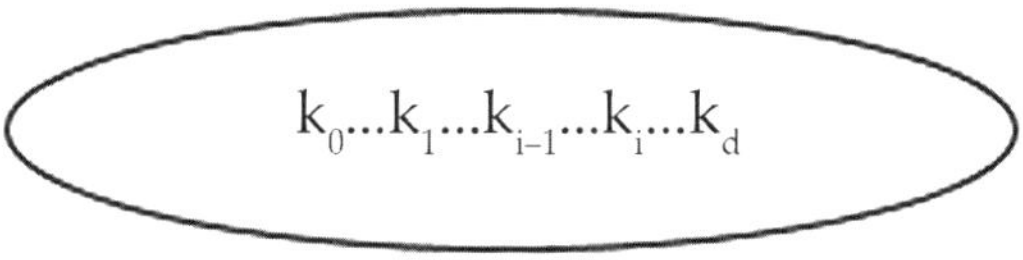

Figure 3.30(a). Multiway Search Trees.

Children of each internal node are "between" the items in that node. If T_i is the sub-tree rooted at child v_i, then all keys in T_i fall between the keys k_{i-1} and k_i, that is, $k_{i-1} \leq T_i \leq k_i$ (Figure 3.30(b)).

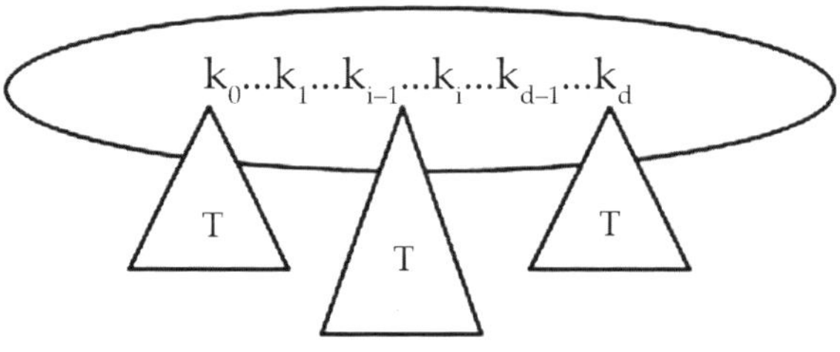

Figure 3.30(b). Sub-tree rooted.

A multi way search tree T storing n items has n+1 external nodes.

3.15. DIGITAL SEARCH TREES

A digital search tree is a binary tree where each node has one element. All nodes in the left sub-tree of a node at level i (root at level 0, its children at level 1, etc.) have an ith bit of 0. Similarly, all nodes in the right sub-tree of a node at level i have an ith bit of 1.

Since we assume no duplicate keys. Hence, tree can have height at most log k, the number of bits in our keys. The search method looks like this:

```
void digital_search (Tree t, Key k)
{
……
digital_search_sub(t.root, k, 0);
……
}
digital_search_sub(Node n, Key k, int b)
{
if (n==null)
printf("not there\n");
if (k == n.key)
return n.val;
if (digit(k,b) == 0)
return digital_search_sub(n.left, k, b+1);
else
return digital_search_sub(n.right, k, b+1);
}
```

Insert follows the same descent strategy and puts the new node where the first null is reached. Delete can find the element, delete it, and recursively move children into their parent's position until every node again has an element.

Digital search trees are not sorted. So, we do not have to replace the element with its successor. In fact, despite efficient insert, lookup, and delete, digital search trees do not have efficient predecessor and successor.

3.16. HASHING

It is a searching technique, which is independent of the number n of elements in the collection of data.

3.16.1. Hash Table

The hash table contains key values with pointers to the corresponding records. The basic idea of a hash table is that we have to place a key value into a location in the hash table, the location will be calculated from the key value itself. This one-one mapping between a key value and index in the hash table is known as hashing.

3.16.2. Hashing Function

The general idea of using the key to determine the address of a record is an excellent idea, but it must be modified so that a great deal of space in not wasted. This modification takes the form of a function H from the set K of keys into the set L of memory addresses, i.e.,

$H: K \rightarrow L$

This function is called the hash function. The two principal criteria for selecting a hash function $H: K \rightarrow L$ are:

a. The function H should be easy and quick to compute; and

b. The function H should distribute the elements of our collection as uniformly as possible to the L slots of the hash table. The key criterion is that there should be a minimum number of collisions.

Following are the some popular hash functions, which can be used in many applications:

1. **The Division Method:** One of the most widely accepted hashing function is the division method, which is defined as follows:

Select a number m larger than the number n of keys in K. The hash function H is defined as:

$H(k) = k(\text{mod } m)$ or $H(k) = k(\text{mod } m) + 1$

The first formula is used when the hash addresses range from 0 to m–1, otherwise 1 to m. Where k∈K, a key value. The operator mod denotes the module arithmetic, which is equal to the remainder of dividing k by m. Let us take an example, if m=13 and k=32 then,

$H(34) = 32(\text{mod } 13) = 6$ or

$H(34) = 32(\text{mod } 13) + 1 = 7$

When using this method, we usually avoid certain values of m. Powers of 2 are usually avoided, for k mod 2^b simply selects the b low order bits of k. Unless we know that all the 2^b possible values of the lower order bits are equally likely, this will not be a good choice, because some bits of the key are not used in the hash function. Prime numbers, which are close to powers of 2, seem to be generally good choices for m.

For example, if we have 4,000 elements, and we have chosen an overflow table organization, but wish to have the probability of collisions quite low, then we might choose m = 4093(4093 is the largest prime less than 4096 = 2^{12}).

2. **Midsquare Method:** In this method, a key is multiplied by itself and the address is calculated by selecting an appropriate number of bits or digits from the middle of the number. This selection usually depends on the size of the hash table. The function is defined as:

$H(k) = m$

where; m is obtained by deleting digits or bits from both ends of k^2.

Let us take an example, consider a key value of four digits of integer type and we require a hash addresses of 3 digits.

k: 1234

k^2: 1522756

H(k): 227

This method gives a good results when applied to certain keys sets but is criticized because of time consuming multiplication operation.

3. **Folding Method:** In this method, key k is partitioned into number of parts, $k_1, k_2, \ldots k_n$, where each of which has the same number of digits as the required address except possible the last part k_n. The parts are added together, ignoring the final carry, to form an address. That is:

$H(k) = k_1 + k_2 + \ldots + k_n$

There are various variations in this method. In fold shifting method, the even number parts $k_2, k_4, \ldots$are reversed and added. In fold shifting method the boundary parts k_1, k_n are reversed before they are added to the other parts. Let us take an example in which the size of the each part of the key is 3.

k: 356942781

parts: $k_1 = 356$ $k_2 = 942$ $k_3 = 781$

Fold shifting: $k_1 = 356$ $k_2 = 249$ $k_3 = 781$

356+249+781 =1386

Fold boundary: $k_1 = 653$ $k_2 = 942$ $k_3 = 187$

653 + 942 + 187 = 1782

This method is also useful in converting multiword keys into a single word so that it can be used by the other hashing function.

3.16.3. Collisions Resolution Techniques

In the small number of cases, where multiple keys map to the same hash address, then elements with different keys may be stored in the same "slot" of the hash table. This situation is called the collision (Table 3.4). Various techniques are used to resolve the collisions:

1. **Linear Probing:** In linear probing, when a collision occurs, the new element is put in the next available spot (by doing a sequential search).

For example,

Insert: 49 18 89 48, Hash table size = 10, so

49% 10 = 9,

18% 10 = 8,

89% 10 = 9,

48% 10 = 8

Table 3.4. Collisions Resolution Techniques

	Insert 1	Insert 2	Insert 3	Insert 4
[0]	–	–	89	89
[1]	–	–	–	48
[2]	–	–	–	–
[3]	–	–	–	–
[4]	–	–	–	–
[5]	–	–	–	–
[6]	–	–	–	–
[7]	–	–	–	–

[8]	–	18	18	18
[9]	49	49	49	49

The problem with linear probing is that records tend to get cluste-red around each other, i.e., once an element is placed in the hash table the chances of it's adjacent element being filled are doubled (i.e., it can either be filled by a collision or directly). If two adjacent elements are filled then the chances of the next element being filled is three times that for an element with no neighbor.

2. **Quadratic Probing:** It is a collision resolution method that eliminates the primary clustering problem of linear probing. In quadratic probing, if there is a collision we first try and insert an element in the next adjacent space (at a distance of +1). If this is full we try a distance of 4 (2^2) then 9 (3^2) and so until we find an empty element. The full index function is of the form:

$(h + i^2)$ % HashTableSize for i = 0, 1, 2, 3, …

where; h is the initial hashed key value.

We take the modulus of the result so the search can wrap around to the beginning of the table. Even so not all the locations in a table may be able to be reached (especially if the table size is a power of 2). This means we may not be able to insert a value even though the table is not full. Generally though, in linear and quadratic probing, the hash table size is deliberately kept considerably larger than the number of expected keys, otherwise the performance of hashing becomes too slow (as the table becomes fuller more collisions occur and more probing is required to insert and retrieve elements) (Table 3.5).

For example,

As before insert: 49 18 89 48, Hash table size = 10

Table 3.5. Insert and retrieve elements

	Insert 1	**Insert 2**	**Insert 3**	**Insert 4**
[0]	–	–	89	89
[1]	–	–	–	–
[2]	–	–	–	48
[3]	–	–	–	–
[4]	–	–	–	–

[5]	–	–	–	–
[6]	–	–	–	–
[7]	–	–	–	–
[8]	–	18	18	18
[9]	49	49	49	49

3. **Double Hashing:** Another method of probing is to use a second hash function to calculate the probing distance. For example, we define a second hash function $Hash_2(Key)$ and we use the return value as the probe value. If this results in a collision we try a distance of 2 * $Hash_2(Key)$, then 3 * $Hash_2(Key)$ and so on. A common second hash function is:

$Hash_2(Key) = R – (Key \% R)$

where; R is a prime number smaller than the hash table size. The full index function is then of the form:

(h + i*(R – (Key % R)) % HashTableSize for i = 0, 1, 2, 3, …

where; h is the initial hashed key value.

4. **Rehashing:** If the table gets too full, the running time for the operations will start taking too long and inserts might fail with quadratic probing.

The standard solution in this case is to build an entirely new hash table approximately twice the size of the original, calculate a new hash value for each key and then insert all keys into the new table (then destroying the old table). This is known as reorganization or rehashing.

5. **Chaining:** In this method, we keep a linked list of all elements that hash to the same value. The hash table itself becomes an array of pointers to list nodes instead of an array of elements that hold actual records. When collisions occur in chaining, elements are simply added to the appropriate linked list.

For example,

Insert: 0 1 4 9 16 25 36 49 64 81,

Hash table size = 10, so

Table 3.6. Hash table

[0]	=>	0	NULL	–	–
[1]	=>	1	=>	81	NULL
[2]	NULL	–	–	–	–
[3]	NULL	–	–	–	–
[4]	=>	4	=>	64	NULL
[5]	=>	25	NULL	–	–
[6]	=>	16	=>	36	NULL
[7]	NULL	–	–	–	–
[8]	NULL	–	–	–	–
[9]	=>	9	=>	49	NULL

3.16.4. Implementation of a Chained Hash Table

The following program hash_chained.c shows the implementation of chaining with keys taken from set of values from the int data type:

```
/* hash_chained.c*/
#include <stdio.h>
#include <stdlib.h>
#define HTABLESIZE 10
struct Node
{
struct Node *Next;
int Data;
};
struct Node *HashTable[HTABLESIZE];
void HashTableCreate();
void HashTableDestroy();
int HashTableInsert(int); // = –1 on failure, =0 if ok
struct Node *HashTableFind(int); // search return data node
int HashTableDelete(int); // =0 on ok, = –1 on fail
int HashFunction(int);
void HashTablePrint(); // Print all elements in table
```

```
void main()
{
int i;
HashTableCreate();
for(i=1;i<200;++i) // Insert values from 1–199
{
HashTableInsert(i);
}
HashTablePrint();        // Print out all of the Hash Table
for(i=50;i<=90;++i) // Remove keys 50–90
{
HashTableDelete(i);
}
HashTablePrint();        // Print out Hash table
HashTableDestroy();   // Destroy the Hash Table
}
void HashTableCreate()
{
int i;
for(i=0;i<HTABLESIZE;++i)
{
HashTable[i]=0;
}
}
void HashTableDestroy()
{
int i;
struct Node *p,*temp;
for(i=0;i<HTABLESIZE;++i)
{
for(p=HashTable[i];p!=0;)
```

```
{
temp=p;
p=p->Next;
free(temp);
}
}
}
int HashTableInsert(int data) // = –1 on failure, =0 if ok
{
int ind;
struct Node *nw;
nw=(struct Node *)malloc(sizeof(struct Node));
if(nw==0)
{
return –1;
}
nw->Data=data;
ind=HashFunction(data);
nw->Next=HashTable[ind];
HashTable[ind]=nw;
return 0;
}
struct Node *HashTableFind(int data) // search return data node
{
struct Node *p;
for(p=HashTable[HashFunction(data)];p!=0;p=p->Next)
{
if(p->Data==data)
{
return p;
}
```

```
}
return 0;
}
int HashTableDelete(int data) // =0 ok, = –1 on fail
{
int ind;
struct Node *p,*temp;
ind=HashFunction(data);
if((p=HashTable[ind])==0)
{
return –1;
}
if(p->Data==data)
{
HashTable[ind]=p->Next;
free(p);
return 0;
}
for(; p->Next!=0; p=p->Next)
{
if(p->Next->Data==data)
{
temp=p->Next;
p->Next=temp->Next;
free(temp);
return 0;
}
}
return –1;
}
int HashFunction(int data)
```

```
{
return data%HTABLESIZE; // Simple Function
}
void HashTablePrint() // Print all elements in table
{
int i;
for(i=0;i<HTABLESIZE;++i)
{
struct Node *p;
printf("Slot %d:,"i);
for(p=HashTable[i];p!=0;p=p->Next)
{
printf(" %d,"p->Data);
}
printf("\n");
}
printf("\n");
}
```

Exercise

- **Q.1.** What is the purpose of writing the more complicated code to do binary searches, when a linear one will not only find the item if it is there, but does not even require the data to be sorted in the first place?
- **Q.2.** On your system, for what list length is a binary search more time efficient than a linear search?
- **Q.3.** Write an algorithm to display the elements of a binary tree in level order, i.e., list the element in the root, followed by the elements in depth 1, then the elements at depth 2, and so on.
- **Q.4.** An in order threaded binary tree is given. Write an algorithm to find the pre order and post order threaded binary tree.

- **Q.5.** Suppose the following sequence list the nodes of a binary tree T in preorder and inorder, respectively:

Preorder: G B Q A C K F P D E R H

Inorder: Q B K C F A G P E D H R

Draw the diagram of the tree.

- **Q.6.** Suppose the following eight numbers are inserted in order into an empty binary search tree T:

50 33 44 22 77 35 60 40

Draw the tree T.

- **Q.7.** Draw the binary expression for the following expression:

$E = (3x - y)(5a + b)^4$

- **Q.8.** Write a function that counts number of nodes in a binary tree.
- **Q.9.** Draw the binary search tree whose elements are inserted in the following order:

50 72 96 107 26 12 11 9 2 10 25 51 16 17 95

- **Q.10.** Write a program, which uses the mid square method to find the 2-digit hash address of a 4-digit employee number key.
- **Q.11.** Draw all 14 binary trees with four nodes.
- **Q.12.** Give the pre order, inorder, post order, and level-order traversals for the following trees:

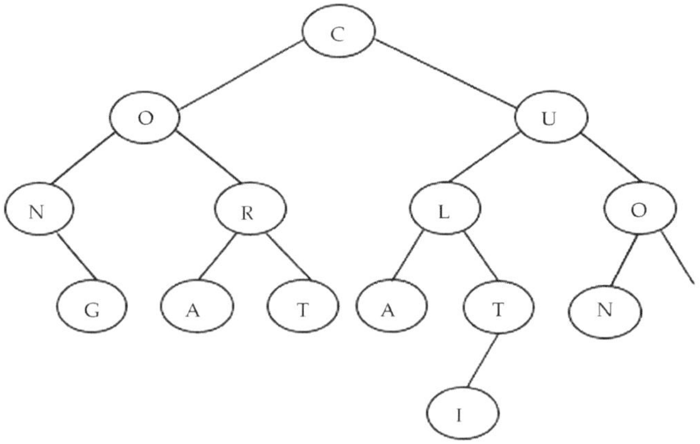

- **Q.13.** Give the pre order, inorder, post order, and level-order traversals for the following trees:

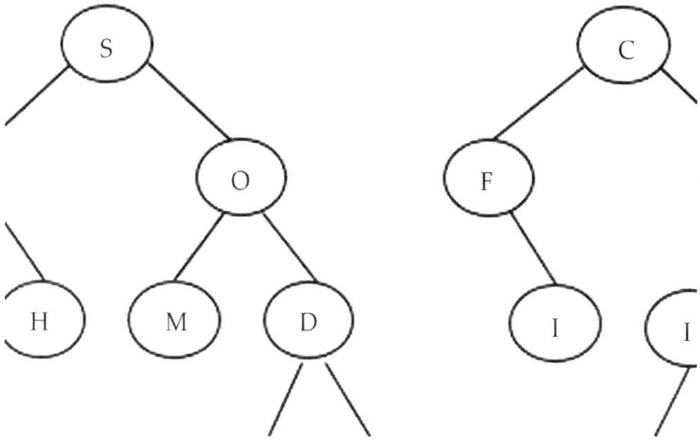

- **Q.14.** Draw the expression tree for the following expressions. Evaluate the tree by evaluating one level at each step.

a. (3+6) × (5%2)

b. ((((8 – 1) – 2) – 3) × 3) + 1

CHAPTER 4

SORTING ALGORITHMS

CONTENTS

4.1. INTRODUCTION

This chapter covers various sorting techniques like- bubble sort, insertion sort, selection sort, quick sort, merge sort, address calculation sort and heap sort. These techniques are discussed with the help of array of integers. Complexity of the algorithm is also discussed at the end of the unit. An exercise at the end of chapter is given.

4.2. SORTING

Sorting is one of the most important operations performed by computers. In the days of magnetic tape storage before modern data-bases, it was almost certainly the most common operation performed by computers as most "database" updating was done by sorting transactions and merging them with a master file. It's still important for presentation of data extracted from databases: most people prefer to get reports sorted into some relevant order before wading through pages of data.

The basic premise behind sorting an array is that, its elements start out in some (presumably) random order and need to be arranged from lowest to highest. If the number of items to be sorted is small, a reader may be able to tell at a glance what the correct order ought to be. If there are a large number of items, a more systematic approach is required. To do this, it is necessary to think about what it means for an array to be sorted. It is easy to see that the list 1, 5, 6, 19, 23, 45, 67, 98, 124, 401 is sorted, whereas the list 4, 1, 90, 34, 100, 45, 23, 82, 11, 0, 600, 345 is not. The property that makes the second one "not sorted" is that, there are adjacent elements that are out of order. The first item is greater than the second instead of less, and likewise the third is greater than the fourth and so on.

Once this observation is made, it is not very hard to devise a sort that precedes by examining adjacent elements to see if they are in order, and swapping them if they are not. The following are the methods, which can be used for performing sorting:

- Bubble sort;
- Selection sort;
- Insertion sort;
- Quick sort;
- Merge sort;

- Address calculation sort;
- Heap sort.

4.2.1. Bubble Sort

In this sorting algorithm, multiple swapping takes place in one pass. Smaller elements move or 'bubble' up to the top of the list, hence the name bubble is given to the algorithm.

This most elementary sorting method proceeds by scanning through the elements one pair at a time, and swapping any adjacent pairs it finds to be out of order. Thus, for the list in the example given below, the first two items are swapped, then the (new) second item is compared to the third (and not swapped,) the third is compared to the fourth, and so on to the end. The list would be altered as follows (comparisons are emphasized):

4, 1, 90, 34, 100, 45, 23, 82, 11, 0, 600, 345

1, *4, 90*, 34, 100, 45, 23, 82, 11, 0, 600, 345

1, 4, *90, 34*, 100, 45, 23, 82, 11, 0, 600, 345

1, 4, 34, *90, 100*, 45, 23, 82, 11, 0, 600, 345

1, 4, 34, 90, *100, 45*, 23, 82, 11, 0, 600, 345

1, 4, 34, 90, 45, *100, 23*, 82, 11, 0, 600, 345

1, 4, 34, 90, 45, 23, *100, 82*, 11, 0, 600, 345

1, 4, 34, 90, 45, 23, 82, *100, 11*, 0, 600, 345

1, 4, 34, 90, 45, 23, 82, 11, *100, 0*, 600, 345

1, 4, 34, 90, 45, 23, 82, 11, 0, *100, 600*, 345

1, 4, 34, 90, 45, 23, 82, 11, 0, 100, *600, 345*

1, 4, 34, 90, 45, 23, 82, 11, 0, 100, 345, 600

Unfortunately, the list is not yet sorted, as there are still several places where adjacent items are out of order. The number 0, for instance, which should be in first slot, is in the ninth slot. Notice, however, that the largest item worked its way to the top position, and indeed, this algorithm will always force this to happen. Thus, if at this point the same strategy is continued, it is only the first n–1 items that need to be scanned. On the second pass, the second largest item will move to its correct position, and on the third pass (stopping at item n–3) the third largest item will be in place. It is this gradual percolation, or bubbling of the larger items to the top end that gives this sorting technique its name.

There are two ways in which the sort can terminate with everything in the right order. It could complete by reaching the n–1th pass and placing the second smallest item in its correct position. Alternately, it could find on some earlier pass that nothing needs to be swapped. That is, all adjacent pairs are already in the correct order. In this case, there is no need to go on to subsequent passes, for the sort is complete already.

If the list started in sorted order, this would happen on the very first pass. If it started in reverse order, it would not happen until the last one.

When this sort was tested, statements were included to print the array after each comparison, and to print the number of swaps on each pass. The original data is given first, and the items that are compared are emphasized.

234 77 0 113 404 94 900 113 15 300 13 135

Pass number 1

77 234 0 113 404 94 900 113 15 300 13 135

77 *0 234* 113 404 94 900 113 15 300 13 135

77 0 *113 234* 404 94 900 113 15 300 13 135

77 0 113 *234 404* 94 900 113 15 300 13 135

77 0 113 234 *94 404* 900 113 15 300 13 135

77 0 113 234 94 *404 900* 113 15 300 13 135

77 0 113 234 94 404 *113 900* 15 300 13 135

77 0 113 234 94 404 113 *15 900* 300 13 135

77 0 113 234 94 404 113 15 *300 900* 13 135

77 0 113 234 94 404 113 15 300 *13 900* 135

77 0 113 234 94 404 113 15 300 13 *135 900*

Swaps on this pass = 9

Pass number 2

0 77 113 234 94 404 113 15 300 13 135 900

0 *77 113* 234 94 404 113 15 300 13 135 900

0 77 *113 234* 94 404 113 15 300 13 135 900

0 77 113 *94 234* 404 113 15 300 13 135 900

0 77 113 94 *234 404* 113 15 300 13 135 900

0 77 113 94 234 *113 404* 15 300 13 135 900

0 77 113 94 234 113 *15 404* 300 13 135 900

0 77 113 94 234 113 15 *300 404* 13 135 900

0 77 113 94 234 113 15 300 *13 404* 135 900

0 77 113 94 234 113 15 300 13 *135 404* 900

Swaps on this pass = 7

Pass number 3

0 77 113 94 234 113 15 300 13 135 404 900

0 *77 113* 94 234 113 15 300 13 135 404 900

0 77 *94 113* 234 113 15 300 13 135 404 900

0 77 94 *113 234* 113 15 300 13 135 404 900

0 77 94 113 *113 234* 15 300 13 135 404 900

0 77 94 113 113 *15 234* 300 13 135 404 900

0 77 94 113 113 15 *234 300* 13 135 404 900

0 77 94 113 113 15 234 *13 300* 135 404 900

0 77 94 113 113 15 234 13 *135 300* 404 900

Swaps on this pass = 5

Pass number 4

0 77 94 113 113 15 234 13 135 300 404 900

0 *77 94* 113 113 15 234 13 135 300 404 900

0 77 *94 113* 113 15 234 13 135 300 404 900

0 77 94 *113 113* 15 234 13 135 300 404 900

0 77 94 113 *15 113* 234 13 135 300 404 900

0 77 94 113 15 *113 234* 13 135 300 404 900

0 77 94 113 15 113 *13 234* 135 300 404 900

0 77 94 113 15 113 13 *135 234* 300 404 900

Swaps on this pass = 3

Pass number 5

0 77 94 113 15 113 13 135 234 300 404 900

0 *77 94* 113 15 113 13 135 234 300 404 900

0 77 *94 113* 15 113 13 135 234 300 404 900

0 77 94 *15 113* 113 13 135 234 300 404 900

0 77 94 15 *113 113* 13 135 234 300 404 900

0 77 94 15 113 *13 113* 135 234 300 404 900

0 77 94 15 113 13 *113 135* 234 300 404 900

Swaps on this pass = 2

Pass number 6

0 77 94 15 113 13 113 135 234 300 404 900

0 *77 94* 15 113 13 113 135 234 300 404 900

0 77 *15 94* 113 13 113 135 234 300 404 900

0 77 15 *94 113* 13 113 135 234 300 404 900

0 77 15 94 *13 113* 113 135 234 300 404 900

0 77 15 94 13 *113 113* 135 234 300 404 900

Swaps on this pass = 2

Pass number 7

0 77 15 94 13 113 113 135 234 300 404 900

0 *15 77* 94 13 113 113 135 234 300 404 900

0 15 *77 94* 13 113 113 135 234 300 404 900

0 15 77 *13 94* 113 113 135 234 300 404 900

0 15 77 13 *94 113* 113 135 234 300 404 900

Swaps on this pass = 2

Pass number 8

0 15 77 13 94 113 113 135 234 300 404 900

0 *15 77* 13 94 113 113 135 234 300 404 900

0 15 *13 77* 94 113 113 135 234 300 404 900

0 15 13 *77 94* 113 113 135 234 300 404 900

Swaps on this pass = 1

Pass number 9

0 15 13 77 94 113 113 135 234 300 404 900

0 *13 15* 77 94 113 113 135 234 300 404 900

0 13 *15 77* 94 113 113 135 234 300 404 900

Swaps on this pass = 1

Pass number 10

0 13 15 77 94 113 113 135 234 300 404 900

0 *13 15* 77 94 113 113 135 234 300 404 900

Swaps on this pass = 0

A. **Algorithm:** The steps to be taken are as follows:

a. Initialize k = n–1

b. Repeat steps (c) to (f) while(k>0)

c. Initialize i = 0

d. Repeat steps (e) to (f) while(i<k)

e. [Compare the i'th element to the i+1'th element]

If(array[i] > array[i+1]) then

f. Set temp = array[i]

array[i] = array[i+1]

array[i+1] = temp

g. End.

B. Equivalent C Function:

```
void BubbleSort(int array[],int n)
{
int i,k,temp;
for(k=n – 1; k > 0; k– –)
{
for(i=0;i<k;++i)
{
if(array[i]>array[i+1])
{
temp=array[i];
array[i]=array[i+1];
array[i+1]=temp;
}
}
}
}
```

C. **Implementation of Bubble Sort Function:** The following program sort_bubble.c implements the bubble sort function using the array of integers:

```
/*sort_bubble.c*/
#include <stdio.h>
#include <stdlib.h>
#define N     100
void Input(int array[],int n);
void BubbleSort(int array[],int n);
void Print(int array[],int n);
void main()
{
int n,array[N];
printf("!!!This program sorts the array of integers using bubble sort algorithm!!!\n");
printf("Please enter how many numbers are there in the array:\n");
scanf("%d,"&n);
Input(array,n);
BubbleSort(array,n);
Print(array,n);
}
// BUBBLE SORT ///////////////
void BubbleSort(int array[],int n)
{
int i,k,temp;
for(k = n – 1; k > 0; k– –)
{
for(i=0;i<k;++i)
{
if(array[i]>array[i+1])
{
temp=array[i];
```

```
array[i]=array[i+1];
array[i+1]=temp;
}
}
}
}
void Input(int array[],int n)
{
int i;
printf("Please enter the number of the array:\n");
for (i=0;i<n;i++)
scanf("%d,"&array[i]);
printf("Array before sorting: ");
for(i=0;i<n;++i)
printf("%d,"array[i]);
printf("\n");
}
void Print(int array[],int n)
{
int i;
printf("Array after sorting: ");
for(i=0;i<n;++i)
{
printf("%d,"array[i]);
}
printf("\n");
}
```

D. **Output of the Program:** !!!This program sorts the array of integers using bubble sort algorithm!!!

Please enter how many numbers are there in the array:

10

Please enter the number of the array:

12

21

32

31

45

34

56

54

67

65

Array before sorting: 12 21 32 31 45 34 56 54 67 65

Array after sorting: 12 21 31 32 34 45 54 56 65 67

E. **Analysis:** The best case involves performing one pass, which requires n–1 comparisons in the outer loop. Hence, the best case is O(n). In worst case, array is in reverse order and the inner loop uses the maximum number of comparisons n–1. Hence, the worst case is $O(n^2)$. The average case is more difficult to analyze. The number of comparisons in the inner loop is (n–1)/2. Hence, the average case is $O(n^2)$.

4.2.2. Selection Sort

It is not difficult to see that some additional efficiency can be obtained for the bubble sort. It uses many swaps to get the largest item into its correct position on each pass, and some of these are wasted. If the scan is modified so that it simply finds the smallest item in the range being scanned and no interchanges are done until the scan is finished, all the intermediate swaps can be eliminated. Then, when the pass is complete, the smallest item can be swapped it with the first item in the array. For instance, starting with the list:

234 77 0 113 404 94 900 115 15 300 13 135

One would find the number 0 to be the smallest on the first pass (as with the bubble sort,) but do only the swap from its present position to the first spot for the pass. This process is called selection sort. Successive passes would produce the lists:

Pass number 1

0 77 234 113 404 94 900 115 15 300 13 135

Pass number 2

0 13 234 113 404 94 900 115 15 300 77 135

Pass number 3

0 13 15 113 404 94 900 115 234 300 77 135

Pass number 4

0 13 15 77 404 94 900 115 234 300 113 135

Pass number 5

0 13 15 77 94 404 900 115 234 300 113 135

Pass number 6

0 13 15 77 94 113 900 115 234 300 404 135

Pass number 7

0 13 15 77 94 113 115 900 234 300 404 135

Pass number 8

0 13 15 77 94 113 115 135 234 300 404 900

Pass number 9

0 13 15 77 94 113 115 135 234 300 404 900

Pass number 10

0 13 15 77 94 113 115 135 234 300 404 900

Pass number 11

0 13 15 77 94 113 115 135 234 300 404 900

A. **Algorithm:** The steps to be taken are as follows:

a. Initialize k = n–1

b. Repeat steps (c) to (g) while(k>0)

c. Initialize pos = 0, i = 1

d. Repeat steps (e) to (f) while(i<=k)

e. [Compare the i'th element to the pos element]

If(array[i] > array[pos]) then

f. Set pos = i

g. Set temp=array[pos];

array[pos]=array[k];

array[k]=temp;

h. End.

B. Equivalent C Function:

```
void SelectionSort(int array[],int n)
{
int i,k,pos,min,temp;
for(k=0;k<n;k++)
{
min = array[k];
pos=k;
for(i=k+1;i<n;++i)
{
if(array[i]<min)
{
min = array[i];
pos=i;
}
}
temp=array[k];
array[k]=array[pos];
array[pos]=temp;
}
}
```

C. **Implementation of Selection Sort Function:** The following program sort_selection.c implements the selection sort function using the array of integers:

```
/*sort_selection.c */
#include <stdio.h>
#include <stdlib.h>
#define N     100
void Input(int array[],int n);
void SelectionSort(int array[],int n);
void Print(int array[],int n);
void main()
```

```
{
int n,array[N];
printf("!!!This program sorts the array of integers using selection sort algorithm!!!\n");
printf("Please enter how many numbers are there in the array:\n");
scanf("%d,"&n);
Input(array,n);
SelectionSort(array,n);
Print(array,n);
}
void SelectionSort(int array[],int n)
{
int i,k,pos,min,temp;
for(k=0;k<n;k++)
{
min = array[k];
pos=k;
for(i=k+1;i<n;++i)
{
if(array[i]<min)
{
min = array[i]; //Find the smallest value
pos=i;
}
}
temp=array[k];
array[k]=array[pos];
array[pos]=temp;
}
}
```

```
void Input(int array[],int n)
{
int i;
printf("Please enter the number of the array:\n");
for (i=0;i<n;i++)
scanf("%d,"&array[i]);
printf("Array before sorting: ");
for(i=0;i<n;++i)
printf("%d,"array[i]);
printf("\n");
}
void Print(int array[],int n)
{
int i;
printf("Array after sorting: ");
for(i=0;i<n;++i)
{
printf("%d,"array[i]);
}
printf("\n");
}
```

D. **Output of the Program:** !!!This program sorts the array of integers using selection sort algorithm!!!

Sorting Algorithms 255

Please enter how many numbers are there in the array:

12

Please enter the number of the array:

234

77

113

404

94

900

113

15

300

13

135

5

Array before sorting: 234 77 113 404 94 900 113 15 300 13 135 5

Array after sorting: 5 *13* 15 77 94 113 113 135 234 300 404 900

E. **Analysis:** During the first pass, in which the record with the smallest key is found, n–1 records are compared. In general for i'th pass of the sort, n-i comparisons are required. The total number of comparisons is therefore, n(n–1)/2. Hence, the number of comparisons is proportional to $O(n^2)$.

4.2.3. Insertion Sort

An insertion sort works by growing a sorted group. The group starts with a single element, and a new element is continuously added by shifting each member of the group until the position where the new element is added. The following example demonstrates an insertion sort on an array of integers:

113 77 0 50 113 114 900 113 15 300 13 135 1

77 113 0 50 113 114 900 113 15 300 13 135 1

0 77 113 50 113 114 900 113 15 300 13 135 1

0 50 77 113 113 114 900 113 15 300 13 135 1

0 50 77 113 113 114 900 113 15 300 13 135 1

0 50 77 113 113 114 900 113 15 300 13 135 1

0 50 77 113 113 114 900 113 15 300 13 135 1

0 50 77 113 113 113 114 900 15 300 13 135 1

0 15 50 77 113 113 113 114 900 300 13 135 1

0 15 50 77 113 113 113 114 300 900 13 135 1

0 13 15 50 77 113 113 113 114 300 900 135 1

0 13 15 50 77 113 113 113 114 135 300 900 1

0 1 13 15 50 77 113 113 113 114 135 300 900

A. **Algorithm:** The steps to be taken are as follows:

a. Initialize k = 1

b. Repeat steps (c) to (g) while(k<n)

c. Set element = array[k]

d. Initialize pos = k–1

e. Repeat steps (f) while(array[pos]>element && pos>=0)

f. Set array[pos+1] = array[pos]

g. Set array[pos+1] = element

h. End.

B. **Equivalent C Function:**

```
void InsertionSort(int array[],int n)
{
int k,element, pos;
for(k=1;k<n;++k)
{
element=array[k];
for(pos=k–1;array[pos]>element && pos>=0;pos– –)
{
array[pos+1]=array[pos];
}
array[pos+1]=element;
}
}
```

C. **Implementation of Insertion Sort Function:** The following program sort_insertion.c implements the insertion sort function using the array of integers:

```
/* sort_insertion.c */
#include <stdio.h>
#include <stdlib.h>
#define N      100
void Input(int array[],int n);
void InsertionSort(int array[],int n);
```

```
void Print(int array[],int n);
void main()
{
int n,array[N];
printf("!!!This program sorts the array of integers using insertion sort algorithm!!!\n");
printf("Please enter how many numbers are there in the array:\n");
scanf("%d,"&n);
Input(array,n);
InsertionSort(array,n);
Print(array,n);
}
// INSERTION SORT ////////////////
void InsertionSort(int array[],int n)
{
int k,element, pos;
for(k=1;k<n;++k)
{
element=array[k];
for(pos=k–1;array[pos]>element && pos>=0;pos– –)
{
array[pos+1]=array[pos];
}
array[pos+1]=element;
}
}
void Input(int array[],int n)
{
int i;
printf("Please enter the number of the array:\n");
for (i=0;i<n;i++)
```

```
scanf("%d,"&array[i]);
printf("Array before sorting: ");
for(i=0;i<n;++i)
printf("%d,"array[i]);
printf("\n");
}
void Print(int array[],int n)
{
int i;
printf("Array after sorting: ");
for(i=0;i<n;++i)
{
printf("%d,"array[i]);
}
printf("\n");
}
```

D. **Output of the Program:** !!!This program sorts the array of integers using insertion sort algorithm!!!

Please enter how many numbers are there in the array:

12

Please enter the number of the array:

113

77

50

113

114

900

113

15

300

13

135

1

Array before sorting:

113 77 50 113 114 900 113 15 300 13 135 1

Array after sorting:

1 13 15 50 77 113 113 113 114 135 300 900

E. **Analysis:** This sorting method is frequently used when the array size is small and linear search is about as efficient as the binary search. The best case requires array to be in order, so that it involves performing only one pass, which requires n–1 comparisons in the outer loop. Hence, the best case is O(n). The worst case is there, if array is in reverse order and the inner loop uses the maximum number of comparisons n–1. Hence, the worst case is $O(n^2)$. The average case is more difficult to analyze. The number of comparisons in the inner loop is (n–1)/2. Hence, the average case is $O(n^2)$.

4.2.4. Quick Sort

The method of sorting by partitioning a list into two sub-lists around some pivot, (where the items in the left sub-list are all less than the pivot, and those in the right sub-list are all greater than the pivot), and then recursively sorting the left and right sub-lists in the same manner is called a quick sort.

The key to realizing steps two and three in the sequence above is to start with the next item after the pivot, and counting forward, discover the first one that is greater than the pivot(i.e., it really belongs to the right sub-list). One then commences examining items from the last in the current list backwards to find the first one that is less than the pivot(i.e., it really belongs to the left sub-list). Since these two items are both now in the wrong sub-list, swap them. Then pick up the count again where it left off and continue, gradually working towards a collision between the two counters. To see this in operation, suppose one begins with the list:

16 7 9 44 2 18 8 53 1 5 17

Isolating item #1 (16) as the pivot, scan from #2 and discover that item #4 (44) is the first one greater than 16. Suspending the count here, begin with item #11 (17) and work backwards. Item #10 (5) is the first one less than 16, so swap it with item #4 to get:

16	7	9	<u>5</u>	2	18	8	53	1	<u>44</u>	17

The underscore marks the two that were swapped and also the places where counting was suspended in the forward and backward scans. Continuing, the next two that must be swapped because they are in the wrong sub-list are item #6 (18) and item #9 (1) so the list becomes:

16	7	9	5	2	<u>1</u>	8	53	<u>18</u>	44	17

The next item found that is greater than 16 is item #8 (53), but at this point, the count from the right passes with the one from the left (at the arrow) without finding another item less than the pivot value. So, there are no more swaps to make in this pass, and the scan has now found the correct place to put the pivot item (at position #7):

16	7	9	5	2	<u>1</u>	8	53	<u>18</u>	44	17

Rather than move everything down and insert it there, observe that the lower items are out of order any way and can be re-positioned later, so it will do to simply swap the pivot item with item #7. This produces:

8	7	9	5	2	<u>1</u>	16	53	<u>18</u>	44	17

The list is written with the 16 isolated, inverted, and separating two sub-lists so as to emphasize the fact of the partition. The item 16 is now in the correct position and should never be touched again. Because of the way in which the correct position for the item 16 was located, everything in the left sub-list is now less than 16, and everything in the right sub-list is greater than 16 (hence the name pivot). Thinking recursively, it is now possible to observe that when the left and right sub-lists are sorted, the entire list will be sorted.

Repeating for the left sub-list yields:

8	7	<u>9</u>	5	2	<u>1</u>	16	53	18	44	17
8	7	1	5	2	9	16	53	18	44	17
2	7	1	5	8	9	16	53	18	44	17

Repeat for the left sub-list of the 8, to obtain:

2	7	1	5	8	9	16	53	18	44	17
2	1	7	5	8	9	16	53	18	44	17
1	2	7	5	8	9	16	53	18	44	17

The left sub-list of the pivot 2 is sorted. When the right sub-list of pivot 2 (two items) is sorted, one has:

1	2	5	7	8	9	16	53	18	44	17

Now, the left sub-list of the last pivot (7) has only one item and it is sorted. Backing up the recursion chain, the right sub-list of the pivot 8 also has only one item (9), it is already sorted. Backing up further, the next list to sort is the right sub-list of the original pivot 16.

1	2	5	7	8	9	16	53	18	44	17
1	2	5	7	8	9	16	17	18	44	53
1	2	5	7	8	9	16	17	18	44	53
1	2	5	7	8	9	16	17	18	44	53
1	2	5	7	8	9	16	17	18	44	53

The last right sub-list of the pivot 18 has only one element and is sorted, so the entire sort is finished. Note that there were even places where one or the other of the two sub-lists was empty and also did not need to be considered.

Having carefully hand-stepped through this sorting method, it is now possible to produce the code for the quick sort. This code will depart a little from the previous conventions for sorts in this chapter, in that, it will assume that it is being called by a client that is already numbering the array [0. n–1]. This assumption is made because the quick sort, being recursive, is its own major client, and already has the array numbered in that manner when it calls itself.

Notice, also the treatment of numbers scanned in either direction that are equal to the pivot. They are left where they are for that scan. Eventually, they will be shuffled adjacent to this pivot when another sub-list is sorted.

A. **Algorithm:** The array[] is an array with n elements. The method of sorting by partitioning a list into two sub-lists around some pivotpos, (where the items in the left sub-list are all less than the pivotpos, and those in the right sub-list are all greater than the pivotpos), and then recursively sorting the left and right sub-lists.

Steps: The steps to be taken are as follows:

a. If n<=1 then return

b. [Otherwise call function partition]

pivotpos = Partition(array,n)

c. [Recursively call the function quick sort for both partitions]

QuickSort(array,pivotpos)

QuickSort(array+pivotpos+1,n-pivotpos–1)

d. End.

B. **Equivalent C Function:**

```
void QuickSort(int array[],int n)
{
int pivotpos;
if(n<=1)
{
return;
}
pivotpos=Partition(array,n);
QuickSort(array,pivotpos);
QuickSort(array+pivotpos+1,n-pivotpos–1);
}
int Partition(int array[],int n)
{
int pivot,left,right,swap;
pivot=array[0]; // First element is pivot
left=0; right=n–1;
for(;;)
{
```

```
while(left<right && array[left]<=pivot)
{
left++;
}
while(left<right && array[right]>pivot)
{
right – –;
}
if(left==right)
{
if(array[right]>pivot)
{
left=left–1;
}
break;
}
swap=array[left];
array[left]=array[right];
array[right]=swap;
}
swap=array[0];
array[0]=array[left];
array[left]=swap;
return left;
}
```

C. **Implementation of Quick Sort Function:** The following program sort_quick.c implements the quick sort function using the array of integers:

```
/* sort_quick.c */
#include <stdio.h>
#include <stdlib.h>
#define N 100
```

```
void QuickSort(int array[],int n); // Quick Sort
int Partition(int array[],int n); // returns index of pivot
void Input(int array[],int n);
void Print(int array[],int n);
void main()
{
int n,array[N];
printf("!!!This program sorts the array of integers using quick sort algorithm!!!\n");
printf("Please enter how many number are there in the array:\n");
scanf("%d,"&n);
Input(array,n);
QuickSort(array,n);
Print(array,n);
}
void Input(int array[],int n)
{
int i;
printf("Please enter the number of the array:\n");
for (i=0;i<n;i++)
scanf("%d,"&array[i]);
printf("array before sorting: ");
for(i=0;i<n;++i)
printf("%d,"array[i]);
printf("\n");
}
void Print(int array[],int n)
{
int i;
printf("array after sorting: ");
for(i=0;i<n;++i)
```

```
{
printf("%d,"array[i]);
}
printf("\n");
}
void QuickSort(int array[],int n)
{
int pivotpos;
if(n<=1)
{
return;
}
pivotpos=Partition(array,n);
QuickSort(array,pivotpos);
QuickSort(array+pivotpos+1,n-pivotpos–1);
}
int Partition(int array[],int n)
{
int pivot,left,right,swap;
pivot=array[0]; // First element is pivot
left=0; right=n–1;
for(;;)
{
while(left<right && array[left]<=pivot)
{
left++;
}
while(left<right && array[right]>pivot)
{
right – –;
```

```
}
if(left==right)
{
if(array[right]>pivot)
{
left=left–1;
}
break;
}
swap=array[left];
array[left]=array[right];
array[right]=swap;
}
swap=array[0];
array[0]=array[left];
array[left]=swap;
return left;
}
```

D. **Output of the Program:** !!!This program sorts the array of integers using quick sort algorithm !!!

```
Please enter how many numbers are there in the array:
12
Please enter the number of the array:
16
7
9
44
2
18
8
53
1
```

5

17

22

Array before sorting: 16 7 9 44 2 18 8 53 1 5 17 22

Array after sorting: 1 2 5 7 8 9 16 17 18 22 44 53

E. **Analysis:** The best case analysis occurs when, the file is always partitioned in half. The analysis becomes O(n log n). The worst case occurs when, at each invocation of the function, the current list is partitioned into two sub-lists with one of them being empty or key element is smallest or largest one. The worst case analysis becomes $O(n^2)$. For the average case, analysis becomes O(n log n).

4.2.5. Merge Sort

The basic idea is that, if we know we have two sorted lists, we can combine them into a single large sorted list by just looking at the first item in each list. Whichever is smaller is moved to the single list being assembled. There is then a new first item in the list from which the item was moved, and the process repeats.

The process overall is thus:

a. Split the original list into two halves;

b. Sort each half (using merge sort);

c. Merge the two sorted halves together into a single sorted list.

Example: The following example performs a merge sort on an array of integers:

34 56 78 12 45 3 99 23

34 56 78 12□ 45 3 99 23
34 56□ 78 12□ 45 3□ 99 23
34 □56□ 78□12□ 45□ 3□ 99□ 23
34 56□ 12 78□ 3 45□ 23 99
12 34 56 78 □3 23 45 99
3 12 23 34 45 56 78 99

A. **Algorithm:** The steps to be taken for merge sort are as follows:

a. [Check the size of the array]

If n=1 then return

b. [Otherwise check the first and last integer]

If(first!=last)then repeat step (c) to (f)

c. [Find the middle integer]

middle = ((last + first)/2)

d. [Recursively sort the left half array]

MergeSort(array,first,middle)

e. [Recursively sort the right half array]

MergeSort(array,middle+1,last)

f. [Merge two ordered sub-arrays]

Merge(array,first,middle,last)

g. End.

B. Equivalent C Function:

```
void MergeSort(int array[],int i,int n)
{
int mid,first,last;
first=i;
last=n;
if(first!=last)
{
mid = (first+last)/2;
MergeSort(array,first,mid);
MergeSort(array,mid+1,last);
Merge(array,first,mid,last);
}
}
void Merge(int array[],int first,int n,int last)
{
int temp[100];
int f = first;
int w = n+1;
int l = last;
int upper;
```

```
while((f<=n)&&(w<=last))
{
if(array[f]<=array[w])
{
temp[l]=array[f];
f++;
}
else
{
temp[l]=array[w];
w++;
}
l++;
}
if(f<=n)
{
for(f=f;f<=n;f++)
{
temp[l] = array[f];
l++;
}
}
else
{
for(w=w;w<=last;w++)
{
temp[l]=array[w];
l++;
}
}
for(upper=first;upper<=last;upper++) // copy result back
```

```
array[upper]=temp[upper];
}
```

C. **Implementation of Merge Sort Function:** The following program sort_merge.c implements the merge sort function using the array of integers:

```
/* sort_merge.c */
#include <stdio.h>
#include <stdlib.h>
#define N       100
void Input(int array[],int n);
void MergeSort(int array[],int i,int n);
void Merge(int array[],int f, int l,int n);
void Print(int array[],int n);
void main()
{
int i=0,n,array[N];
printf("!!!This program sorts the array of integers using merge sort algorithm!!!\n");
printf("Please enter how many number are there in the array:\n");
scanf("%d,"&n);
input(array,n);
MergeSort(array,i,n–1);
Print(array,n);
}
void Input(int array[],int n)
{
int i;
printf("Please enter the number of the array:\n");
for (i=0;i<n;i++)
scanf("%d,"&array[i]);
printf("Array before sorting: ");
for(i=0;i<n;++i)
```

```
printf("%d,"array[i]);
}
void Print(int array[],int n)
{
int i;
printf("Array after sorting: ");
for(i=0;i<n;++i)
{
printf("%d,"array[i]);
}
printf("\n");
}
void MergeSort(int array[],int i,int n)
{
int mid,first,last;
first=i;
last=n;
if(first!=last)
{
mid = (first+last)/2;
MergeSort(array,first,mid);
MergeSort(array,mid+1,last);
Merge(array,first,mid,last);
}
}
void Merge(int array[],int first,int n,int last)
{
int temp[100];
int f = first;
int w = n+1;
int l = last;
```

```
int upper;
while((f<=n)&&(w<=last))
{
if(array[f]<=array[w])
{
temp[l]=array[f];
f++;
}
else
{
temp[l]=array[w];
w++;
}
l++;
}
if(f<=n)
{
for(f=f;f<=n;f++)
{
temp[l] = array[f];
l++;
}
}
else
{
for(w=w;w<=last;w++)
{
temp[l]=array[w];
l++;
}
}
```

```
for(upper=first;upper<=last;upper++) // copy result back
array[upper]=temp[upper];
}
```

D. Output of the Program: !!!This program sorts the array of integers using merge sort algorithm!!!

Please enter how many numbers are there in the array:

8

Please enter the number of the array:

34

56

78

12

45

3

99

23

Array before sorting: 34 56 78 12 45 3 99 23

Array after sorting: 3 12 23 34 45 56 78 99

E. Analysis: In this method, since log n passes are required in the sort, the total number of comparisons required are O(n log n) in all three cases, i.e., best case, average case and worst case. To execute the algorithm, extra space needed is equal to the number of elements in the list, i.e., space complexity is O(n). One of the drawbacks of this method is the large auxiliary area required.

4.2.6. Address Calculation Sort

This method uses hash function for sorting. Depending on the result of the hash function the key is applied into the one of the linked lists. Each set of keys, which hash into the same address, is called equivalence class. Each equivalence is represented by a linked list. In case, if there is a collision, the new key is placed into one of the linked lists.

For applying a hash function to the sorting process, we assume that a hashing function T with the property that:

z1 < z2 □ T(z1) <= T(z2)

When such a function is used to hash a particular key into a particular address to which previous keys have already been hashed, the new key is placed in the set of colliding records to preserve the order of the keys. Function, which follows above property, is called a non-decreasing or order-preserving, hashing function. Finally concatenate the nonempty linked lists into one. Let us consider the sample key set:

34 56 78 12 45 3 90 23 74 61 84

Now apply the above hashing function in which all keys within the ranges 1–15, 16–30, 31–45, 46–60, 60–75, and 75–90 are each hashed into a different set. As a result, we have six ordered sets as shown in Table 4.1.

Table 4.1. Address Calculating Sorting

Set	**Keys in the Set**						
1–15	3	→	12				
16–30	23						
30–45	34 56	→	45				
46–60	61						
61–75	78	→	74				
75–90		→	84	→	90		

These six ordered sets are merged to obtained the desired sorted list.

We can use the separate chaining method of collision resolution with a separate hash table to represent the sorting process.

Table 4.2 shows the variables, which can be used for implementing address calculation sort algorithm.

Table 4.2. Variables and Their Function

Variable	**Function**
n(integer)	Size of the hash table
HEAD(pointer)	Address of the first record in the sorted table
HASH_ TABLE(pointer)	Vector of pointers representing the hash table
HASH(integer)	Hashing function
RECORD(record)	Overflow area record

K(integer)	Key of a record
DATA(string)	Other relevant information in a record
LINK(pointer)	Location of the next record in the list
KEY(integer)	Key of the input record
INFO(string)	Other relevant information of the input record
RANDOM(integer)	Hash address of input record
NEW(pointer)	Address of newly created overflow record

A. **Algorithm:** This algorithm sorts the records based on address calculation using a hash table with a separate overflow area. The sorted table generated is in the form of a linked list.

Steps: The steps to be taken are as follows:

a. [Initialize hash table entries]

Repeat for(i=1;i<=n;i++)

HASH_TABLE[i] = NULL

b. [Input and insert records into the appropriate linked lists]

Repeat step (c) to (d) until all records input

c. [Read and hash a record]

Read(KEY,INFO)

NEW ← RECORD

K(NEW) ← KEY

DATA(NEW) ← INFO

LINK(NEW) ← NULL

RANDOM ← HASH(KEY)

d. [Insert record into appropriate linked list]

if (HASH_TABLE[RANODM] = NULL)

(Insert record into empty linked list)

LINK(NEW) ← HASH_TABLE[RANDOM]

HASH_ATBLE[RANDOM] ←NEW

else (Insert record in middle or at end of linked list)

P ← HASH_TABLE[RANDOM]

S ←LINK(P)

Repeat while S ≠ NULL and K(S) < KEY

P ← S

S ← LINK(S)

LINK(P) ← NEW

LINK(NEW) ←S

e. [Find first nonempty linked list]

i ← 1

Repeat while HASH_TABLE[i] = NULL and i<n

i ← i +1

HEAD ← HASH_TABLE[I]

j ← i + 1

f. [Concatenate the nonempty linked lists]

Repeat while j ≤ n

If HASH_TABLE[j] ≠ NULL then

(Find tail of the linked list)

P ←HASH_TABLE[i]

Repeat while LINK(P) ≠ NULL

P ← LINK(P)

(Link tail of this linked list to the head of the next)

LINK(P) ← HASH_TABLE[j]

i ← j

j ← i + 1

g. End.

B. Analysis: In the best case, the hashing function is uniformly distributed. The address calculation sort performs in a linear fashion as each key is assigned to its proper linked list and some extra work is required to place the key within the linked list. In such case, the sort is O(n). In the worst case, when all keys are mapped to the same location, significant work is to be done to place a key properly within the linked list and the sort is $O(n^2)$.

4.2.7. Heap Sort

The basic approach of heap sort is to turn an unordered list into a heap, and then to keep dequeuing elements from the heap until it is empty. Because, a deletion always causes the next highest element to be moved to the root, the process of dequeuing will produce an ordered list. The space advantage of heap sort is obtained by placing each element, we delete from the heap, at the end of the unsorted section of the list (in a similar way to selection sort's strategy of swapping values to the beginning of the list). In this way, we do not have to create another array to place the sorted elements (merge sort requires such an array).

However, the first phase of a heap sort involves building the heap from an unordered list. We can take the advantage of the fact that no deletions will intervene to create a more efficient insert routine that again reorders a single array instead of copying from one array to another.

4.2.7.1. Building a Heap

We can build a heap by starting with the middle element of an unordered array and treating that element as the root of a sub-tree within the heap, we try and insert the element in its correct order in the sub-tree(moving down from the sub-tree root). Because, we are moving values up the heap as we search for the correct position for our element, we are correctly ordering other elements with respect to the element, we are adding. For this reason, we can start in the middle of an unordered list and work backwards to the root and at the end of the process, we have created a valid heap. This means, we perform n/2 insertions instead of n as we had been using our earlier insertion routine (Figure 4.1).

For example, consider the unordered list:

1	2	3	4	5	6	7	8
12	34	17	33	19	22	11	10

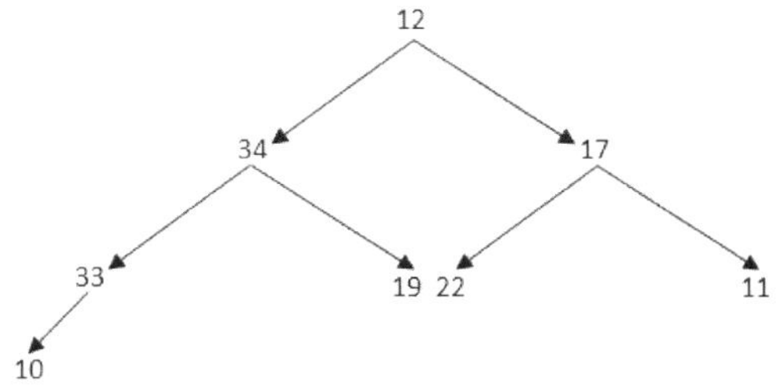

Figure 4.1. Insertion of heap.

We start with the middle element (**33**) and try to insert it within its own sub-tree. It is already in a correct position (**33 > 10**), so we continue by moving back to **17**. As **17 < 22** we move **22** up and replace it with **17** (Figure 4.2):

1	2	3	4	5	6	7	8
12	34	22	33	19	17	11	10

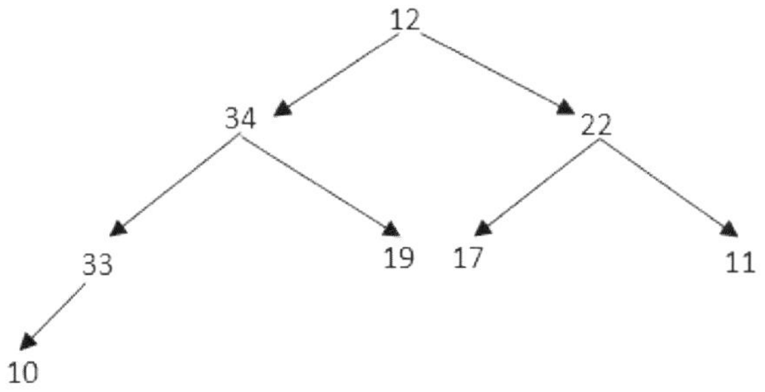

Figure 4.2. Replace Element.

Next, we move back to **34** which is > both **33** and **19**, so nothing need be done and finally, we test **12** which is < **34** so we move **34** up. As **12** is also greater than **33**, **33** goes up and **12** replaces it to produce the final heap (Figure 4.3):

1	2	3	4	5	6	7	8
34	33	22	12	19	17	11	10

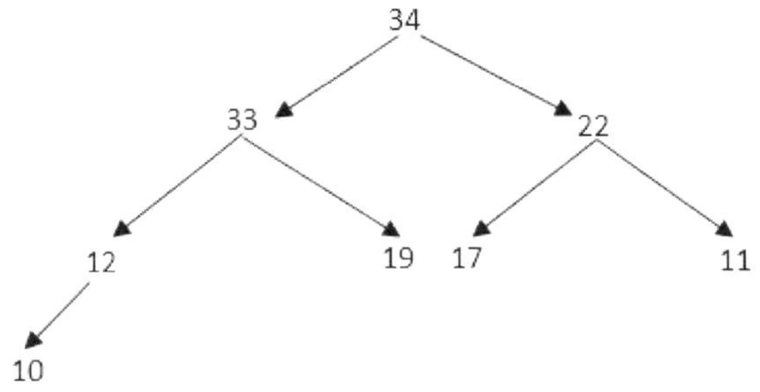

Figure 4.3. Produce the final heap.

4.2.7.2. Sorting a Heap

The strategy is to copy **34** to the end of the list (so it replaces **10**) and then try to insert **10** in the tree, starting at the root. So, after removing **34** the tree would be as follows (Figure 4.4):

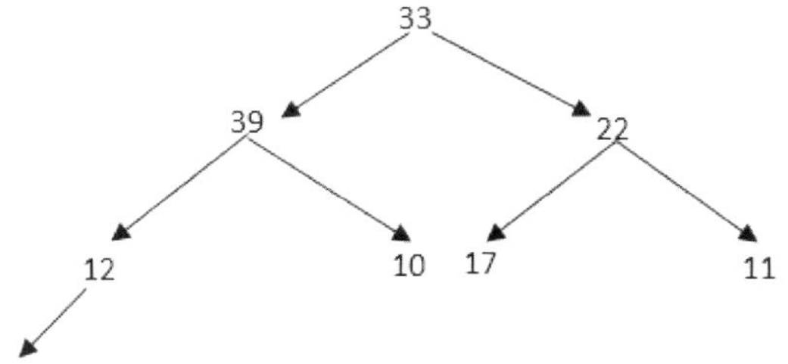

Figure 4.4. Sorting a Heap.

1	2	3	4	5	6	7	8
33	19	22	12	10	17	11	34

We would now take **33** and place it in the position currently occupied by **11**, and then try inserting **11** at the root (Figure 4.5):

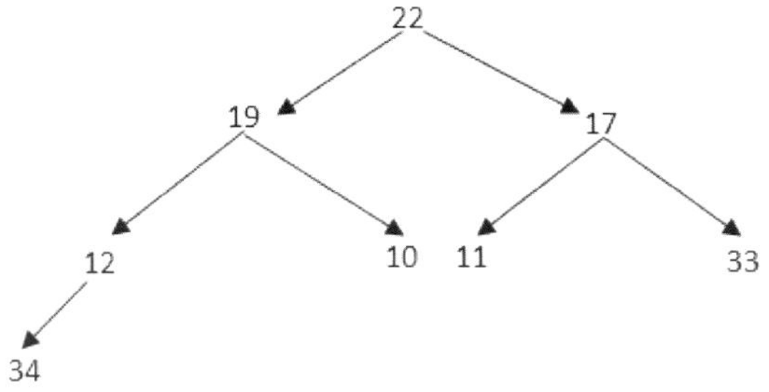

Figure 4.5. Replace the heap.

1	2	3	4	5	6	7	8
22	19	17	12	10	11	33	34

Now take **22** and place it in the position currently occupied by **11**, and then try inserting **11** at the root (Figure 4.6):

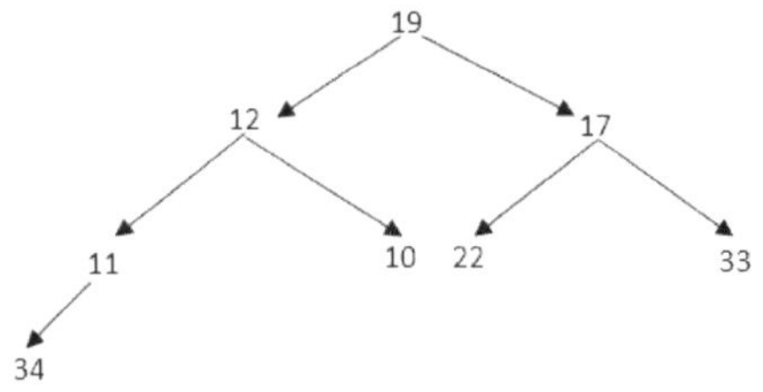

Figure 4.6. Replace the heap.

1	2	3	4	5	6	7	8
19	12	17	11	10	22	33	34

Repeat the process taking **19** and place it in the position currently occupied by **10**, and then try inserting **10** at the root (Figure 4.7):

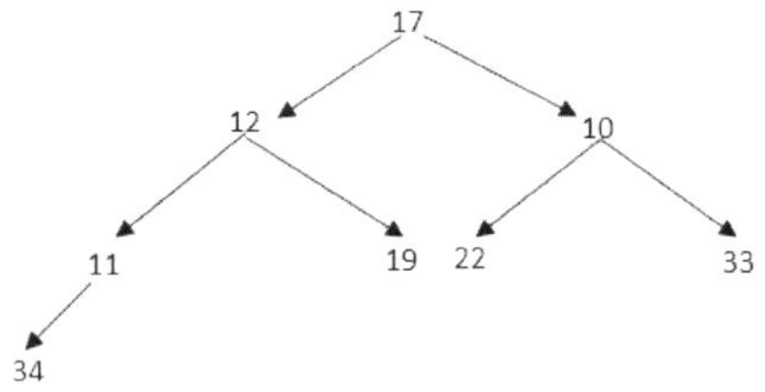

Figure 4.7. Heap Insertion at the root.

1	2	3	4	5	6	7	8
17	12	10	11	19	22	33	34

Repeat the process, take **17** and place it in the position currently occupied by **11**, and then try inserting **11** at the root (Figure 4.8):

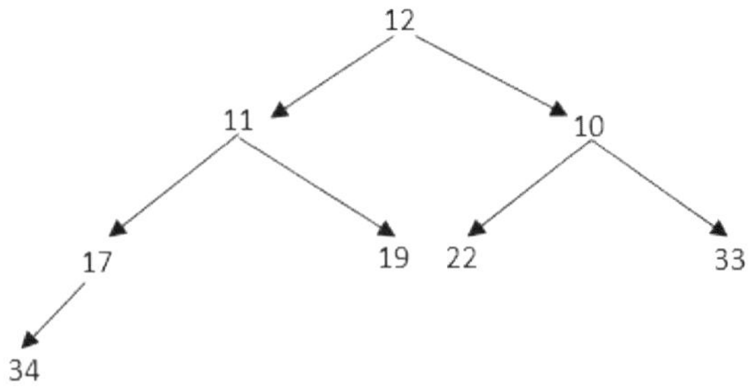

Figure 4.8. Heap Insertion at the root.

1	2	3	4	5	6	7	8
12	11	10	17	19	22	33	34

Repeat the process, take **12** and place it in the position currently occupied by **10**, and then try inserting **10** at the root (Figure 4.9):

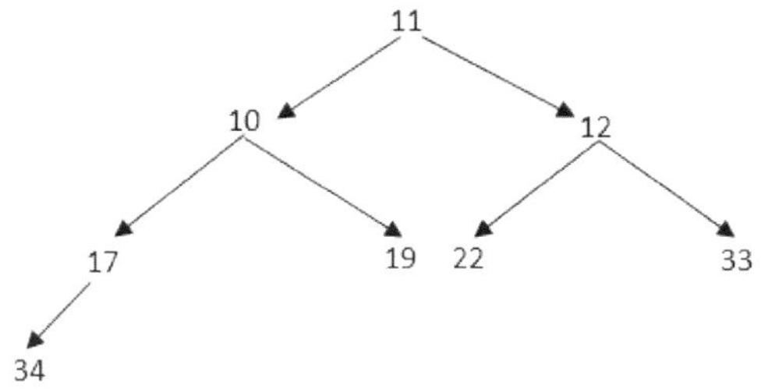

Figure 4.9. Heap Insertion at the root.

1	2	3	4	5	6	7	8
11	10	12	17	19	22	33	34

Repeat the process, take **11** and place it in the position currently occupied by **10**, and then try inserting **10** at the root (Figure 4.10):

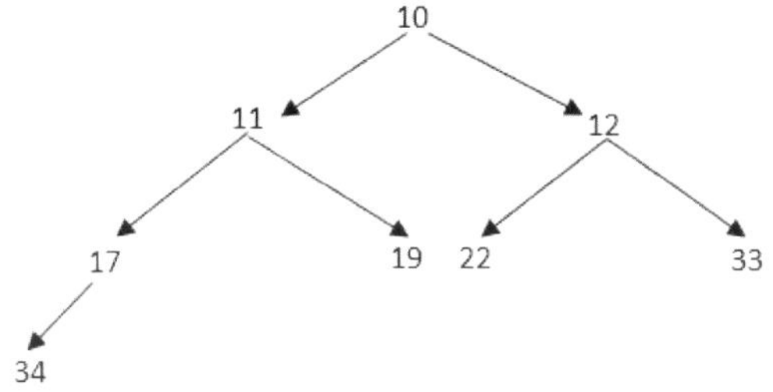

Figure 4.10. Heap Insertion at the root.

1	2	3	4	5	6	7	8
10	11	12	17	19	22	33	34

It is clear that by repeating this strategy, we will finally arrive at a sorted list.

A. Equivalent C Function:

```
void InsertFromHeap (int pos,int array[],int n)
{
```

```
int k,right,left,max,temp;
for(k=pos;;)
{
left=2*k+1;
right=left+1;
if(left>=n)
{
return;
}
else
if(right>=n)
{
max=left;
}
else
if(array[left]>array[right])
{
```

Sorting Algorithms 277

```
max=left;
}
else
{
max=right;
}
if(array[k]>array[max])
{
return;
}
temp=array[k];
array[k]=array[max];
array[max]=temp;
```

```
k=max;
}
}
void HeapSort(int array[],int n)        // Perform heap sort
{
int i,temp;
for(i=n/2;i>=0; – –i)    // Heapify-Theta(n)
{
InsertFromHeap(i,array,n);
} // Time Complexity: Theta(n)
for(i=n–1;i>0;i– –) // Time Complexity: Theta(n*lg(n));
{
temp=array[0];
array[0]=array[i];
array[i]=temp;
InsertFromHeap(0,array,i);
}
}
```

B. **Implementation of Heap Sort Function:** The following program sort_heap.c implements the heap sort function using the array of integers:

```
/* sort_heap.c */
#include <stdio.h>
#include <stdlib.h>
#define N      100
void Input(int array[],int n);
void InsertFromHeap(int pos,int array[],int n);
void HeapSort(int array[],int n);       // Perform heap sort
void Print(int array[],int n);
void main()
{
int n,array[N];
```

```
printf("!!!This program sorts the array of integers using heap sort algorithm!!!\n");
printf("Please enter how many numbers are there in the array:\n");
scanf("%d,"&n);
Input(array,n);
HeapSort(array,n);
Print(array,n);
}
void InsertFromHeap(int pos,int array[],int n)
{
int k,right,left,max,temp;
for(k=pos;;)
{
left=2*k+1;
right=left+1;
if(left>=n)
{
return;
}
else
if(right>=n)
{
max=left;
}
else
if(array[left]>array[right])
{
max=left;
}
else
{
```

```
max=right;
}
if(array[k]>array[max])
{
return;
}
temp=array[k];
array[k]=array[max];
array[max]=temp;
k=max;
}
}
void HeapSort(int array[],int n)
{
int i,temp;
for(i=n/2;i>=0; – –i)
{
InsertFromHeap(i,array,n);
}
for(i = n–1; I > 0; i– –)
{
temp=array[0];
array[0]=array[i];
array[i]=temp;
InsertFromHeap(0,array,i);
}
}
void Input(int array[],int n)
{
int i;
printf("Please enter the number of the array:\n");
```

```
for (i=0;i<n;i++)
scanf("%d,"&array[i]);
printf("Array before sorting: ");
for(i=0;i<n;++i)
printf("%d,"array[i]);
printf("\n");
}
void Print(int array[],int n)
{
int i;
printf("Array after sorting: ");
for(i=0;i<n;++i)
{
printf("%d,"array[i]);
}
printf("\n");
}
```

4.3. COMPLEXITY OF THE ALGORITHM

An algorithm is a well-defined set of steps for solving a particular problem. Our task is to develop efficient algorithms for the processing of data. The analysis of an algorithm is a major task in computer science. In order to compare algorithm, we must have some criteria to measure the efficiency of our algorithm. The time and space are the two measures for an efficient algorithm.

The time is measured by counting the number of key operations. In sorting algorithms, for example, the number of comparisons. The space is measured by counting the maximum of memory needed by the algorithm.

The complexity of an algorithm is the function, which gives the running time and/or storage space requirement of the algorithm in terms of the size of the input data. The storage space required by an algorithm is simply a multiple of the data size.

The complexity of the sorting algorithm measures the running time as a function of the number n of items to be sorted. Normally, the complexity function measures only the number of comparisons, since the number of other operations is at most a constant factor of the number of comparisons. Table 4.3 shows the complexity of the various sorting algorithms:

Table 4.3. Complexity of Sorting Methods

Sorting Method	Best Case	Average Case	Worst Case
Bubble sort	$O(n^2)$	$O(n^2)$	$O(n^2)$
Selection sort	$O(n^2)$	$O(n^2)$	$O(n^2)$
Inserted sort	O(n)	$O(n^2)$	$O(n^2)$
Quick sort	O(n log n)	O(n log n)	$O(n^2)$
Merge sort	O(n log n)	O(n log n)	O(n log n)
Address calculation sort	O(n)	O(n log n)	$O(n^2)$
Heap sort	O(n log n)	O(n log n)	O(n log n)

Exercise

- **Q.1.** What is the purpose of writing the more complicated code to do binary searches, when a linear one will not only find the item if it is there, but does not even require the data to be sorted in the first place?
- **Q.2.** Rewrite the bubble sort and the merge sort to produce the list in reverse order (largest to smallest).
- **Q.3.** Implement a shell sort and a quick sort for the type cardinal (as in the text) and the type real. Which factors make the performances different for the type real? What conclusions can you draw?
- **Q.4.** Write a program that will read an array of strings from a disk file, sort it, and write it back.
- **Q.5.** Modify the shell sort as finally shown in the text to use a stored array for the k-sequence. To begin with, have the program ask you for the sequence from the keyboard. Test various sequences and try to find an optimum one. Once you have this, organize your work in modules as with your k-sequence safely tucked away in the implementation part.
- **Q.6.** Suppose instead of using the middle item for the pivot in a quick sort, one uses the median of the left, middle, and right items instead. Write and test this modification, determining whether or

not there is a performance increase or decrease for random and already sorted arrays.

- **Q.7.** Implement a merge sort to combine the contents of two previously created files into a single file, without holding the entire sorted array in memory.
- **Q.8.** Write a recursive algorithm for merge sort and show how merge sort sorts the sequence 4,31,1,6,7,2,4,9.
- **Q.9.** Write a recursive algorithm for quick sort and show quick sort would sort the array 4,31,1,6,9,3,5,8.
- **Q.10.** Implement selection sort algorithm for linked lists. What is the time and space complexity?
- **Q.11.** Implement merge sort algorithm to merge two linked lists. Sort the concatenated list. What is its time complexity?

CHAPTER 5

GRAPHS

CONTENTS

5.1. INTRODUCTION

This chapter covers graphs, along with their related definitions like- definition of graph, adjacent vertices, paths, cycles, and trees etc. Various types of graphs like- directed, undirected, connected, strongly connected, weakly connected, unconnected, simple, and multi graphs etc., are discussed. Graph representation includes: adjacency matrix, adjacency list and adjacency multilists. In traversal schemes, depth first search and breadth first searches are discussed. Shortest path problem with dijkstra algorithm is discussed. Minimum spanning tree with their prim's and kruskal's algorithm are also covered.

5.2. GRAPH

A graph G is a set of vertices(nodes) V and a set of edges(arcs) E, which connect them. Vertices on the graph are shown as points or circles and edges are drawn as arcs or line segments.

We write:

$G = (V,E)$

where; V is the finite and non empty set of vertices and the set of edges:

$E = \{(v_i,v_j)\}$

where; v_i and v_j are pair of vertices in V. Therefore, V(G), read as V of G, is a set of vertices, and E(G), read as E of G, is a set of edges. A graph may be pictorially represented as shown in Figure 5.1.

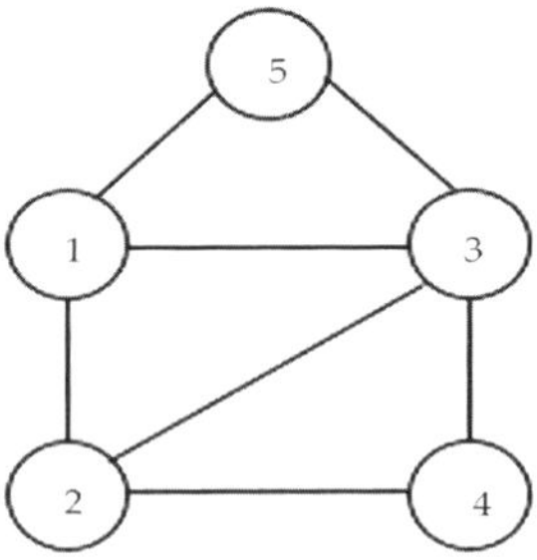

Figure 5.1. A graph.

We have numbered the nodes as 1, 2, 3, 4, and 5. Therefore,

V(G) = (1,2,3,4,5)

and E(G) = {(1,2), (1,3), (1,5), (2,3), (2,4), (3,4), (3,5)}

5.3. ADJACENT VERTICES

Two vertices are said to be adjacent if there is an edge between them, i.e., vertex v1 is said to be adjacent to a vertex v2 if there is an edge (v1, v2) or (v2, v1).

The adjacent vertices of graph shown in Figure 5.2 are tabulated in Table 5.1.

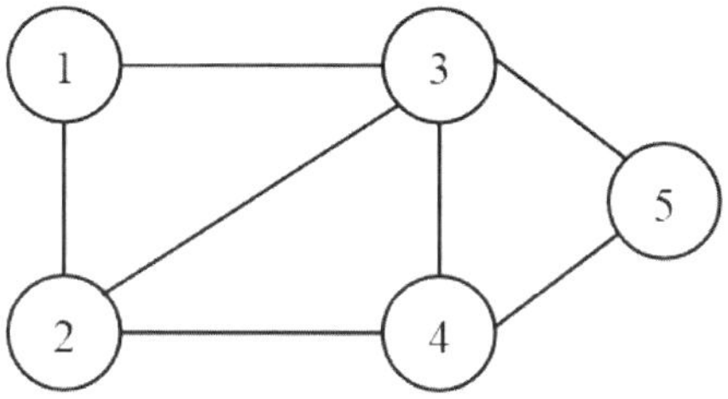

Figure 5.2. Adjacent Vertices.

Table 5.1. Adjacent Vertices

Vertex	Adjacent Vertices
1	2,3
2	1,3,4
3	1,4,5
4	2,3,5
5	3,4

5.4. PATHS

A path P of length k, through a graph is a sequence of connected vertices, each adjacent to the next. If v_0 is the initial vertex and v_k is the terminal vertex, the path from v_0 to v_k is the sequence of vertices so that v_0 is adjacent to v_1, v_1 is adjacent to v_2 … and v_{k-1} is adjacent to v_k. The number of edges on the path is called path length.

Once again, consider the graph as shown in the Figure 5.2. Some of the paths and lengths are tabulated in Table 5.2.

Table 5.2 Paths and lengths

Initial Vertex	Terminal Vertex	Path	Length
1	4	1,2,4 1,3,4 1,3,5,4 1,2,3,4	2 2 3 3
2	5	2,4,5 2,3,5 2,3,4,5 2,1,3,5	2 2 3 3

5.5. CYCLES

A cycle is a path in which first and last vertices are the same. A graph contains no cycles, if there is no path of non-zero length through the graph, $P = \langle v_0, v_1, \ldots, v_k \rangle$ such that $v_0 = v_k$.

Let us consider the graph shown in the Figure 5.2. We may notice that there is a path, which starts at vertex 1 and finishes at vertex 1, i.e., path 1,2,4,5,3,1. Such a path is called a cycle.

5.6. VARIOUS TYPES OF GRAPHS

The graphs are classified in the following categories:

1. **Directed Graph:** A graph in which every edge is directed is called a directed graph or a digraph.

In a directed graph, each edge is an ordered pair of vertices, i.e., a directed pair represents each edge. If E = (v,w), then v is the tail or initial vertex of the edge and w is the head or final vertex of the edge. Subsequently (v,w) and (w,v) represent two different edges.

A directed graph may be pictorially represented as given in Figure 5.3. An arrow indicates the direction.

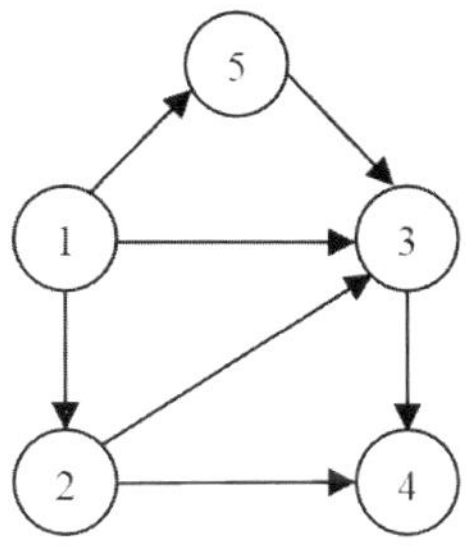

Figure 5.3. A directed graph.

The set of vertices V(G) = (1,2,3,4,5} and the set of edges E(G) = {(1,2), (1,3), (1,5), (2,3), (2,4), (3,4), (5,3)}.

2. **Undirected Graph:** A graph in which there is no direction between two vertices is called an undirected graph. In an undirected graph, pair of vertices representing any edge is unordered. There can be two ways of representation of edges. Thus, (v,w) and (w,v) represent the same edge.

An undirected graph may be pictorially represented as shown in Figure 5.4.

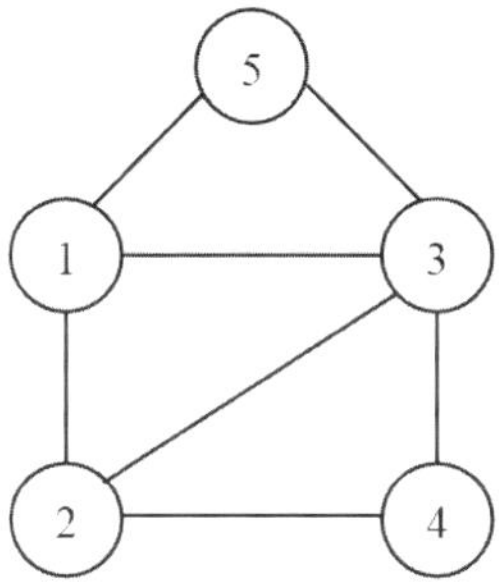

Figure 5.4. An undirected graph.

We have numbered the nodes as 1, 2, 3, 4, and 5. Therefore, V(G) = (1,2,3,4,5) and E(G) = {(1,2),(1,3), (1,5), (2,3), (2,4), (3,4), (3,5)}.

You may notice that the edge incident with node 1 and node 5 is written as (1,5); we could also have written (5,1) instead of (1,5). The same applies to all the other edges. Therefore, we may say that ordering of vertices is not significant here. So, we can also represent the set of edges as:

E(G) ={(2,1),(3,1), (5,1), (3,2), (4,2), (4,3), (5,3)}

3. **Connected Graph:** A graph is called connected, if there exists a path from any vertex to any other vertex, i.e., every pair of its vertices is connected. The Figure 5.4 depicts a connected graph, as there exist a path from any vertex to any other vertex. A connected graph may consist of only one or more than one connected components.

i. **Strongly Connected Graph:** Two vertices are strongly connected, if they are connected in both directions to one another. A digraph is called strongly connected, if every pair of its vertices is strongly connected.

Let us consider a directed graph as shown in Figure 5.5. It is a strongly connected graph because every pair of vertices is strongly connected, i.e., they are connected in both directions to one another. Table 5.3, sets the paths between pair of vertices.

Table 5.3 Sets the paths between pair of vertices

Pair of Vertices	Path
1,2	1->2
1,3	1->2->4->3
1,4	1->2->4
1,5	1->5
2,1	2->4->3->1
2,3	2->4->3
2,4	2->4
2,5	2->4->3->5
3,1	3->1
3,2	3->2
3,4	3->2->4
3,5	3->5
4,1	4->3->1
4,2	4->3->2
4,3	4->3
4,5	4->3->5
5,1	5->1
5,2	5->1->2
5,3	5->1->2->4->3
5,4	5->1->2->4

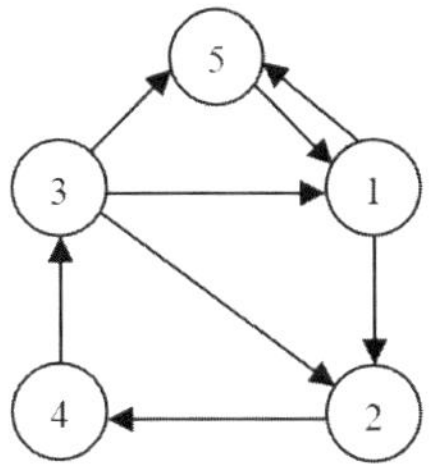

Figure 5.5. Strongly connected graph.

ii. **Weakly Connected Graph:** Two vertices are weakly connected, if they are not connected in both directions to one another. A digraph is called weakly connected, if every pair of its vertices is not strongly connected.

The directed graph in Figure 5.6 is weakly connected. There does not exist a directed path from vertex 2 to vertex 1; also from vertex 5 to other vertices; and so on. Therefore, it is a weakly connected graph.

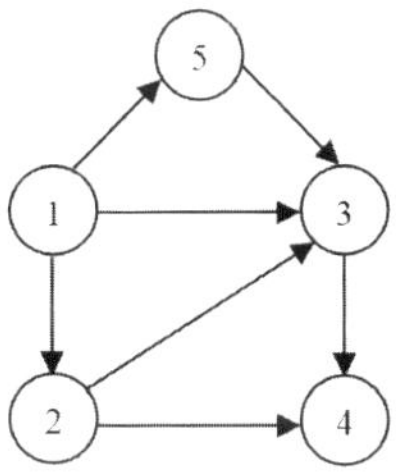

Figure 5.6. A weakly directed graph.

4. **Unconnected Graph:** A graph is called an unconnected graph, if there exist at least two vertices with no path between them. Figure 5.7 is an example of unconnected graph.

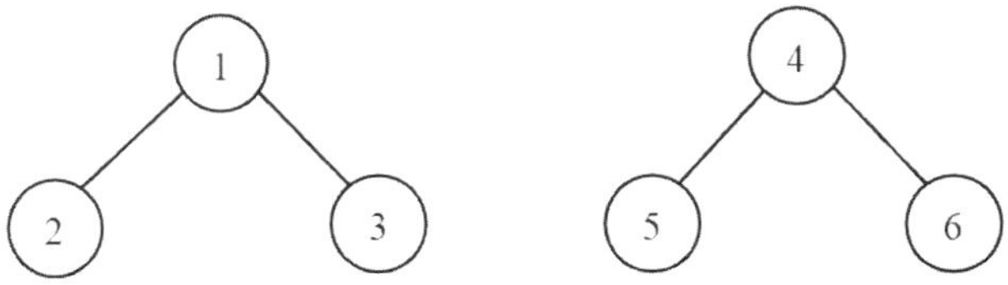

Figure 5.7. Unconnected graph.

It is an unconnected graph. We may say that these are two graphs and not one. Look at the figure in its totality and apply the definition of graph. Does it satisfy the definition of a graph? It does. Therefore, it is one graph having two unconnected components. Since, there are unconnected components, it is an unconnected graph.

5. **Simple and Multi Graph:** A graph is said to be simple, if only one edge is directed from any one vertex to any other vertex. Otherwise it is called multi graph. Figure 5.8 shows such graphs.

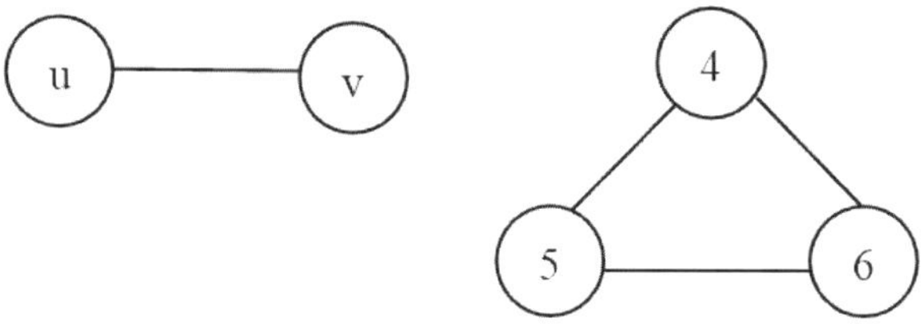

Figure 5.8. Simple and multi graph.

5.7. TREES

A Tree is a special type of graph. A graph is called a tree, if it has two properties:

- It is connected; and
- There are no cycles in the graph.

Figure 5.9 shows a graph called tree.

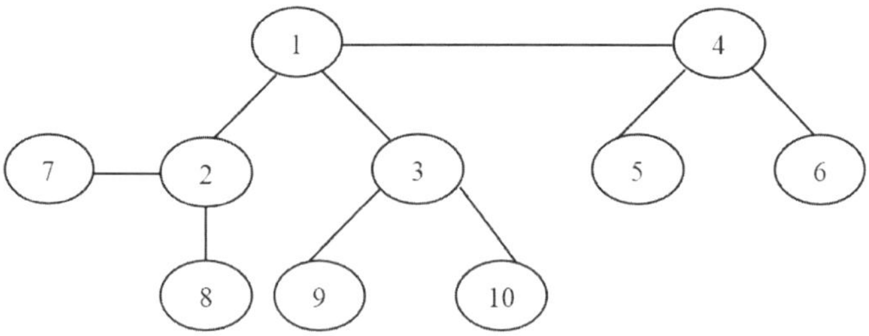

Figure 5.9. Trees.

5.8. GRAPH REPRESENTATIONS

Graph is a mathematical structure and finds its application in many areas of interest in which problems need to be solved using computers. Thus, this mathematical structure must be represented as some kind of data structures. The following representations are used for representations of graph:

5.8.1. Adjacency Matrix

Suppose G=(V,E) is a graph with n vertices(nodes) and suppose the nodes of the graph have been ordered and are called v_1, v_2,..., v_n. Then the adjacency matrix A of graph G, is an nxn matrix of bits, such that:

1 if there is an edge from vi to vj, i.e., vi is adjacent to vj

Aij = 0 if there is no such edge.

The matrix likes A, which contains entries of only 0 and 1, is called a bit matrix or a boolean matrix. The adjacency matrix A of the graph G does depend on the ordering of the nodes of G; i.e., a different ordering of the nodes may result in a different adjacency matrix. However, the resulting matrix from two different ordering can be interchanged from one to another by interchanging rows and columns.

5.8.1.1. Adjacency Matrix for Undirected Graph

The adjacency matrix A of an undirected graph G will be a symmetric matrix, i.e., Aij = Aji for every i and j.

Let us take an undirected graph shown in Figure 5.10. The adjacency matrix for the graph is tabulated in Table 5.4.

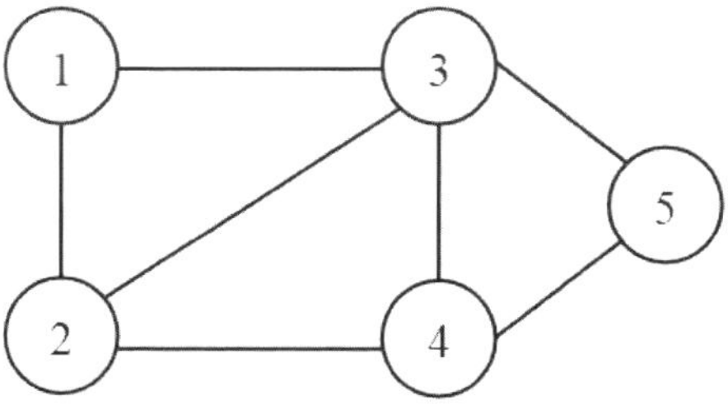

Figure 5.10. Adjacency Matrix.

Table 5.4. Adjacency Matrix

Vertex	**1**	**2**	**3**	**4**	**5**
1	0	1	1	0	1
2	1	0	1	1	0
3	1	1	0	1	1
4	0	1	1	0	0
5	1	0	1	0	0

We may observe that the adjacency matrix for an undirected graph is symmetric, as the lower and upper triangles are the same. Also, all the diagonal elements are zero.

5.8.1.2. Adjacency Matrix for Directed Graph

The adjacency matrix A of a directed graph G will be a matrix, in which Aij != Aji unless there are two edges, one in either direction, between i and j.

Let us take a directed graph shown in Figure 5.11. The adjacency matrix for the graph is tabulated in Table 5.5.

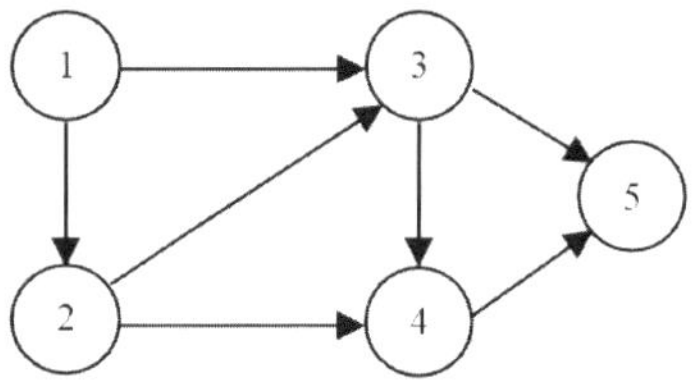

Figure 5.11. Adjacency Matrix for Directed Graph.

Table 5.5. Adjacency Matrix for Directed Graph

Vertex	**1**	**2**	**3**	**4**	**5**
1	0	1	1	0	0
2	0	0	1	1	0
3	0	0	0	1	1
4	0	0	0	0	1
5	0	0	0	0	0

The total number of 1's account for the number of edges in the digraph. The number of 1's in each row gives the out degree of the corresponding vertex.

In C language, adjacency matrix can be implemented as a 2-dimensional array of type **int**. We may have a declaration like:

```
#DEFINE vertex 20
typedef struct graph_tag{
int n;
int adjmat[vertex][vertex];
}graph;
```

where; n is the number of nodes in the graph.

adjmat[vertex][vertex] =1 if vertex are adjacent

adjmat[vertex][vertex] =0 otherwise

5.8.2. Adjacency List Representation

Adjacency lists are lists of nodes that are connected to a given node. For each node, a linked list of nodes connected to it can be set up.

In this representation, we store a graph as a linked structure. We store all the vertices in a list and then for each vertex, we have a linked list of its adjacent vertices. Let us consider the directed graph G given in Figure 5.12.

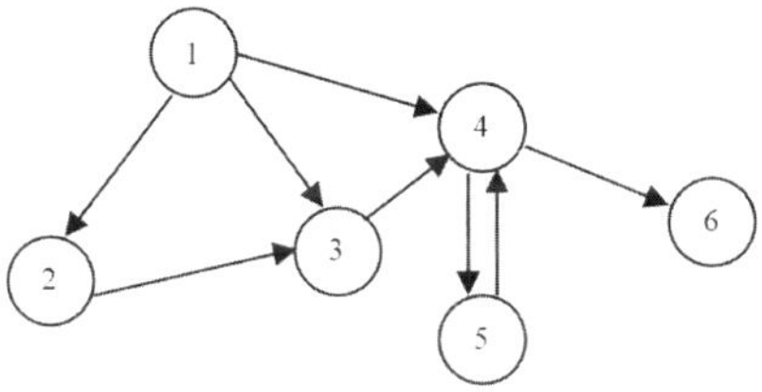

Figure 5.12. Adjacency List Representation.

The adjacency list representation needs a list of all of its nodes and for each node a linked list of its adjacent nodes (Figure 5.13). Therefore,

1	2	3	4	5	6

1	→	2	→	3	→	4
2	→	3				
3	→	4				
4	→	5	→	6		
5	→	4				
6						

Figure 5.13. Adjacency list structure for graph.

The adjacent vertices may appear in the adjacency list in arbitrary order. Also, an arrow from 2 to 3 in the list linked to 1, does not mean that 2 and 3 are adjacent.

5.8.3. Adjacency Multilists

In some situations, it is necessary to be able to determine the second entry for a particular edge and mark that edge as have been examined. It can be accomplished easily, if the adjacency list is actually maintained as multilist.

It is a list in which nodes may be shared among several lists. There is exactly one node for each edge and this node is on the adjacency list for each of the two vertices it is incident to.

- **Declaration for Adjacency Multilists:** The following is the declaration of the adjacency multilists:

```
#define MAX_VERTICES 20
typedef struct edge *edge_pointer;
typedef struct edge {
short int marked;
int vertex1, vertex2;
edge_pointer path1, path2;
};
edge_pointer graph[MAX_VERTICES];
```

5.9. MINIMUM PATH PROBLEM

In many applications, we are often required to find a shortest path, i.e., a path having the minimum weight between two vertices. It turns out that it is just as easy to solve the more general problem of starting at one vertex called the source and finding the shortest path to every other vertex instead of just one destination vertex.

We have seen in the graph traversals that we can travel through edges of the graph. It is very much likely in applications that these edges have some weights attached to it. This weight may reflect distance, time or some other quantity that corresponds to the cost we incur when we travel through that edge.

For example, in the graph in Figure 5.14, we can go from 1 to 5 through 3 at a cost of 7 or through 2 and 4 at a cost of 11.

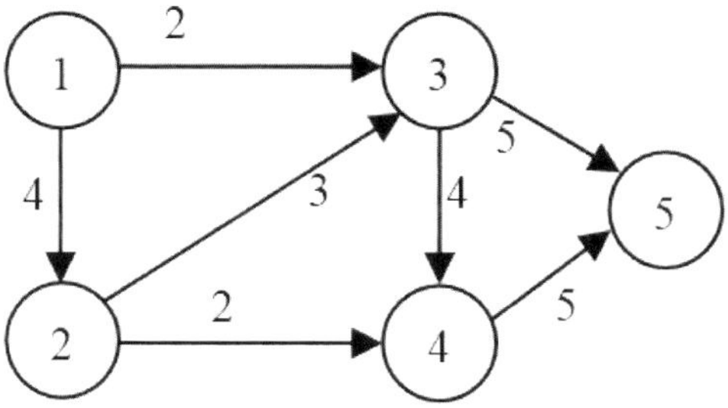

Figure 5.14. Minimum Path Problem.

We can use the following algorithm to find the minimum path for directed graph in which every edge has a non-negative weight attached.

5.10. TRAVERSAL SCHEMES OF A GRAPH

A graph traversal means visiting all the nodes of the graph. Graph traversal may be needed in many application areas and there may be many methods for visiting the vertices of the graph. Two graph traversal methods are:

5.10.1. Depth First Traversal

In this method, we start with vertex say, v. An adjacent vertex is selected and a depth first search is initiated from it. For example, let v_1, v_2. vk are adjacent vertices to vertex v. We may select any vertex from this list. Say, we select v_1. Now all the adjacent vertices to v_1 are identified and all of those are visited; next v_2 is selected and all its adjacent vertices visited and so on. This process continues till all the vertices are visited. It is possible that we reach a traversed vertex second time. Therefore, we have to set a flag somewhere to check, if the vertex is already visited. Let us consider a graph shown in Figure 5.15.

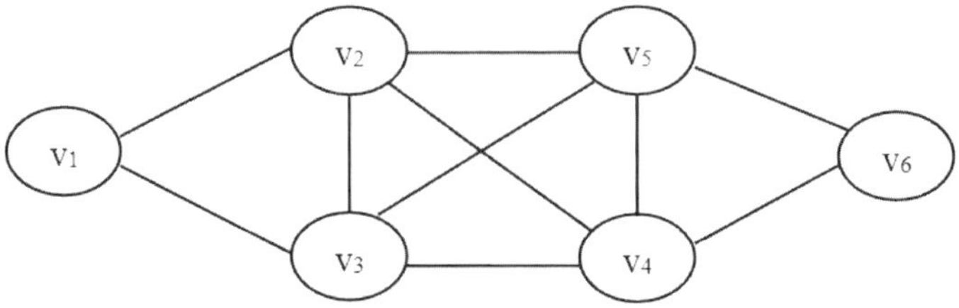

Figure 5.15. Graph for DFS.

Table 5.6 tabulates the adjacency matrix of graph 5.15.

Table 5.6. The adjacency matrix of graph

Vertex	v_1	v_2	v_3	v_4	v_5	v_6
v_1	0	1	1	0	0	0
v_2	1	0	1	1	1	0
v_3	1	1	0	1	1	0
v_4	0	1	1	0	1	1
v_5	0	1	1	1	0	1
v_6	0	0	0	1	1	0

Table 5.7 shows the process of visiting each vertex in the graph shown in the Figure 5.15.

Table 5.7. Process of visiting each vertex in the graph

Vertices Visited	Adjacency Vertices	Next Non-Visited Vertex
v_1	v_2, v_3	v_2
v_1, v_2	v_1, v_3, v_4, v_5	v_3
v_1, v_2, v_3	v_1, v_2, v_4, v_5	v_4
v_1, v_2, v_3, v_4	v_2, v_3, v_5, v_6	v_5
v_1, v_2, v_3, v_4, v_5	v_2, v_3, v_4, v_6	v_6
$v_1, v_2, v_3, v_4, v_5, v_6$	v_4, v_5	NULL

Let us start with v_1. Its adjacent vertices are v_2 and v_3. Let us pick v_2. Its adjacent vertices are v_1, v_3, v_4, and v_5. v_1 is already visited. Let us pick v_3. Its adjacent vertices are v_1, v_2, v_4, and v_5. v_1 and v_2 are 20 already visited. Let us visit v_4. Its adjacent vertices are v_2, v_3, v_5, and v_6. v_2 and v_3 are already visited.

Let us traverse v_5. Its adjacent vertices are v_2, v_3, v_4, and v_6. v_2, v_3 and v_4 are already visited. So, visit v_6. We had v_4 and v_5 both are visited. Therefore, we back track. Now, we have visited all the vertices. Therefore, the sequence of traversal is: v_1, v_2, v_3, v_4, v_5, v_6. This is not a unique or the only sequence possible for using this traversal method.

- **Declaration:** The following is the structure declaration for depth first search algorithm:

```
#define v 10
typedef int adj_matrix[v][v];
typedef struct t_graph{
int nodes[v];
int n_nodes;
int *visited;
adj_matrix am;
}graph;
```

where; nodes represent the traversal order of the vertices of the graph, n_ nodes represent the total nodes in the graph, visited is the flag, which is used to indicate whether the vertex of the graph is visited or not and am is used to represent the adjacent matrix of the graph. The following is the algorithm which implements the depth first search process of traversing a node within the graph(G).

A. **Algorithm:** Following are the steps for depth first search:

a. [Initialize the counter with zero for storing the arrival vertices of the graph]

Set index = 0

b. [Enter the vertices in the graph]

Read(n_nodes)

c. [Initialize all vertices in the array with FALSE to indicate the absence of visits to the vertices]

Repeat step (d) for(i=1;i<n_nodes;i++)

d. Set visited[i] = FALSE

e. [Read adjacent matrix of the graph, enter 1 in the array for all adjacent vertices j of vertex i and 0 for not]

Repeat step (f) for(i=1;i<n_nodes;v++),

for(j=1;j<n_nodes;j++)

f. Read am[i][j]

g. [Check each vertex of the graph whether it is visited or not]

Repeat step from (h) for(i=1;i<n_nodes;i++)

h. If(!visited(i)) then

Call function visit(g,i)

i. [Print the adjacent matrix of the graph]

Repeat step (m) for(i=1;i<n_nodes;v++),

for(j=1;j<n_nodes;j++)

j. Write a[i][j]

k. [Print the sequence of traversal of a given graph]

Repeat step (o) for(i=1;i<n_nodes;v++)

l. Write nodes[i]

m. [Definition of the function DFS]

void visit(g, i)

n. Set visited[i] = TRUE

Set nodes[++index] = i

o. [Check all the vertices adjacent to the vertex i]

Repeat step (p) for(j=1;j<n_nodes;j++)

p. If(am[i][j] == 1) then

If(!visited(j)) then

Call visit(g, j) recursively

q. End.

B. Equivalent Function in C:

```
void DFS(graph *g)
{
int i,j,k;
/*Initialize all the vertices of the graph with FALSE to indicate the
absence of visits to the vertices*/
for(k=1;k<=g->n_nodes;k++)
g->visited[k] = FALSE;
```

294 Data Structures

```
/* Read the adjacent matrix of the graph*/
for(i=1;i<=g->n_nodes;i++)
{
for(j=1;j<=g->n_nodes;j++)
{
scanf("%d,"&g->am[i][j]);
}
}
/*check the vertex of the graph is visited or not */
for(k=1;k<=g->n_nodes;k++)
{
if (!g->visited[k])
/* Call function visit */
visit(g, k);
}
/* Print the adjacency matrix of the graph !!*/
for(i=1;i<=g->n_nodes;i++)
{
for(k=1;k<=g->n_nodes;k++)
{
printf("%d\t,"g->am[i][k]);
}
printf("\n");
}
/*The sequence of traversal of a given graph in DFS */
i=0;
while(i<g->n_nodes)
{
printf("%d\t,"g->nodes[++i]);
```

```
}
}
void visit(graph *g, int k)
{
int j;
/*assign the vertex of the graph is visited */
g->visited[k] = TRUE;
g->nodes[++search_index] = k;
/* Search for visited vertex */
for(j=1;j<=g->n_nodes;j++)
{
/* Check adjacent vertex of the vertex */
if(g->am[k][j] == 1)
{
/*check the vertex of the graph is visited or not */
if (!g->visited[j])
/* Call recursively function vists */
visit(g, j);
}
}
}
```

C. **Implementation of the Depth First Search Method:** The following program graph_dfs.c performs the traversal operation of the graph using depth first search method. A depth first traverse of a graph uses an additional array to flag nodes that it has visited already:

```
/*graph_dfs.c*/
#include<stdio.h>
#define v 10
#define FALSE 0
#define TRUE 1
typedef int adj_matrix[v][v];
```

```
typedef struct  t_graph{
int nodes[v];
int n_nodes;
int *visited;
adj_matrix am;
}graph;
void DFS(graph *);
void visit(graph *,int);
static int search_index=0;
void main()
{
graph g;
printf("This program performs the traversal of graph using depth first search method!!\n");
printf("Please enter the nodes in the graph\n");
scanf("%d,"&g.n_nodes);
DFS(&g);
}
void DFS(graph *g)
{
int i,j,k;
for(k=1;k<=g->n_nodes;k++)
```

296 Data Structures

```
g->visited[k] = FALSE;
for(i=1;i<=g->n_nodes;i++)
{
for(j=1;j<=g->n_nodes;j++)
{
printf("Please enter data of vertex %d for(%d,%d):\n,"i,i,j);
printf("Please enter 1 for adjacent vertex and 0 for not\n");
scanf("%d,"&g->am[i][j]);
```

```
}
}
for(k=1;k<=g->n_nodes;k++)
{
if (!g->visited[k])
visit(g, k);
}
printf("!!ADJACENCY MATRIX!!\n");
for(i=1;i<=g->n_nodes;i++)
{
for(k=1;k<=g->n_nodes;k++)
{
printf("%d\t,"g->am[i][k]);
}
printf("\n");
}
i=0;
printf("!!The sequence of traversal of a given graph in DFS is!!\n");
while(i<g->n_nodes)
{
printf("%d\t,"g->nodes[++i]);
}
}
void visit(graph *g, int k)
{
int j;
g->visited[k] = TRUE;
g->nodes[++search_index] = k;
for(j=1;j<=g->n_nodes;j++)
{
if(g->am[k][j] == 1)
```

Graphs 297

```
{
if (!g->visited[j])
visit(g, j);
}
}
}
```

D. **Output of the Program:** This program performs the traversal of graph using depth first search method!!

```
Please enter the nodes in the graph
6
Please enter data of vertex 1 for(1,1):
Please enter 1 for adjacent vertex and 0 for not
0
Please enter data of vertex 1 for(1,2):
Please enter 1 for adjacent vertex and 0 for not
1
Please enter data of vertex 1 for(1,3):
Please enter 1 for adjacent vertex and 0 for not
1
Please enter data of vertex 1 for(1,4):
Please enter 1 for adjacent vertex and 0 for not
0
Please enter data of vertex 1 for(1,5):
Please enter 1 for adjacent vertex and 0 for not
0
Please enter data of vertex 1 for(1,6):
Please enter 1 for adjacent vertex and 0 for not
0
Please enter data of vertex 2 for(2,1):
Please enter 1 for adjacent vertex and 0 for not
1
```

```
Please enter data of vertex 2 for(2,2):
Please enter 1 for adjacent vertex and 0 for not
0
Please enter data of vertex 2 for(2,3):
Please enter 1 for adjacent vertex and 0 for not
1
Please enter data of vertex 2 for(2,4):
Please enter 1 for adjacent vertex and 0 for not
1
Please enter data of vertex 2 for(2,5):
Please enter 1 for adjacent vertex and 0 for not
1
Please enter data of vertex 2 for(2,6):
Please enter 1 for adjacent vertex and 0 for not
0
Please enter data of vertex 3 for(3,1):
Please enter 1 for adjacent vertex and 0 for not
1
Please enter data of vertex 3 for(3,2):
Please enter 1 for adjacent vertex and 0 for not
1
Please enter data of vertex 3 for(3,3):
0
Please enter data of vertex 3 for(3,4):
Please enter 1 for adjacent vertex and 0 for not
1
Please enter data of vertex 3 for(3,5):
Please enter 1 for adjacent vertex and 0 for not
1
Please enter data of vertex 3 for(3,6):
Please enter 1 for adjacent vertex and 0 for not
```

0

Please enter data of vertex 4 for(4,1):

Please enter 1 for adjacent vertex and 0 for not

0

Please enter data of vertex 4 for(4,2):

Please enter 1 for adjacent vertex and 0 for not

1

Please enter data of vertex 4 for(4,3):

Please enter 1 for adjacent vertex and 0 for not

1

Please enter data of vertex 4 for(4,4):

Please enter 1 for adjacent vertex and 0 for not

0

Please enter data of vertex 4 for(4,5):

Please enter 1 for adjacent vertex and 0 for not

1

Please enter data of vertex 4 for(4,6):

Please enter 1 for adjacent vertex and 0 for not

1

Please enter data of vertex 5 for(5,1):

Please enter 1 for adjacent vertex and 0 for not

0

Please enter data of vertex 5 for(5,2):

Please enter 1 for adjacent vertex and 0 for not

1

Please enter data of vertex 5 for(5,3):

Please enter 1 for adjacent vertex and 0 for not

1

Please enter data of vertex 5 for(5,4):

Please enter 1 for adjacent vertex and 0 for not

1

```
Please enter data of vertex 5 for(5,5):
Please enter 1 for adjacent vertex and 0 for not
0
Please enter data of vertex 5 for(5,6):
Please enter 1 for adjacent vertex and 0 for not
1
Please enter data of vertex 6 for(6,1):
Please enter 1 for adjacent vertex and 0 for not
0
Please enter data of vertex 6 for(6,2):
Please enter 1 for adjacent vertex and 0 for not
0
Please enter data of vertex 6 for(6,3):
Please enter 1 for adjacent vertex and 0 for not
0
Please enter data of vertex 6 for(6,4):
Please enter 1 for adjacent vertex and 0 for not
1
Please enter data of vertex 6 for(6,5):
Please enter 1 for adjacent vertex and 0 for not
1
Please enter data of vertex 6 for(6,6):
Please enter 1 for adjacent vertex and 0 for not
0
!!ADJACENCY MATRIX!!
0 1 1 0 0 0
1 0 1 1 1 0
1 1 0 1 1 0
0 1 1 0 1 1
0 1 1 1 0 1
```

0 0 0 1 1 0

!!The sequence of traversal of a given graph in DFS is!!

1 2 3 4 5 6

5.10.2. Breadth First Traversal

In this method, we start with vertex say, v. Visit v and then visit all the adjacent vertices of the vertex v and then visit all the unvisited vertices adjacent to these and so on. This process continues till all the vertices are visited. It is possible that we reach a traversed vertex second time. Therefore, we have to set a flag somewhere to check, if the vertex is already visited. Let us consider a graph shown in Figure 5.16.

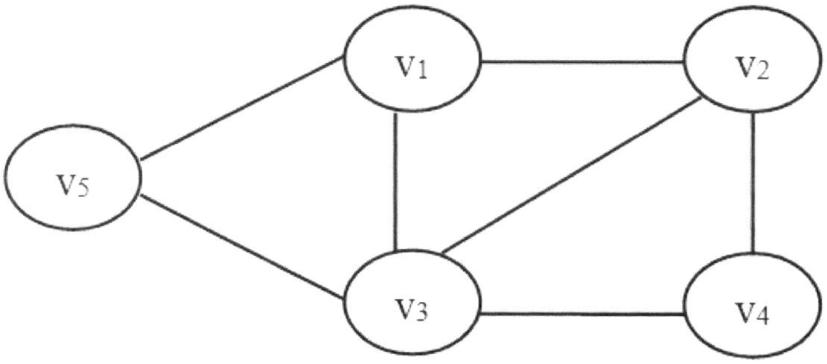

Figure 5.16. Graph for BFS.

Table 5.8 tabulates the adjacency matrix of graph shown in Figure 5.16.

Table 5.8. Adjacency matrix

Vertex	v_1	v_2	v_3	v_4	v_5
v_1	0	1	1	0	1
v_2	1	0	1	1	0
v_3	1	1	0	1	1
v_4	0	1	1	0	0
v_5	1	0	1	0	0

We start with vertex say, v_1. Its adjacent vertices are v_2, v_3, and v_5. We visit all one by one. The list of visited vertices is v_1, v_3, v_4, and v_5. Now, we pick one of these, say v_2. Its adjacent vertices are v_1, v_3, and v_4. The unvisited adjacent vertex to v_2 is v_4. We visit v_4. We go back to the remaining visited vertices of v_1. There are no more unvisited adjacent vertices of v_3, v_4, and v_5. Therefore, the sequence of traversal is: v_1, v_2, v_3, v_5, v_4.

- **Declaration:** The following is the structure declaration for breath first search algorithm;

```
#define v 10
typedef int adj_matrix[v][v];
typedef struct t_graph{
int n_nodes;
int *visited;
adj_matrix am;
}graph;
```

where; n_nodes represent the total nodes in the graph, visited is the flag, which is used to indicate whether the vertex of the graph is visited or not and am is used to represent the adjacent matrix of the graph. The following is the algorithm, which implements the breath first search process of traversing a node within the graph(G).

A. Algorithm: Following are the steps for breadth first search algorithm:

a. [Initialize the counter with zero for storing the arrival vertices of the graph]

Set index = 0

b. [Enter the vertices in the graph]

Read(n_nodes)

c. [Initialize all vertices in the array with FALSE to indicate the absence of visits to the vertices]

Repeat step (d) for(i=1;i<n_nodes;i++)

d. Set visited[i] = FALSE

e. [Read adjacent matrix of the graph, enter 1 in the array for all adjacent vertices j of vertex i and 0 for not]

Repeat step (f) for(i=1;i<n_nodes;v++),

for(j=1;j<n_nodes;j++)

f. Read am[i][j]

g. [Check each vertex of the graph whether it is visited or not]

Repeat step from (h) to (n) for(i=1;i<n_nodes;i++)

h. If(!visited(i)) then

Call insert_queue(q, i)

i. [Check all the vertices adjacent to the vertex i]

Repeat step from (j) to (n) while(front!=rear)

j. Set k = delete_queue(q)

k. Set visited[i] = TRUE

l. [Check adjacent vertex of the graph whether it is visited or not]

Repeat step from (m) to (n) for(j=1;j<n_nodes;j++)

m. If(am[i][j] == 0) then

continue

n. [Check all the vertices adjacent to the vertex i]

If(!visited(j)) then

Set visited[j] = TRUE,

Call insert_queue(q, j)

o. [Print the adjacent matrix of the graph]

Repeat step (m) for(i=1;i<n_nodes;v++),

for(j=1;j<n_nodes;j++)

p. Write a[i][j]

q. [Print the sequence of traversal of a given graph]

Repeat step (o) for(i=1;i<n_nodes;v++)

r. Write q[i]

s. End.

B. Equivalent Function in C

```
void BFS(graph *g)
{
int k,i,j;
/*Initialize all the vertices of the graph with FALSE to indicate the absence of visits to the vertices*/
for(k=1;k<=g->n_nodes;k++)
g->visited[k] = FALSE;
/* Read the adjacent matrix of the graph*/
```

```
for(i=1;i<=g->n_nodes;i++)
{
for(j=1;j<=g->n_nodes;j++)
{
scanf("%d,"&g->am[i][j]);
}
}
/*check the vertex of the graph is visited or not */
for(k=1;k<=g->n_nodes;k++)
{
if (!g->visited[k])
{
/* Insert visited vertex in the queue */
insert_queue(q,k);
do
{
/* Delete vertex from the queue */
k = delete_queue(q);
/*assign the vertex of the graph is visited*/
g->visited[k] = TRUE;
for(j=1;j<=g->n_nodes;j++)
{
/* Check adjacent vertex of the vertex */
if(g->am[k][j] == 0)
continue;
/*check the vertex of the graph is visited or not */
if (!g->visited[j])
{
/*assign the vertex of the graph is visited */
g->visited[j] = TRUE;
/* Insert visited vertex in the queue */
```

```
insert_queue(q, j);
}
}
}while(front!=rear);
}
}
/* Print the adjacency matrix of the graph !!*/
for(i=1;i<=g->n_nodes;i++)
{
for(k=1;k<=g->n_nodes;k++)
{
printf("%d\t,"g->am[i][k]);
}
printf("\n");
}
/*The sequence of traversal of a given graph in BFS is*/
i=0;
while(i<g->n_nodes)
{
printf("%d\t,"q[++i]);
}
}
```

C. **Implementation of the Breath First Search Method:** The following program graph_bfs.c performs the traversal operation of the graph using breath first search method. A breath first traverse of a graph uses an additional array to flag nodes that it has visited already:

```
/*graph_bfs.c*/
#include<stdio.h>
#define v 10
#define FALSE 0
#define TRUE 1
```

```
typedef int adj_matrix[v][v];
typedef struct t_graph{
int n_nodes;
int *visited;
304 Data Structures
adj_matrix am;
}graph;
void BFS(graph *);
void insert_queue(int[],int);
int delete_queue(int[]);
int front=1,rear=1;
int q[v];
void main()
{
graph g;
printf("This program performs the traversal of graph using breath first search method!!\n");
printf("Please enter the nodes in the graph\n");
scanf("%d,"&g.n_nodes);
BFS(&g);
}
void BFS(graph *g)
{
int k,i,j;
for(k=1;k<=g->n_nodes;k++)
g->visited[k] = FALSE;
for(i=1;i<=g->n_nodes;i++)
{
for(j=1;j<=g->n_nodes;j++)
{
printf("Please enter data of vertex %d for(%d,%d):\n,"i,i,j);
```

```
printf("Please enter 1 for adjacent vertex and 0 for not\n");
scanf("%d,"&g->am[i][j]);
}
}
for(k=1;k<=g->n_nodes;k++)
{
if (!g->visited[k])
{
insert_queue(q,k);
do
{
k = delete_queue(q);
g->visited[k] = TRUE;
for(j=1;j<=g->n_nodes;j++)
{
if(g->am[k][j] == 0)
continue;
if (!g->visited[j])
{
g->visited[j] = TRUE;
insert_queue(q, j);
}
}
}while(front!=rear);
}
}
printf("!!ADJACENCY MATRIX!!\n");
for(i=1;i<=g->n_nodes;i++)
{
for(k=1;k<=g->n_nodes;k++)
{
```

```
printf("%d\t,"g->am[i][k]);
}
printf("\n");
}
i=0;
printf("!!The sequence of traversal of a given graph in BFS is!!\n");
while(i<g->n_nodes)
{
printf("%d\t,"q[++i]);
}
}
void insert_queue(int q[], int k)
{
q[rear] = k;
rear++;
}
int delete_queue(int q[])
{
int item;
item = q[front];
front++;
if(front==v)
{
front=1;
rear=1;
}
return(item);
}
```

D. **Output of the Program:** This program performs the traversal of graph using breath first search method!!

Please enter the nodes in the graph

5

```
Please enter data of vertex 1 for(1,1):
Please enter 1 for adjacent vertex and 0 for not
0
Please enter data of vertex 1 for(1,2):
Please enter 1 for adjacent vertex and 0 for not
1
Please enter data of vertex 1 for(1,3):
Please enter 1 for adjacent vertex and 0 for not
1
Please enter data of vertex 1 for(1,4):
Please enter 1 for adjacent vertex and 0 for not
0
Please enter data of vertex 1 for(1,5):
Please enter 1 for adjacent vertex and 0 for not
1
Please enter data of vertex 2 for(2,1):
Please enter 1 for adjacent vertex and 0 for not
1
Please enter data of vertex 2 for(2,2):
Please enter 1 for adjacent vertex and 0 for not
0
Please enter data of vertex 2 for(2,3):
Please enter 1 for adjacent vertex and 0 for not
1
Please enter data of vertex 2 for(2,4):
Please enter 1 for adjacent vertex and 0 for not
1
Please enter data of vertex 2 for(2,5):
Please enter 1 for adjacent vertex and 0 for not
0
```

Please enter data of vertex 3 for(3,1):

1

Please enter data of vertex 3 for(3,2):

Please enter 1 for adjacent vertex and 0 for not

1

Please enter data of vertex 3 for(3,3):

Please enter 1 for adjacent vertex and 0 for not

0

Please enter data of vertex 3 for(3,4):

Please enter 1 for adjacent vertex and 0 for not

1

Please enter data of vertex 3 for(3,5):

Please enter 1 for adjacent vertex and 0 for not

1

Please enter data of vertex 4 for(4,1):

Please enter 1 for adjacent vertex and 0 for not

0

Please enter data of vertex 4 for(4,2):

Please enter 1 for adjacent vertex and 0 for not

1

Please enter data of vertex 4 for(4,3):

Please enter 1 for adjacent vertex and 0 for not

1

Please enter data of vertex 4 for(4,4):

Please enter 1 for adjacent vertex and 0 for not

0

Please enter data of vertex 4 for(4,5):

Please enter 1 for adjacent vertex and 0 for not

0

Please enter 1 for adjacent vertex and 0 for not

Please enter data of vertex 5 for(5,1):

Please enter 1 for adjacent vertex and 0 for not

1

Please enter data of vertex 5 for(5,2):

Please enter 1 for adjacent vertex and 0 for not

0

Please enter data of vertex 5 for(5,3):

Please enter 1 for adjacent vertex and 0 for not

1

Please enter data of vertex 5 for(5,4):

Please enter 1 for adjacent vertex and 0 for not

0

Please enter data of vertex 5 for(5,5):

Please enter 1 for adjacent vertex and 0 for not

0

!!Adjacency matrix!!

0 1 1 0 1

1 0 1 1 0

1 1 0 1 1

0 1 1 0 0

1 0 1 0 0

!!The sequence of traversal of a given graph in BFS is!!

1 2 3 5 4

5.11. SPANNING TREES

A spanning tree of a connected graph G is a connected sub-graph of G having no cycles. Every connected graph has a spanning tree. Let us formally define a spanning tree. A tree T is a spanning tree of a connected graph G(V,E) such that:

- Every vertex of G belongs to an edge in T;
- The edges in T form a tree.

Let us see how we construct a spanning tree for a given graph. Take any vertex v as an initial partial tree and add edges one by one so that each edge joins a new vertex to the partial tree. In general, if there are n vertices in the graph we shall construct a spanning tree in (n – 1) steps, i.e., (n – 1) edges are needed to be added. For example, the following graph has four distinct spanning trees (Figures 5.17 and 5.18):

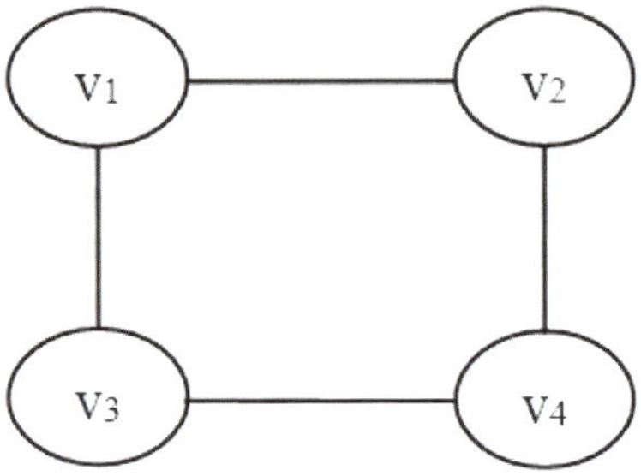

Figure 5.17. Graph has four distinct spanning trees.

Spanning Trees:

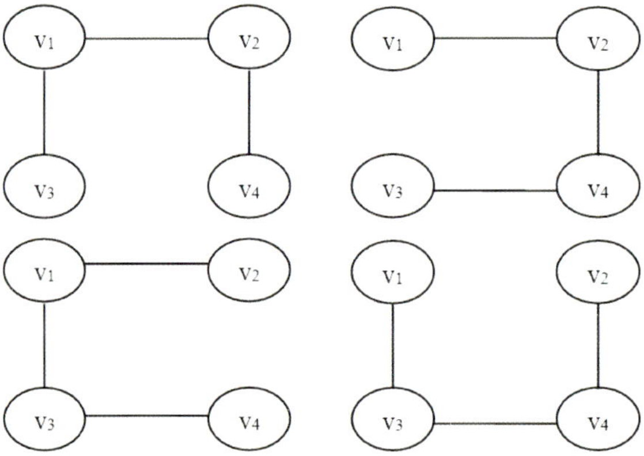

Graphs 309

Figure 5.18. Graph has four distinct spanning trees.

5.12. APPLICATIONS OF GRAPH

Graph is an important data structure whose extensive applications are known in almost all application areas. Nowadays, many applications related with computation can be managed efficiently with graph structures. In this section we have discussed two of them.

5.12.1. Minimum Spanning Tree Problem

Suppose the edges of the graph have weights or lengths. The weight of a tree is just the sum of weights of its edges. Obviously, different trees have different lengths. The cost of the spanning tree is the sum of the cost of all edges in the tree. We usually want to find a spanning tree of minimum cost.

Among all the spanning trees of a weighted and connected graph, the one (possibly more) with the least total weight is called a minimum spanning tree (MST).

- **Computer Networks:** Vertices in the graph might represent computer installations, edges represent connections between computers.

We want to allow messages from any computer to get to any other, possibly with routing through an intermediate computer, with minimum cost in connections.

- **Airline Routes:** Vertices in the graph are cities, and edges are routes between cities. We want to service a connected set of cities, with minimum cost.

The minimum spanning tree problem is the simplest, and one of the most central models in the field of combinatorial problem. It has inspired the development of many other problem domains in discrete optimization. In many systems, such as highways, computer networks, telephone lines, television cables, etc., we face such a problem: we need to design a simplest network(spanning tree) that will connect geographically dispersed system components so that they can communicate with each other and the total construction cost is minimized. This is only a situation where the minimum spanning tree problem can be applied directly. Actually, there are lots of indirect applications of the minimum spanning tree problem, such as, optimal message passing, all-pairs mini-max path, reducing data storage, cluster analysis, etc.

Suppose we have a group of islands that we wish to link with bridges so that it is possible to travel from one island to any other in the group. Further suppose that (as usual) our government wishes to spend the absolute minimum amount on this project (because other factors like the cost of using, maintaining, etc., these bridges will probably be the responsibility of some future government). The engineers are able to produce a cost for a bridge linking each possible pair of islands. The set of bridges, which will enable one to travel from any island to any other at minimum capital cost to the government, is the minimum spanning tree and for finding the minimum spanning tree is the minimum spanning tree problem. The following are the algorithms, which can be used for finding the minimum spanning tree:

5.12.1.1. Prims Algorithm

This algorithm for finding a minimal cost spanning tree in a connected graph is very easy to follow. It begins by adding the lowest cost edge and its two end points to the solution set. It then loops adding the lowest cost edge that connects a vertex in the solution set to one outside it. It also adds the end point of this edge that is not already in the solution set. The algorithm terminates when all vertices are in the solution set. The edges and vertices in the solution set at this point constitute a minimal cost spanning tree of the input graph.

This method does not require listing of all nodes in increasing order of weights and does not require to check at each step whether a newly selected node forms a circuit or not. The prim's algorithm can be easily implemented using the adjacency matrix representation of a graph.

- **Declaration:** The following is the structure declaration for prim's algorithm:

```
#define v 10
typedef struct t_tree     {
int n_nodes;
int path[v];
int tree[v][v];
int selected[v];
int adj_matrix[v][v];
}tree;
```

where; n_nodes represent the total nodes in the tree, selected is the flag, which is used to indicate whether the vertex of the graph is visited or not, adj_matrix is used to represent the cost from one vertex to another, tree is an array, which stores the output of the minimum spanning tree in an adjacency matrix and path represent the path of the minimum spanning tree. The following is the algorithm, which implements the prim's algorithm of tree (T):

A. **Algorithm:** Following are the steps for prim's algorithm.

a. [Read the vertices in the graph]

Read(n_nodes)

b. [Read adjacent matrix of the graph. The weight will be taken infinity, if there is no direct path between one vertex to another vertex, we have used 1500 for infinity, enter cost 0 for vertex to itself]

Repeat step (c) for(i=0;i<n_nodes;v++),

for(j=0;j<n_nodes;j++)

c. Read adj_matrix[i][j]

d. [Write the adjacent matrix of the graph]

Repeat for(i=0;i<n_nodes;i++)

Repeat for(j=0;j<n_nodes;j++)

Print(adj_matrix[i][j])

e. [Initially none of the vertices are selected]

for(i=0;i<n_nodes;i++)

Set selected[i] = FALSE

f. [Initially enters 0 in the minimum spanning tree matrix]

for(i=0;i<n_nodes;i++)

for(j=0;j<n_nodes;j++)

Set tree[i][j]=0

g. [Select the vertex 0 as the starting vertex]

Set selected[0]=TRUE,

path[0]=0,

length = 1

h. [Find the nearest neighbor vertex of one of selected vertices]

Repeat step (i) to (n) while(length<=n_nodes)

i. Set min = INFINITY

j. Repeat step(k) to (m)for(i=0;i<n_nodes;i++)

k. If(selected[i]==TRUE) then

l. Repeat step(m) for(j=0;j<n_nodes;j++)

m. If(selected[j]==FALSE) then

If(adj_matrix[i][j] <min) then

Set min = adj_matrix[i][j],

u = i,

w = j,

n. [Include the nearest neighbor into the tree]

Set tree[u][w] = 1,

selected[w] = TRUE,

path[++k] = w,

length = length + 1

o. [Write the minimum spanning tree adjacency matrix]

Repeat for(i=0;i<n_nodes;i++)

Repeat for(j=0;j<n_nodes;j++)

Print(tree[i][j])

p. [Write the shortest path from the source to all vertices]

Repeat for(i=0;i<k;i++)

Print(path[i])

q. End.

B. Equivalent Function in C

```
void prim(tree *t)
{
int i,j,k=0,w,u,p,min;
/* Read the cost matrix */
for(i=0;i<t->n_nodes;i++)
{
for(j=0;j<t->n_nodes;j++)
{
scanf("%d,"&t->adj_matrix[i][j]);
}
}
```

```
/*THE ADJACENT MATRIX OF THE GRAPH IS: */
for(i=0;i<t->n_nodes;i++)
{
for(j=0;j<t->n_nodes;j++)
{
printf("%5d\t,"t->adj_matrix[i][j]);
}
printf("\n");
}
/* Initially none of the vertices are selected */
for(i=0;i<t->n_nodes;i++)
{
t->selected[i] = FALSE;
}
/* Initially enters 0 in the minimum spanning tree matrix */
for(i=0;i<t->n_nodes;i++)
{
for(j=0;j<t->n_nodes;j++)
{
t->tree[i][j]=0;
}
}
/* Select the vertex 0 as the starting vertex */
t->selected[0]=TRUE;
t->path[0]=0;
length = 1;
/*Find the nearest neighbor vertex of one of the selected vertices*/
while(length<=t->n_nodes)
{
min = INFINITY;
for(i=0;i<t->n_nodes;i++)
```

```
{
if(t->selected[i]==TRUE)
{
for(j=0;j<t->n_nodes;j++)
{
if(t->selected[j]==FALSE)
{
if(t->adj_matrix[i][j] <min)
{
min = t->adj_matrix[i][j];
u = i;
w = j;
}
}
}
}
}
/* Include the nearest neighbor into the tree */
t->tree[u][w] = 1;
t->selected[w] = TRUE;
t->path[++k] = w;
length++;
} /* End of While loop */
/* the minimum spanning tree adjacency matrix is*/
for(i=0;i<t->n_nodes;i++)
{
for(j=0;j<t->n_nodes;j++)
{
printf("%5d\t,"t->tree[i][j]);
}
}
```

```
/* print the shortest path from the source to all vertices */
for(i=0;i<k;i++)
printf("%d\t,"t->path[i]);
}
```

5.12.1.2. Operation of Prim's Algorithm

Let us take an undirected weighted graph and its weighted adjacency matrix as shown in Figure 5.19. The following sequence of diagrams depicts the operation of prim's algorithm:

Source Graph

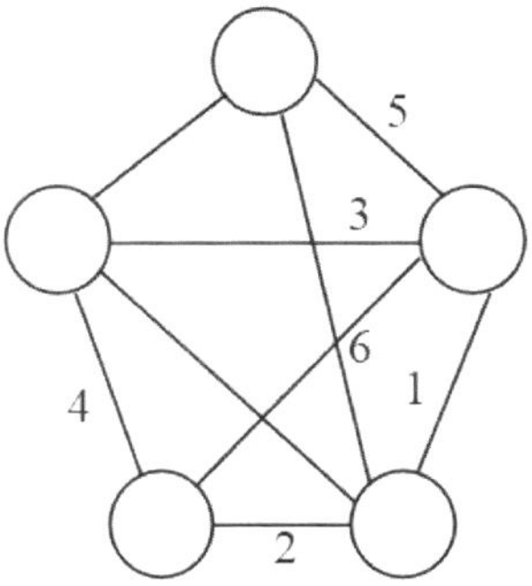

Adjacency Matrix

	0	1	2	3	4
0	–	5	3	–	2
1	5	–	1	6	6
2	3	1	–	2	10
3	–	6	2	–	4
4	2	6	10	4	–

Initial Tree

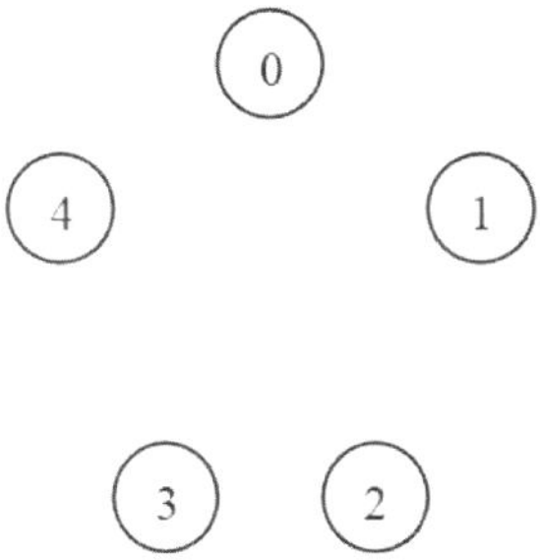

We start with source node 0.

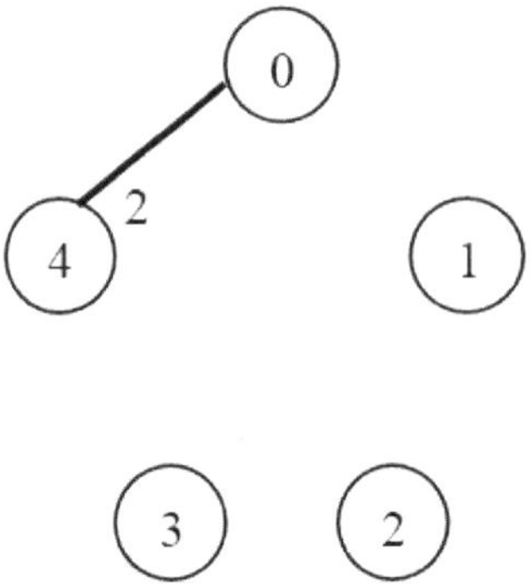	Choose the closest node to 0. We locate the vertex closest to it, i.e., we find a vertex from the adjacent vertices of 0 for which the length of the edge is minimum. 4, 2 and 1 are the adjacent vertices of 0. Vertex 4 has the minimum length(04)=2. Therefore, we choose 4.
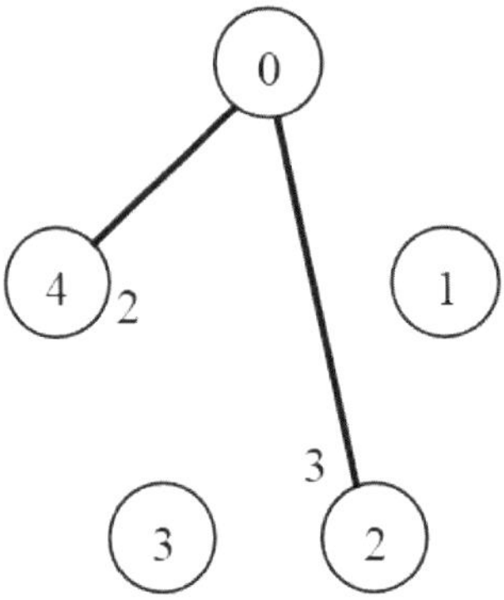	Now we look for all the adjacent vertices excluding the just earlier vertex of newly added vertex and the remaining adjacent vertices of earlier vertices, i.e., we have 1, 2 and 3 (as adjacent vertices of 4) and 1, 2 (as remaining adjacent vertex of 0). Now we again compare the length of the paths from source vertex to these unattached vertices. We find the length(02)=3 is the minimum. Therefore, we choose vertex 2.
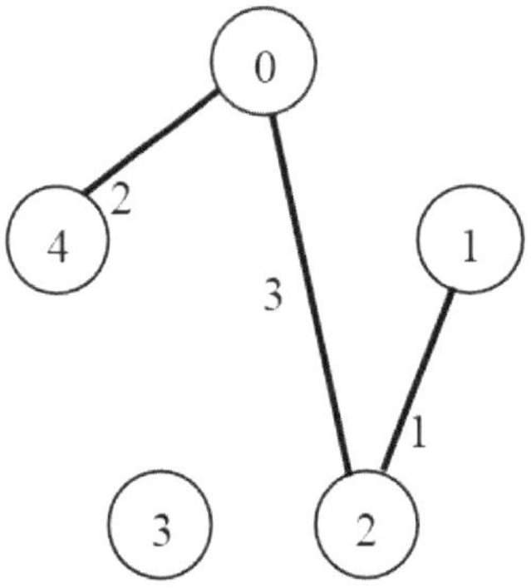	Now we have 1 and 3 (as adjacent vertices of 2) 3 and 1 (as remaining adjacent vertex of 4) and 1 (as remaining adjacent vertex of 0). Now we again compare the length of the paths from source vertex to these unattached vertices. We find the length(21)=1 is the minimum. Therefore, we choose vertex 1.

Final Stage	
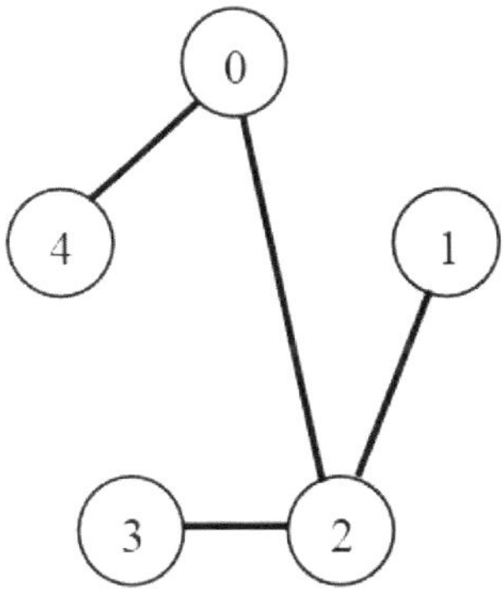	Now we have 3 (as adjacent vertices of 1) 3 (as remaining adjacent vertex of 2) and 3 (as remaining adjacent vertex of 4). Now we again compare the length of the paths from source vertex to these unattached vertices, We find the length(23)=2 is the minimum. Therefore, we choose vertex 3. The total length of the tree can be calculated as 8.

Figure 5.19. Sequence of diagrams depicts the operation of Prim's algorithm.

A. **Implementation of the Prim's Algorithm:** The program tree_prim.c finds the minimum spanning tree of the given undirected graph using prim's algorithm. The distances will be taken infinity if there is no direct path from one vertex to another vertex. We have used 1500 for infinity, we can use constant INT_MAX defined in <limits.h>. If there is no arrowhead from a vertex to itself the distance is taken as 0.

```
/*tree_prim.c*/
#include<stdio.h>
#include<limits.h>
#define INFINITY INT_MAX
#define v 10
#define FALSE 0
#define TRUE 1
typedef struct t_tree    {
int n_nodes;
int path[v];
int tree[v][v];
int selected[v];
int adj_matrix[v][v];
}tree;
void prim(tree *);
```

```
void main()
{
tree t;
printf("This program finds the minimum spanning tree of a undirected graph using prim's algorithm!!\n");
printf("Please enter how many edges in the graph:\n");
scanf("%d,"&t.n_nodes);
prim(&t);
}
void prim(tree *t)
{
int i,j,k=0,w,u,min,length;
for(i=0;i<t->n_nodes;i++)
{
for(j=0;j<t->n_nodes;j++)
{
printf("Please enter weight for visiting edge %d to edge %d:,"i,j);
scanf("%d,"&t->adj_matrix[i][j]);
}
}
printf("THE ADJACENT MATRIX OF THE GRAPH IS\n");
for(i=0;i<t->n_nodes;i++)
{
for(j=0;j<t->n_nodes;j++)
{
printf("%5d\t,"t->adj_matrix[i][j]);
}
printf("\n");
}
for(i=0;i<t->n_nodes;i++)
{
```

```
t->selected[i] = FALSE;
}
for(i=0;i<t->n_nodes;i++)
for(j=0;j<t->n_nodes;j++)
{
t->tree[i][j]=0;
}
}
t->selected[0]=TRUE;
t->path[0]=0;
length = 1;
while(length<=t->n_nodes)
{
min = INFINITY;
for(i=0;i<t->n_nodes;i++)
{
if(t->selected[i]==TRUE)
{
for(j=0;j<t->n_nodes;j++)
{
if(t->selected[j]==FALSE)
{
if(t->adj_matrix[i][j] <min)
{
min = t->adj_matrix[i][j];
u = i;
w = j;
}
}
}
}
```

```
}
t->tree[u][w] = 1;
t->selected[w] = TRUE;
t->path[++k] = w;
length++;
}
printf("THE MINIMUM SPANNING TREE ADJANCENCY MATRIX IS\n");
for(i=0;i<t->n_nodes;i++)
{
for(j=0;j<t->n_nodes;j++)
{
printf("%5d\t,"t->tree[i][j]);
}
printf("\n");
}
/* print the shortest path from the source to all vertices */
printf("The minimum spanning tree path using prim's algorithm is\n");
for(i=0;i<k;i++)
printf("%d\t,"t->path[i]);
printf("\n");
}
```

B. **Output of the Program:** This program finds the minimum spanning tree of a undirected graph using prim's algorithm!!

Please enter how many edges in the graph:

5

Please enter weight for visiting edge 0 to edge 0: 0

Please enter weight for visiting edge 0 to edge 1: 5

Please enter weight for visiting edge 0 to edge 2: 3

Please enter weight for visiting edge 0 to edge 3: 1500

Please enter weight for visiting edge 0 to edge 4: 2

Please enter weight for visiting edge 1 to edge 0: 5

Please enter weight for visiting edge 1 to edge 1: 0

Please enter weight for visiting edge 1 to edge 2: 1

Please enter weight for visiting edge 1 to edge 3: 6

Please enter weight for visiting edge 1 to edge 4: 6

Please enter weight for visiting edge 2 to edge 0: 3

Please enter weight for visiting edge 2 to edge 1: 1

Please enter weight for visiting edge 2 to edge 2: 0

Please enter weight for visiting edge 2 to edge 3: 2

Please enter weight for visiting edge 2 to edge 4: 10

Please enter weight for visiting edge 3 to edge 0: 1500

Please enter weight for visiting edge 3 to edge 1: 6

Please enter weight for visiting edge 3 to edge 2: 2

Please enter weight for visiting edge 3 to edge 3: 0

Please enter weight for visiting edge 3 to edge 4: 4

Please enter weight for visiting edge 4 to edge 0: 2

Please enter weight for visiting edge 4 to edge 1: 6

Please enter weight for visiting edge 4 to edge 2: 10

Please enter weight for visiting edge 4 to edge 3: 4

Please enter weight for visiting edge 4 to edge 4: 0

The adjacent matrix of the graph is

0 5 3 1500 2

5 0 1 6 6

3 1 0 2 10

1500 6 2 0 4

2 6 10 4 0

The minimum spanning tree adjancency matrix is

0 0 1 0 1

0 0 0 0 0

0 1 0 1 0

0 0 0 0 0

0 0 0 0 0

The minimum spanning tree path using prim's algorithm is

0 4 2 1 3

5.12.1.3. Kruskal's Algorithm

The kruskal algorithm starts with a forest, which consists of n single node trees(no edges). In every step of the algorithm, two different trees of this forest are connected to a bigger tree. Therefore, we keep having less and bigger tree in our forest until we end up in a tree which is the minimum spanning tree. In every step, we choose the side with the least cost, if the chosen side connects nodes, which belong to the same tree. The side is rejected and not examined again because it could produce a circle, which will destroy our tree. Either this side or the next one in order of least cost will connect nodes of different trees and this way we connecting two small trees into a bigger one.

A. Algorithm: Let us take an undirected weighted graph G with n vertices. Let the spanning tree T is initially empty. E is the array that contains the edges of the graph G in the increasing order of weights.

Steps: The following are the steps for kruskal algorithm:

a. The forest is constructed with each node in a separate tree.

b. Initialize spanning tree T is empty, i.e., T= 0.

c. List all the edges of the graph G in the increasing order of weights in the array E.

d. Repeat step (e) to (h) until the tree T contains n–1 edges or E is not empty.

e. Extract the cheapest edge e_{ij} from E.

f. Delete this edge e_{ij} from E

$E = E - \{e_{ij}\}$

g. If e_{ij} does not create a cycle add e_{ij} to T.

h. Otherwise reject e_{ij}.

i. If T contains less than n–1 edges and the list E is empty than no spanning tree is possible for the graph G, otherwise return the minimum spanning tree T.

5.12.1.4. Operation of Kruskal Algorithm

The following sequence of diagrams illustrates Kruskal's algorithm in operation. Let us consider the undirected graph G shown in Figure 5.20.

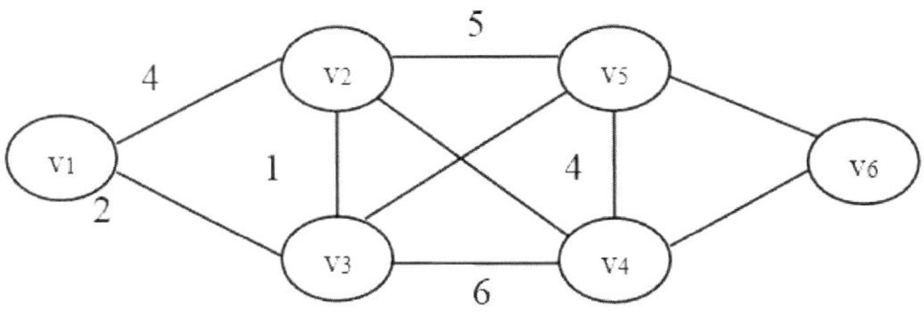

Figure 5.20. Sequence of Kruskal Algorithm.

Construct forest with each node in a separate tree (Figure 5.21):

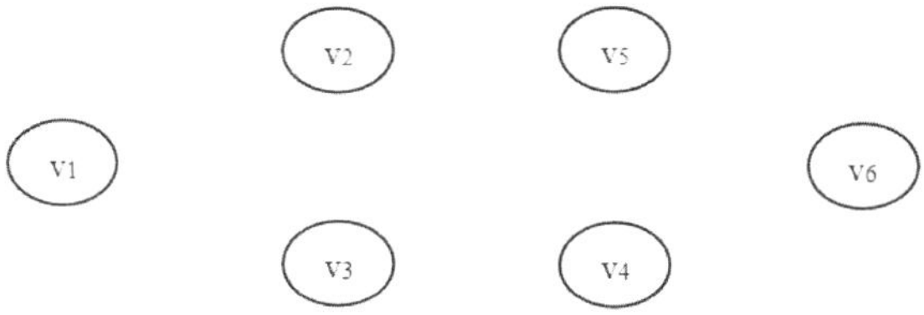

Figure 5.21. A separate tree.

List all the edges of the graph G in the increasing order of weights in the array E. E = 1 1 2 2 3 3 4 4 5 6

Extract the cheapest edge from E, i.e., v_2–v_3 and v_4–$v_{6.}$ Delete these edges from E and add it into spanning tree because, it will not create cycle. Now, the remaining edges are E = 2 2 3 3 4 4 5 6 (Figure 5.22).

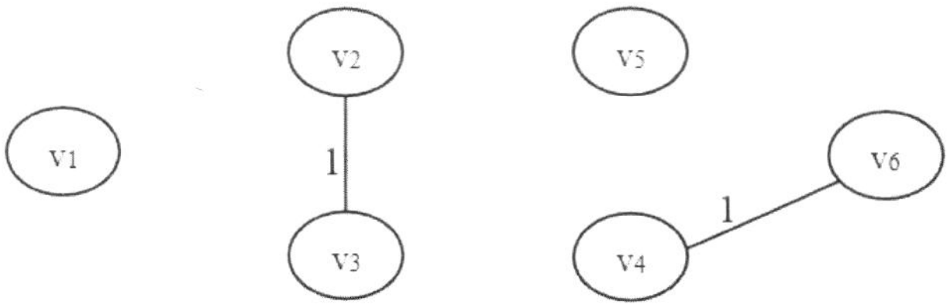

Figure 5.22. Spanning tree.

Extract the next cheapest edge from E, i.e., v_1–v_3 or v_2–$v_{4.}$ Delete these edges from E and add it into spanning tree because, it will not create cycle. Now, E = 3 3 4 4 5 6 (Figure 5.23).

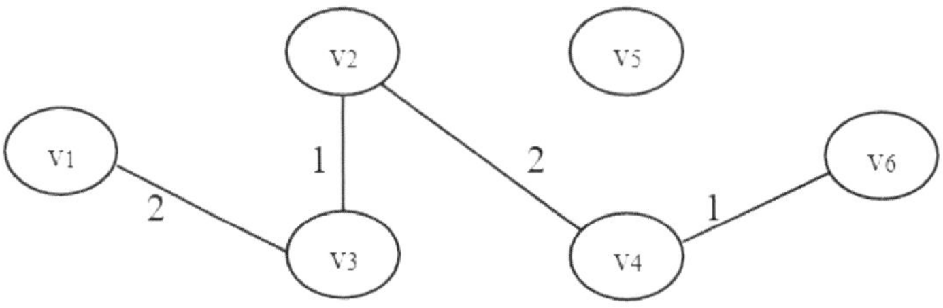

Figure 5.23. Delete these edges from panning tree.

Now extract the next cheapest edge from E, i.e., v_5–v_6 or v_3–$v_{5.}$ Delete these from E and add it v_5–v_6 into spanning tree because, it will not create cycle discard v_3–v_5 because, it will create cycle. Now, E=4 4 5 6 (Figure 5.24)

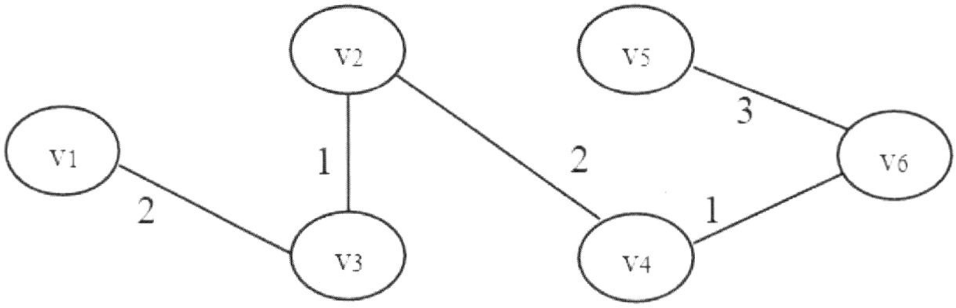

Figure 5.24. Spanning tree not create cycle.

Now spanning tree contains n–1 edges and the remaining edges create cycle so discard these edges and stop the process. The resulting spanning tree i

Now spanning tree contains n–1 edges and the remaining edges create cycle so discard these edges and stop the process. The resulting spanning tree is the minimum spanning tree with total weight 9 shown in Figure 5.24.

5.12.2. Shortest Path Problem

The problem of a graph for finding a path between two vertices V_1 and V_2 in such a way that this path will satisfy some criteria of optimization is called shortest path problem. This is solved using a technique called Dijkstra's algorithm.

5.12.2.1. Dijkstra's Algorithm

E.W. Dijkstra's discovered Dijkstra's algorithm, to solve the problem of finding the shortest path from a point on a graph (the source) to a destination. It turns out that one can find the shortest paths from a given source to all points on a graph in the same time, hence this problem is sometimes called the single-source shortest path problem.

- **Declaration:** The following is the structure declaration for dijkstra's algorithm:

```
#define v 10
typedef struct t_graph {
int n_nodes;
int D[v];
int visited[v];
int path[v];
int adj_matrix[v][v];
}graph;
```

where; n_nodes represent the total nodes in the graph, visited is the flag, which is used to indicate whether the vertex of the graph is visited or not, cost is used to represent the cost from one vertex to another, path represent the shortest path from source to other vertices and D is the array of best estimates of shortest path to each vertex of the graph. The following is the algorithm, which implements the Dijkstra's algorithm within the graph(G):

A. Algorithm: The following steps are taken for Dijkstra's algorithm:

a. [Read the of vertices in the graph]

Read(n_nodes)

b. [Read adjacent cost matrix of the graph. The cost will be taken infinity, if there is no direct path between one vertex to another vertices, we have used 1500 for infinity, enter cost 0 for vertex to itself]

Repeat step (c) for(i=1;i<n_nodes;v++),

for(j=1;j<n_nodes;j++)

c. Read cost[i][j]

d. [Assign source vertex is visited and enters this vertex in the array of best estimate **D** and shortest path array **path**]

Set visited[0]=TRUE,

D[0]=0,

path[0] = 0

e. [Set remaining vertices are unvisited and assigns the cost of remaining vertices from source vertex, into the array of best estimate **D**]

for(u=1;u<n_nodes;u++)

Set visited[u] = FALSE,

D[u] = cost[0][u]

f. Repeat step (g) to (j) for(i=1;i<n_nodes;i++)

Set min = INFINITY

g. [Find the closest vertex u to vertex 0]

for(w=1;w<n_nodes;w++)

if(!visited[w])

if(D[w] <min)

Set u = w,

min = D[w]

h. [Add vertex u to the set of visited vertices]

Set visited[u] = TRUE;

i. [Update the remaining costs in D]

for(w=1;w<n_nodes;w++)

if(!visited[w])

if((min + cost[u][w])< D[w])

D[w] = min + cost[u][w]

path[k] = u

j. [Write the shortest path from the source to all other vertices]

for(p=0;p<=k;++p)

write path[p]

k++

k. End.

B. Equivalent Function in C

void dijkstra(graph *g)

```
{
int i,j,k=0,w,u,p,min;
/* Read the cost matrix */
for(i=0;i<g->n_nodes;i++)
{
for(j=0;j<g->n_nodes;j++)
{
scanf("%d,"&g->cost[i][j]);
}
}
/*THE ADJACENT COST MATRIX IS: */
for(i=0;i<g->n_nodes;i++)
{
for(j=0;j<g->n_nodes;j++)
{
printf("%5d\t,"g->cost[i][j]);
}
printf("\n");
}
/* Assign the source vertex 0 in the set of visited vertices */
g->visited[0]=TRUE;
g->D[0]=0;
g->path[0] = 0;
printf("%d\n,"g->path[0]);
k++;
for(u=1;u<g->n_nodes;u++)
{
g->visited[u] = FALSE;
g->D[u] = g->cost[0][u];
}
/* Start the main loop, add one vertex u to S on each pass */
```

```
for(i=1;i<g->n_nodes;i++)
{
min = INFINITY;
/* Find the closest vertices u to vertex 0 */
for(w=1;w<g->n_nodes;w++)
{
if(!g->visited[w])
if(g->D[w] <min)
{
u = w;
min = g->D[w];
}
}
/* Add u to the set S */
g->visited[u] = TRUE;
/* Update the remaining distances in D */
for(w=1;w<g->n_nodes;w++)
if(!g->visited[w])
if(min + g->cost[u][w]<g->D[w])
g->D[w] = min + g->cost[u][w];
g->path[k] = u;
/* print the shortest path from the source to other vertices */
for(p=0;p<=k;++p)
printf("%d\t,"g->path[p]);
k++;
printf("\n");
}
}
```

5.12.2.2. Operation of Dijkstra's Algorithm

The following sequence of diagrams illustrates the operation of Dijkstra's algorithm (Figure 5.25):

<table>
<tr>
<td>

Source

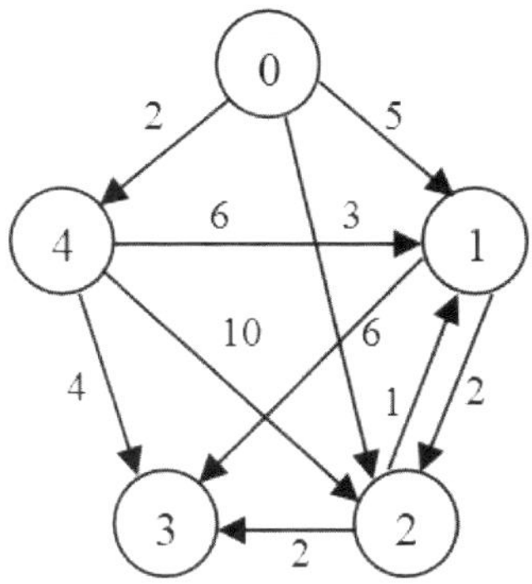

</td>
<td>In initial graph we start with source vertex 0.</td>
</tr>
<tr>
<td>

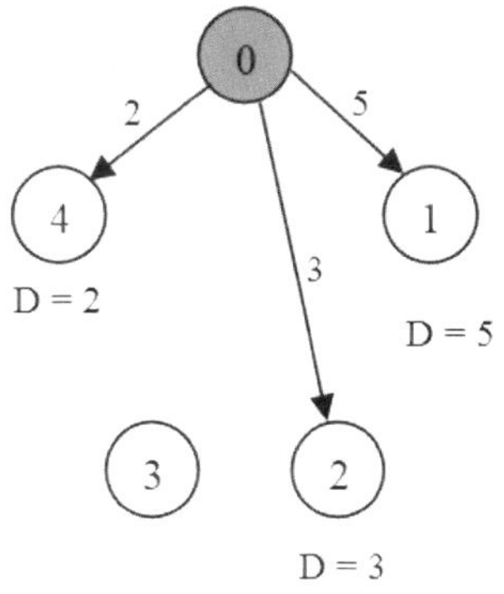

</td>
<td>Choose the closest node to 0. We locate the vertex closest to it, i.e., we find a vertex from the adjacent vertices of 0 for which the length of the edge is minimum. 4, 2 and 1 are the adjacent vertices of 0. Vertex 4 has the minimum length(04)=2. Therefore, we choose 4.</td>
</tr>
<tr>
<td>

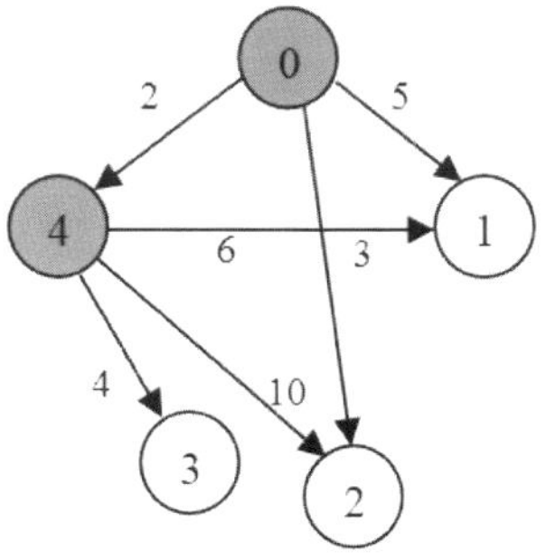

</td>
<td>Now we have 1, 2 and 3 (as adjacent vertices of 4) and 1, 2 (as remaining adjacent vertex of 0). Now we again compare the length of the paths from source vertex to these unattached vertices, i.e., compare length(01)=5, length(02)=3,length(041)=8,length(042)=12 and length(043)=6. We find the length(02)=2 is the minimum. Therefore, we choose vertex 2.</td>
</tr>
</table>

<table>
<tr>
<td>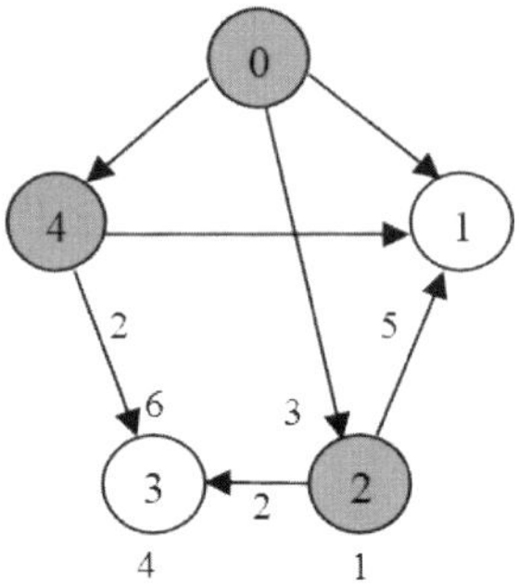</td>
<td>Now we have 1 and 3 (as adjacent vertices of 2) 3 and 1 (as remaining adjacent vertex of 4) and 1 (as remaining adjacent vertex of 0).
Now we again compare the length of the paths from source vertex to these unattached vertices, i.e., compare length(021)= 4,length(023)=5,length(041)=8, length(043)=6 and length(01)=5. We find the length(021)=4 is the minimum. Therefore, we choose vertex 1.</td>
</tr>
<tr>
<td>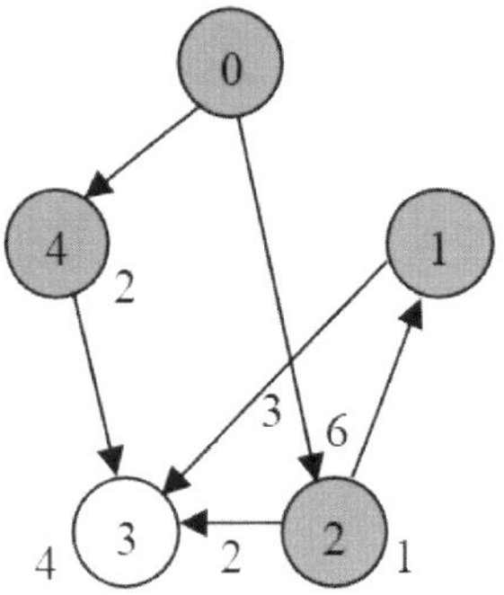</td>
<td>Now we have 3 (as adjacent vertices of 1) 3 (as remaining adjacent vertex of 2) and 3 (as remaining adjacent vertex of 4).
Now we again compare the length of the paths from source vertex to these unattached vertices, i.e., compare length(0213)=10, length(023)=5, length(043)=6. We find the length(023) is the minimum. Therefore, we choose vertex 3.</td>
</tr>
<tr>
<td>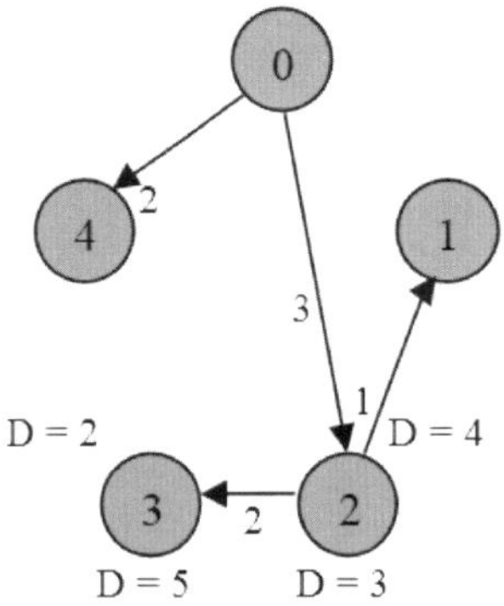</td>
<td>Therefore, the shortest paths from source vertex 0 to all the other vertices are:
0
0 4
0 4 2
0 4 2 1
0 4 2 1
3</td>
</tr>
</table>

Figure 5.25. Sequence of diagrams illustrates the operation of Dijkstra's algorithm.

A. **Implementation of the Dijkstra's Algorithm:** The program tree_dijkstra.c finds the shortest path of the given directed graph using Dijkstra's algorithm. The distances will be taken infinity if there is no direct path from one vertex to another vertex. We have used 1500 for infinity, we can use constant INT_MAX defined in <limits.h>. If there is no arrowhead from a vertex to itself the distance is taken as 0.

326 Data Structures

```
/*tree_dijkstra.c*/
#include<stdio.h>
#include<limits.h>
#define INFINITY INT_MAX
#define v 10
#define FALSE 0
#define TRUE 1
typedef struct t_graph  {
int n_nodes;
int path[v];
int D[v];
int visited[v];
int adj_matrix[v][v];
}graph;
void dijkstra(graph *);
void main()
{
graph g;
printf("This program finds the shortest path of a directed graph using Dijkstra's algorithm!!\n");
printf("Please enter how many vertices in the graph:\n");
scanf("%d,"&g.n_nodes);
dijkstra(&g);
}
void dijkstra(graph *g)
```

```
{
int i,j,k=0,w,u,p,min;
for(i=0;i<g->n_nodes;i++)
{
for(j=0;j<g->n_nodes;j++)
{
printf("Please enter cost for visiting vertex %d to vertex %d:,"i,j);
scanf("%d,"&g->cost[i][j]);
}
}
printf("THE ADJACENT COST MATRIX IS: \n");
for(i=0;i<g->n_nodes;i++)
{
for(j=0;j<g->n_nodes;j++)
{
printf("%5d\t,"g->cost[i][j]);
}
printf("\n");
}
printf("The shortest path of the graph is:\n");
g->visited[0]=TRUE;
g->D[0]=0;
g->path[0] = 0;
printf("%d\n,"g->path[0]);
k++;
for(u=1;u<g->n_nodes;u++)
{
g->visited[u] = FALSE;
g->D[u] = g->cost[0][u];
}
for(i=1;i<g->n_nodes;i++)
```

```
{
min = INFINITY;
for(w=1;w<g->n_nodes;w++)
{
if(!g->visited[w])
if(g->D[w] <min)
{
u = w;
min = g->D[w];
}
}
g->visited[u] = TRUE;
for(w=1;w<g->n_nodes;w++)
if(!g->visited[w])
if(min + g->cost[u][w]<g->D[w])
g->D[w] = min + g->cost[u][w];
g->path[k] = u;
for(p=0;p<=k;++p)
printf("%d\t,"g->path[p]);
k++;
printf("\n");
}
}
```

B. Output of the Program: This program finds the shortest path of a directed graph using Dijkstra's algorithm!!

Please enter how many vertices in the graph:

5

Please enter cost for visiting vertex 0 to vertex 0: 0

Please enter cost for visiting vertex 0 to vertex 1: 5

Please enter cost for visiting vertex 0 to vertex 2: 3

Please enter cost for visiting vertex 0 to vertex 3: 1500

Please enter cost for visiting vertex 0 to vertex 4: 2

Please enter cost for visiting vertex 1 to vertex 0: 1500
Please enter cost for visiting vertex 1 to vertex 1: 0
Please enter cost for visiting vertex 1 to vertex 2: 2
Please enter cost for visiting vertex 1 to vertex 3: 6
Please enter cost for visiting vertex 1 to vertex 4: 1500
Please enter cost for visiting vertex 2 to vertex 0: 1500
Please enter cost for visiting vertex 2 to vertex 1: 1
Please enter cost for visiting vertex 2 to vertex 2: 0
Please enter cost for visiting vertex 2 to vertex 3: 2
Please enter cost for visiting vertex 2 to vertex 4: 1500
Please enter cost for visiting vertex 3 to vertex 0: 1500
Please enter cost for visiting vertex 3 to vertex 1: 1500
Please enter cost for visiting vertex 3 to vertex 2: 1500
Please enter cost for visiting vertex 3 to vertex 3: 0
Please enter cost for visiting vertex 3 to vertex 4: 1500
Please enter cost for visiting vertex 4 to vertex 0: 1500
Please enter cost for visiting vertex 4 to vertex 1: 6
Please enter cost for visiting vertex 4 to vertex 2: 10
Please enter cost for visiting vertex 4 to vertex 3: 4
Please enter cost for visiting vertex 4 to vertex 4: 0
THE adjacent cost matrix is:

0	5	3	1500	2
1500	0	2	6	1500
1500	1	0	2	1500
1500	1500	1500	0	1500
1500	6	10	4	0

The shortest path of the graph is:
0
0 4
0 4 2
0 4 2 1
0 4 2 1 3

Exercise

- **Q.1.** Write a C program for kruskal's minimum spanning tree algorithm.
- **Q.2.** Give an example of a connected graph such that removal of any edge results in a graph that is not connected.
- **Q.3.** Consider the graph given in the figure below:

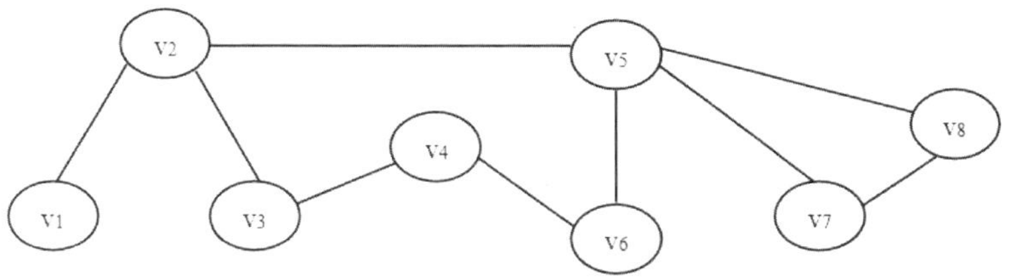

a. Is there a path from A to Z that passes through each vertex exactly once?

b. What is the maximum number of vertices one can visit once in going from A to Z?

- **Q.4.** Find the degree of each vertex of the graph given below:

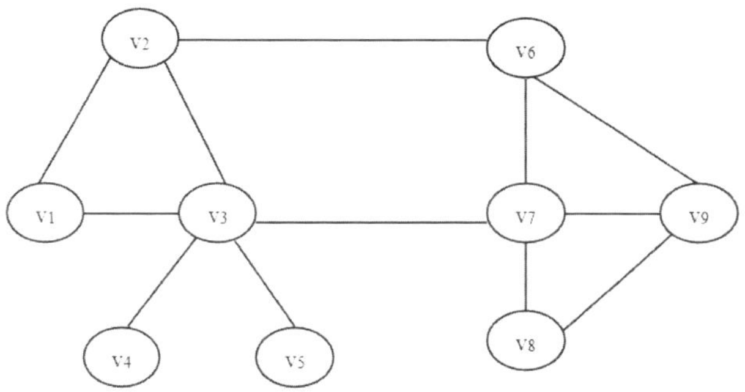

Is it possible to trace the above graph, beginning, and ending at the same point, without lifting your pencil from the paper and without retracing lines? Justify your answer.

- **Q.5.** In the given graph:

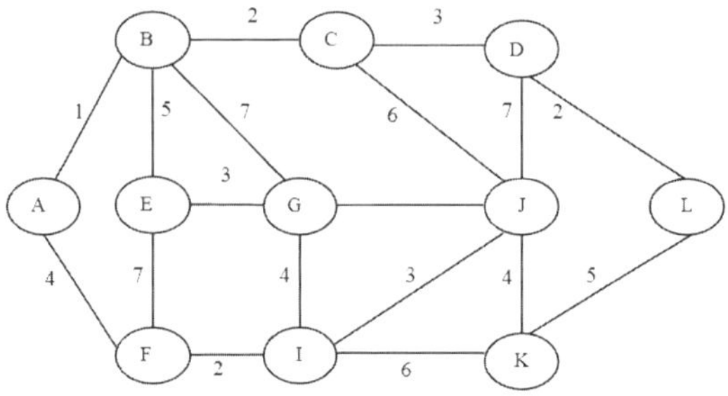

Find the length of the shortest path and the shortest path between:

i. A and F;
ii. A and Z;
iii. D and H.

- **Q.6.** Write a program that accepts adjacency matrix as an input and outputs a list of edges given as pairs of positive integers.
- **Q.7.** Draw minimum cost spanning tree for the graph given below and also find its cost.

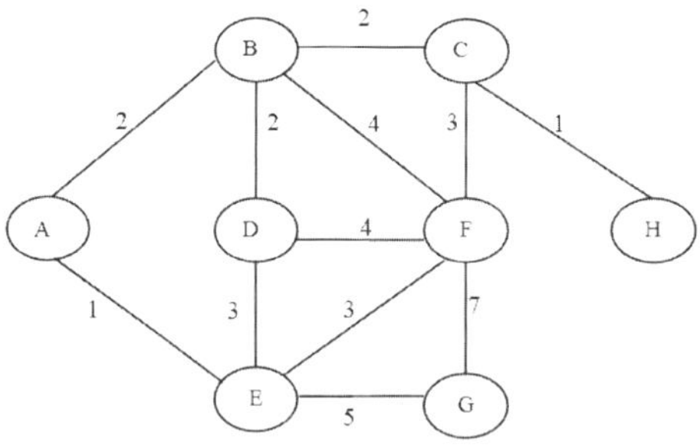

- **Q.8.** Find the shortest paths from source vertex to all the vertices for the graph given in the above figure using dijkstra's algorithm.
- **Q.9.** Show the visiting of all the nodes of the given graph using DFS and BFS traversal schemes.

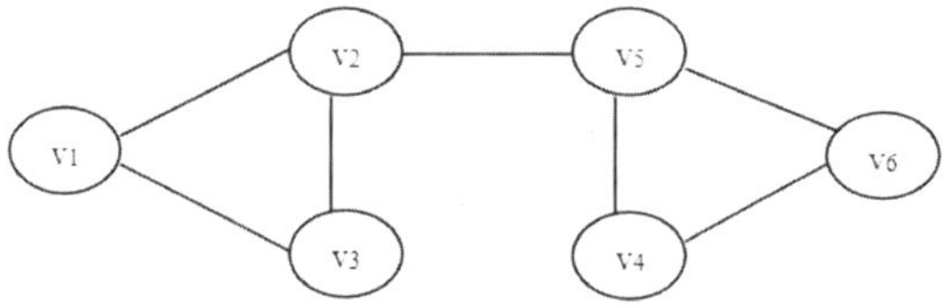

CHAPTER 6

ALGORITHM AND ITS ANALYSIS

CONTENTS

An algorithm was developed by an Arab mathematician. It is chalked out step-by-step approach to solve a given problem. It is represented in an English like language and has some mathematical symbols like- >, >, <, = etc. To solve a given problem or to write a program you approach towards solution of the problem in a systematic, disciplined, non-adhoc, step-by-step way is called Algorithmic approach

We represent an algorithm using a pseudo language that is a combination of the constructs of a programming language together with informal English statements.

The ordered set of instructions required to solve a problem is known as an algorithm. The characteristics of a good algorithm are:

1. **Precision:** The steps are precisely stated (defined).
2. **Uniqueness:** Results of each step are uniquely defined and only depend on the input and the result of the preceding steps.
3. **Finiteness:** The algorithm stops after a finite number of instructions are executed.
4. **Input:** The algorithm receives input.
5. **Output:** The algorithm produces output.
6. **Generality:** The algorithm applies to a set of inputs.

Example: Write an algorithm to find out number is odd or even?

- **Step 1:** start
- **Step 2:** input number
- **Step 3:** rem = number mod 2
- **Step 4:** if rem =0 then

print " even number"

else

Print "Odd number"

Endif

- **Step 5:** Stop

6.1. ANALYSIS OF ALGORITHM

In theoretical analysis of algorithms, it is common to estimate their complexity in the asymptotic sense, i.e., to estimate the complexity function for arbitrarily large input. The term "analysis of algorithms" was coined by Donald Knuth.

Algorithm analysis is an important part of computational complexity theory, which provides theoretical estimation for the required resources of an algorithm to solve a specific computational problem. Most algorithms are designed to work with inputs of arbitrary length. Analysis of algorithms is the determination of the amount of time and space resources required to execute it.

Usually, the efficiency or running time of an algorithm is stated as a function relating the input length to the number of steps, known as time complexity, or volume of memory, known as space complexity.

Analysis of algorithm is the process of analyzing the problem-solving capability of the algorithm in terms of the time and size required (the size of memory for storage while implementation). However, the main concern of analysis of algorithms is the required time or performance. Generally, we perform the following types of analysis:

1. **Worst-Case:** The maximum number of steps taken on any instance of size a.
2. **Best-Case:** The minimum number of steps taken on any instance of size a.
3. **Average Case:** An average number of steps taken on any instance of size a.
4. **Amortized:** A sequence of operations applied to the input of size a averaged over time.

To solve a problem, we need to consider time as well as space complexity as the program may run on a system where memory is limited but adequate space is available or may be vice-versa. In this context, if we compare bubble sort and merge sort. Bubble sort does not require additional memory, but merge sort requires additional space. Though time complexity of bubble sort is higher compared to merge sort, we may need to apply bubble sort if the program needs to run in an environment, where memory is very limited.

CHAPTER 7

DATA STRUCTURE LABORATORY

CONTENTS

EXPT. No. 1. Write a Program to Implement Insertion and Deletion in One Dimensional Array at Specified Position.

- **Aim:** To implement a program of Insertion and Deletion in one Dimensional Array at specified position.
- **Theory:** Insertion operation is used to insert a new element at specific position in to one dimensional array. In order to insert a new element into one dimensional array we have to create space for new element. Suppose there are N elements in an array and we want to insert a new element between first and second element. We have to move last N–1 elements down in order to create space for the new element.

7.1. ALGORITHM FOR INSERTION IN ONE DIMENSIONAL ARRAY

Let A be a Linear Array (unordered) with N elements and LOC is a positive integer such that LOC<=N. Following is the algorithm where ITEM is inserted into the LOC position of Array A

- **Step 1:** TEMP = N–1

LOC = LOC–1

- **Step 2:** Repeat Step 3 While TEMP ≥ LOC
- **Step 3:** A[TEMP+1] = A[TEMP]

TEMP=TEMP–1

- **Step 4:** A[LOC] = ITEM
- **Step 5:** N = N+1

7.2. ALGORITHM FOR DELETION IN ONE DIMENSIONAL ARRAY

This operation is used to delete an element from specific position from one dimensional array. In order to delete an element from one dimensional array first we have to delete element from specified position and then shift remaining elements upwards to take vacant space of the deleted element.

- **Step 1:** POS = POS–1

TEMP = POS

- **Step 2:** Return A[POS]
- **Step 3:** Repeat step4 while TEMP ≤ N–1
- **Step 4:** A[TEMP] = A[TEMP+1]

TEMP = TEMP+1

- **Step 5:** N = N–1
- Program:

```
#include<iostream.h>
#include<conio.h>
void main()
{
clrscr();
int a[10],i,no,pos,n,pos1;
cout<<"\n enter how many element u want to enter in array";
cin>>n;
cout<<"\n enter element in array ";
for(i=1;i<=n;i++)
cin>>a[i];
cout<<"\n element in array are";
for(i=1;i<=n;i++)
cout<<a[i]<<" ";
cout<<"\n enter position to insert new no";
cin>>pos;
cout<<"\n enter new no";
cin>>no;
for(i=n;i>pos;i– –)
a[i]=a[i–1];
a[pos]=no;
cout<<"\n element in array after insertion of new no";
for(i=1;i<=n;i++)
cout<<a[i]<<" ";
cout<<"\n enter position to delete no";
```

```
cin>>pos1;
for(i=pos;i<=n;i++)
a[i]=a[i+1];
cout<<"\n element in array after deletion of no";
for(i=1;i<n;i++)
cout<<a[i]<<" ";
getch();
}
```

Ø **Output:**

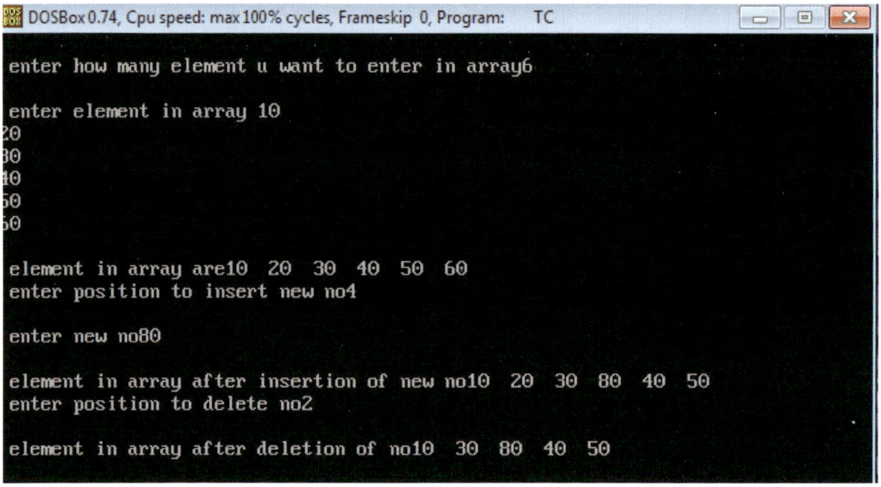

- Viva Questions:
- What are the advantages of one dimensional array?
- What are the disadvantages of one dimensional array?
- What is static time compilation?

EXPT. No. 2. Write a Program to Implement Matrix Addition and Subtraction.

- **Aim:** To implement a program of matrix addition and subtraction
- **Theory:** Algorithm for matrix addition and subtraction
- **Matrices Addition:** The addition of two matrices A_{m*n} and B_{m*n} gives a matrix C_{m*n}. The elements of C are sum of corresponding elements in A and B which can be shown as:

$$\begin{bmatrix} 1 & 2 \\ 4 & 5 \end{bmatrix} + \begin{bmatrix} 5 & 6 \\ 8 & 9 \end{bmatrix} = \begin{bmatrix} 6 & 8 \\ 12 & 14 \end{bmatrix}$$

The algorithm for addition of matrices can be written as:

for i in 1 to m

for j in 1 to n

$c_{ij} = a_{ij} + b_{ij}$

- Key Points:
- Addition of matrices is commutative which means A+B = B+A
- Addition of matrices is associative which means A+(B+C) = (A+B)+C
- The order of matrices A, B, and A+B is always same
- If order of A and B is different, A+B can't be computed
- The complexity of addition operation is O(m*n) where m*n is order of matrices
- **Matrices Subtraction:** The subtraction of two matrices A_{m*n} and B_{m*n} gives a matrix C_{m*n}. The elements of C are difference of corresponding elements in A and B which can be represented as:

$$\begin{bmatrix} 5 & 6 \\ 8 & 9 \end{bmatrix} - \begin{bmatrix} 1 & 2 \\ 4 & 5 \end{bmatrix} = \begin{bmatrix} 4 & 4 \\ 4 & 4 \end{bmatrix}$$

The algorithm for subtraction of matrices can be written as:

for i in 1 to m

for j in 1 to n

$c_{ij} = a_{ij}-b_{ij}$

- **Key Points:**
- Subtraction of matrices is non-commutative which means A–B ≠ B–A
- Subtraction of matrices is non-associative which means A–(B–C) ≠ (A–B)–C
- The order of matrices A, B, and A-B is always same
- If order of A and B is different, A-B can't be computed

The complexity of subtraction operation is O(m*n) where m*n is order of matrices

Program:

```
#include<iostream.h>
#include<conio.h>
void main()
{
clrscr();
int a[2][2],b[2][2],c[2][2],d[2][2],i,j;
cout<<"\n enter the element in 1 array";
for(i=1;i<=2;i++)
{
for(j=1;j<=2;j++)
{
cin>>a[i][j];
}
}
cout<<"\n enter the element in 2 array";
for(i=1;i<=2;i++)
{
for(j=1;j<=2;j++)
{
cin>>b[i][j];
}
}
cout<<"\n matrix addition is";
for(i=1;i<=2;i++)
{
for(j=1;j<=2;j++)
{
c[i][j]=a[i][j]+b[i][j];
```

```
}
}
for(i=1;i<=2;i++)
{
for(j=1;j<=2;j++)
{
cout<< c[i][j]<<" ";
}
cout<<"\n";
}
cout<<"\n matrix subraction is";
for(i=1;i<=2;i++)
{
for(j=1;j<=2;j++)
{
d[i][j]=a[i][j]-b[i][j];
}
}
for(i=1;i<=2;i++)
{
for(j=1;j<=2;j++)
{
cout<< d[i][j]<<" ";
}
cout<<"\n";
}
getch();
}
```

- Output:

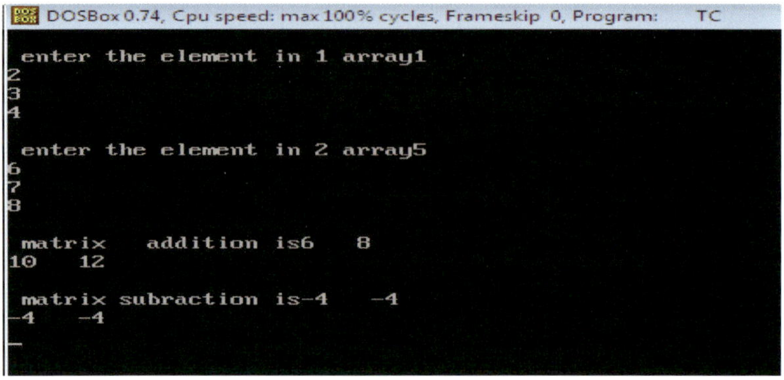

- Viva Questions:
- What is the running time complexity of Matrix Addition?
- What is the running time complexity of Matrix Subtraction?

EXPT. No. 3 Write a Program to Implement Matrix Multiplication.

- **Aim:** To implement a program of matrix multiplication.
- **Theory:** Matrix multiplication falls into two general categories:

Matrix C and D below cannot be multiplied together because the number of columns in C does not equal the number of rows in D. In this case, the multiplication of these two matrices is not defined

- **Algorithm for Matrix Multiplication:**

Matmul(a,b,m,n,p)

for(i=1 to m)

for(j = 1 to)

c[i][j] =0; for(k = 1 to n)

c[i][j] =c[i][j]+a[i][k]*b[k][j]

exit

Ø **Program:**

```
#include<stdio.h>
#include<conio.h>
void main( )
{
int a[2][2], b[2][2],s[2][2];
int i,j,k;
clrscr();
```

```
printf("Enter first matrix:\n");
for(i=1;i<=2;i++)
{
for(j=1;j<=2;j++)
{
printf("Enter%d%d\n,"i,j); scanf("%d,"&a[i][j]);
}
}
printf("Enter second matrix:\n"); for(i=1;i<=2;i++)
{
for(j=1;j<=2;j++)
{
printf("Enter %d%d\n,"i,j); scanf("%d,"&b[i][j]);
}
}
for(i=1;i<=2;i++)
{
for(j=1;j<=2;j++)
{s[i][j]=0;
for(k=1;k<=2;k++)
{
s[i][j] =s[i][j]+a[i][k]*b[k][j];
}
}
}
printf("Matrix Multiplication Is: \n"); for(i=1;i<=2;i++)
{
for (j=1;j<=2;j++)
{
printf("%d\n,"s[i][j]);
}
```

```
}
getch();
```

Ø **Output:**

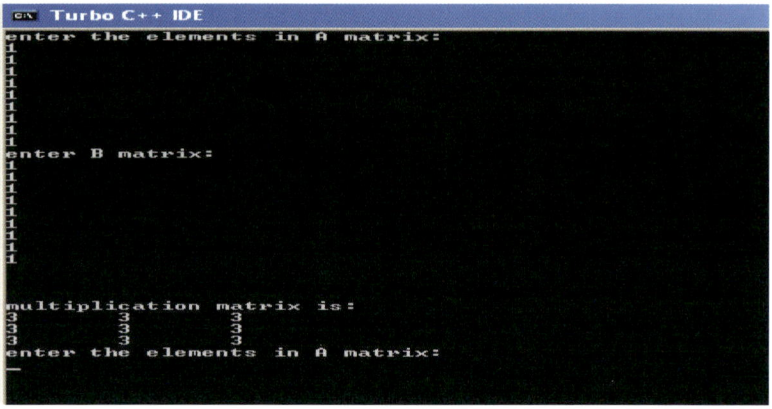

- **Viva Questions:**

1. Consider the two matrices P and Q which are 10 x 20 and 20 x 30 matrices respectively. What is the number of multiplications required to multiply the two matrices?
2. Consider the brute force implementation in which we find all the possible ways of multiplying the given set of n matrices. What is the time complexity of this implementation?
3. Which of the following is the recurrence relation for the matrix chain multiplication problem where mat[i–1] * mat[i] gives the dimension of the ith matrix?
4. What is the time complexity of the above dynamic programming implementation of the matrix chain problem?
5. Which of the following methods can be used to solve the matrix chain multiplication problem?

EXPT. No. 4. Write a Program to Implement Stack Using Array.

- **Aim:** To implement a program of stack using array.
- **Theory:** A stack is a container of objects that are inserted and removed according to the last-in first-out (LIFO) principle. In the pushdown stacks only two operations are allowed: push the item into the stack, and pop the item out of the stack. A stack is a limited access data structure – elements can be added and removed from the stack only at the top. Push adds an item to the top of the stack, pop removes the item from the top. A helpful

analogy is to think of a stack of books; you can remove only the top book, also you can add a new book on the top.

- **Algorithm for PUSH Operation:**

begin procedure push:

stack, data if stack is full

return null

endif

top ← top + 1

stack[top] ← data

end procedure

- **Algorithm for Pop Operation:**

begin procedure pop: stack

if stack is empty

return null

endif

data ← stack[top]

top ← top – 1 return data

end procedure

- Program:

```
#include<iostream.h>
#include<conio.h>
#define MAXSIZE 100
void push();
void pop();
void display();
int top = –1;
int a[MAXSIZE];
void main()
{
int ch;
clrscr();
do
```

```
{
cout<<"\n1.push";
cout<<"\n2.pop";
cout<<"\n3.Display";
cout<<"\n4.Quit";
cout<<"\nEnter your choice: ";
cin>>ch;
switch(ch)
{
case 1: push();break;
case 2: pop();break;
case 3:display();break;
case 4:return;
default:cout<<"Wrong choice";
}
}
while(ch!=4);
getch();
}
void push()
{
if(top==MAXSIZE–1)
cout<<"stack is full";
else
{
int no;
cout<<"enter the no";
cin>>no;
top=top+1;
```

```
a[top]=no;
}
}
void pop()
{
int no;
if(top== –1)
cout<<"stack is empty";
else
{
no=a[top];
cout<<"deleted element is"<<no;
top=top–1;
}
}
void display()
{
if(top==–1)
cout<<"stack is empty";
else
{
cout<<"status of stack is";
for(int i=0;i<=top;i++)
cout<<"\n"<<a[i];
}
}
```

- Output:

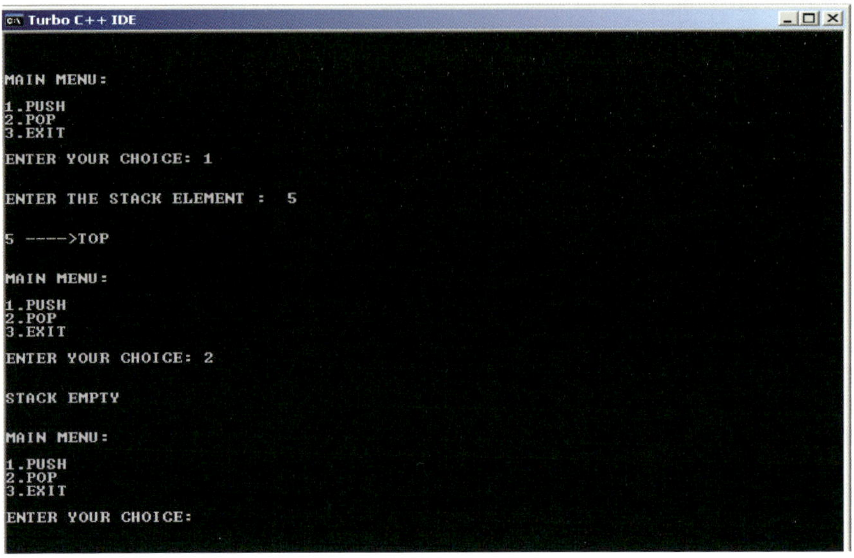

- **Viva Questions:**

1. What is a stack?
2. What are the applications of stack?
3. Explain push algorithm of stack?
4. Explain pop algorithm of stack?
5. Explain algorithm of 2 stack in a single array?

EXPT. No. 5. Write a Program to Implement Queue Using Array.

- **Aim:** To implement a program of queue using array.
- **Theory:** A queue is an ordered collection of items where the addition of new items happens at one end, called the "rear," and the removal of existing items occurs at the other end, commonly called the "front." As an element enters the queue it starts at the rear and makes its way toward the front, waiting until that time when it is the next element to be removed.

The most recently added item in the queue must wait at the end of the collection. The item that has been in the collection the longest is at the front. This ordering principle is sometimes called FIFO, first-in first-out. It is also known as "first-come first-served.

- **Algorithm for Insertion in Queue:**

procedure enqueue(data)

if queue is full

return overflow
endif
rear ← rear + 1
queue[rear] ← data
return true
end procedure

- **Algorithm for Deletion in Queue:**

procedure dequeue
if queue is
return underflow
end if
data = queue[front]
front ← front + 1
return true
end procedure

- Program:

```
#include<iostream.h>
#include<conio.h>
#define MAXSIZE 100
void insert();
void del();
void display();
int front =–1;
int rear=–1;
int a[MAXSIZE];
void main()
{
int ch;
clrscr();
do
{
```

```
cout<<"\n1.Insert";
cout<<"\n2.Delete";
cout<<"\n3.Display";
cout<<"\n4.Quit";
cout<<"\nEnter your choice: ";
cin>>ch;
switch(ch)
{
case 1: insert();break;
case 2: del();break;
case 3:display();
break;
case 4:return;
default:cout<<"Wrong choice";
}
}
while(ch!=4);
getch();
}
void insert()
{
if(rear>=MAXSIZE)
cout<<"queue is full";
else
{
int no;
cout<<"enter the no";
cin>>no;
if(front==-1)
front=rear=0;
else
```

```
rear=rear+1;
a[rear]=no;
}
}
void del()
{
int no;
if(front==–1)
cout<<"queue is empty";
else
{
no=a[front];
cout<<"deleted element is"<<no;
if(front==rear)
front=rear=–1;
else
front=front+1;
}
}
void display()
{
if(front==–1)
cout<<"queue is empty";
else
{
cout<<"status of queue is";
for(int i=front;i<=rear;i++)
cout<<"\n"<<a[i];
}
}
```

- Output:

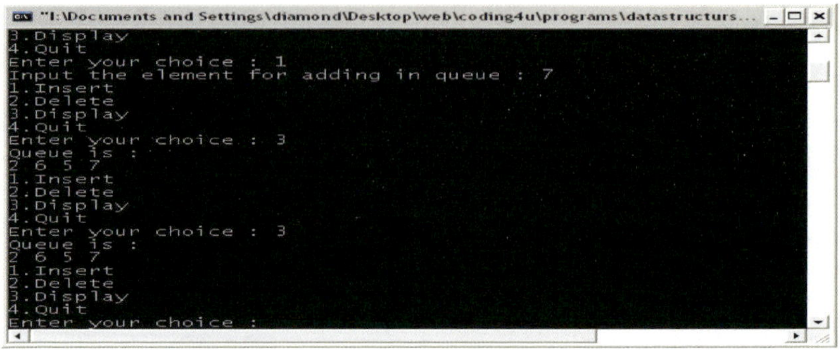

- **Viva Questions:**

1. What is queue?
2. What is circular queue?
3. What are the applications of queue?
4. Explain insertion algorithm of queue?
5. Explain deletion algorithm of queue?
6. What is overflow and underflow condition for queue?

EXPT. No. 6. Write a Program to Implement Singly Linked List.

- **Aim:** To implement a program of singly linked list.
- **Theory:** Linked list is a collection of Nodes. Each node having two parts. First part represents value of the node and second part represents an address of the next node. If Next node is not present then it contains NULL value.

Consider following presentation of linked list:

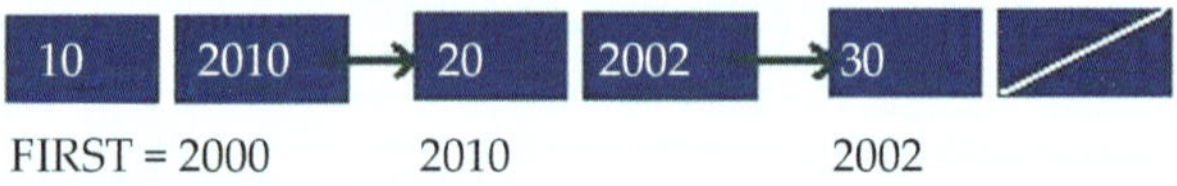

In above presentation FIRST is a pointer which always contains an address of first node in the linked list. If linked list is empty then value of FIRST pointer is NULL.

In Linked List nodes are logically adjacent but physically not adjacent to each other. Because address of first node is 2000, address of second node is 2010 and address of third node is 2002.

- **Algorithm of Insertion:**

In a single linked list, the insertion operation can be performed in three ways. They are as follows:

Inserting At Beginning of the list

Inserting At End of the list

Inserting At Specific location in the list

- Inserting at Beginning of the List:

We can use the following steps to insert a new node at beginning of the single linked list

- **Step 1:** Create a newNode with given value.
- **Step 2:** Check whether list is Empty (head == NULL)
- **Step 3:** If it is Empty then, set newNode→next = NULL and head = newNode.
- **Step 4:** If it is Not Empty then, set newNode→next = head and head = newNode.
- **Inserting at End of the List:** We can use the following steps to insert a new node at end of the single linked list:
- **Step 1:** Create a newNode with given value and newNode → next as NULL.
- **Step 2:** Check whether list is Empty (head == NULL).
- **Step 3:** If it is Empty then, set head = newNode.
- **Step 4:** If it is Not Empty then, define a node pointer temp and initialize with head.
- **Step 5:** Keep moving the temp to its next node until it reaches to the last node in the list (until temp → next is equal to NULL).
- **Step 6:** Set temp → next = newNode.
- **Inserting At Specific Location in the List (After a Node):** We can use the following steps to insert a new node after a node in the single linked list:
- **Step 1:** Create a newNode with given value.
- **Step 2:** Check whether list is Empty (head == NULL)
- **Step 3:** If it is Empty then, set newNode → next = NULL and head = newNode.

- **Step 4:** If it is Not Empty then, define a node pointer temp and initialize with head.
- **Step 5:** Keep moving the temp to its next node until it reaches to the node after which we want to insert the new Node (until temp1 → data is equal to location, here location is the node value after which we want to insert the new Node).
- **Step 6:** Every time check whether temp is reached to last node or not. If it is reached to last node then display 'Given node is not found in the list!!! Insertion not possible!!!' and terminate the function. Otherwise move the temp to next node.
- **Step 7:** Finally, Set 'newNode → next = temp → next' and 'temp → next = newNode'
- **Algorithm of Deletion:** In a single linked list, the deletion operation can be performed in three ways. They are as follows:
- Deleting from beginning of the list;
- Deleting from end of the list;
- Deleting a specific node.
- **Deleting from Beginning of the List:** We can use the following steps to delete a node from beginning of the single linked list:
- **Step 1:** Check whether list is Empty (head == NULL)
- **Step 2:** If it is Empty then, display 'List is Empty!!! Deletion is not possible' and terminate the function.
- **Step 3:** If it is Not Empty then, define a Node pointer 'temp' and initialize with head.
- **Step 4:** Check whether list is having only one node (temp → next == NULL)
- **Step 5:** If it is TRUE then set head = NULL and delete temp (Setting Empty list conditions)
- **Step 6:** If it is FALSE then set head = temp → next, and delete temp.

We can use the following steps to delete a node from end of the single linked list:

- **Step 1:** Check whether list is Empty (head == NULL)
- **Step 2:** If it is Empty then, display 'List is Empty!!! Deletion is not possible' and terminate the function.

- **Step 3:** If it is Not Empty then, define two Node pointers 'temp1' and 'temp2' and initialize 'temp1' with head.
- **Step 4:** Check whether list has only one Node (temp1 → next == NULL)
- **Step 5:** If it is TRUE. Then, set head = NULL and delete temp1. And terminate the function. (Setting Empty list condition)
- **Step 6:** If it is FALSE. Then, set 'temp2 = temp1 ' and move temp1 to its next node. Repeat the same until it reaches to the last node in the list. (until temp1 → next == NULL)
- **Step 7:** Finally, Set temp2 → next = NULL and delete temp1.
- **Deleting a Specific Node from the List:** We can use the following steps to delete a specific node from the single linked list:
- **Step 1:** Check whether list is Empty (head == NULL)
- **Step 2:** If it is Empty then, display 'List is Empty!!! Deletion is not possible' and terminate the function.
- **Step 3:** If it is Not Empty then, define two Node pointers 'temp1' and 'temp2' and initialize 'temp1' with head.
- **Step 4:** Keep moving the temp1 until it reaches to the exact node to be deleted or to the last node. And every time set 'temp2 = temp1' before moving the 'temp1' to its next node.
- **Step 5:** If it is reached to the last node then display 'Given node not found in the list! Deletion not possible!!!.' And terminate the function.
- **Step 6:** If it is reached to the exact node which we want to delete, then check whether list is having only one node or not
- **Step 7:** If list has only one node and that is the node to be deleted, then set head = NULL and delete temp1 (free(temp1)).
- **Step 8:** If list contains multiple nodes, then check whether temp1 is the first node in the list
- (temp1 == head).
- **Step 9:** If temp1 is the first node then move the head to the next node (head = head → next) and delete temp1.
- **Step 10:** If temp1 is not first node then check whether it is last node in the list (temp1 → next == NULL).
- **Step 11:** If temp1 is last node then set temp2 → next = NULL and delete temp1 (free(temp1)).

- **Step 12:** If temp1 is not first node and not last node then set temp2 → next = temp1 → next and delete

temp1 (free(temp1)).

- Program:

```
#include<iostream.h>
#include<conio.h>
#include<malloc.h>
void insert1();void insert2();void insert3();
void del1();void del2();void del3();
void display();
struct node
{int data;
struct node *add;
} *start=NULL;
void main()
{
int ch;
clrscr();
do
{
cout<<"\n1.Insert at Beginning ";
cout<<"\n2.Insert at End ";
cout<<"\n3.Insert at Specified Position";
cout<<"\n4.Delete at Beginning ";
cout<<"\n5.Delete at End ";
cout<<"\n6.Delete at Specified Position";
cout<<"\n7.Display";
cout<<"\n8.Quit";
cout<<"\nEnter your choice: ";
cin>>ch;
switch(ch)
{
```

```
case 1: insert1();break;
case 2: insert2();break;
case 3: insert3();break;
case 4: del1();break;
case 5: del2();break;
case 6: del3();break;
case 7:display();break;
case 8:return;
default:cout<<"Wrong choice";
}
}while(ch!=8);
getch();
}
void insert1()
{
struct node *ptr;
int no;
ptr = (struct node *)malloc(sizeof(struct node));
cout<<"enter the no: ";
cin>>no;
ptr->data=no;
if(start==NULL)
ptr->add=NULL;
else
ptr->add=start;
start=ptr;
}
void insert2()
{
struct node *ptr,*temp; int no;
ptr = (struct node *)malloc(sizeof(struct node));
```

```
cout<<"enter the no: ";
cin>>no;
ptr->data=no;
ptr->add=NULL;
if(start==NULL)
start=ptr;
else
{
temp=start;
while(temp->add!=NULL)
{
temp=temp->add;
}
temp->add=ptr;
}
}
void insert3()
{
struct node *ptr,*temp,*temp1;
int no,i,loc;
temp=start;
cout<<"enter the position";
cin>>loc;
for(i=1;i<loc;i++)
{
temp1=temp;
temp=temp->add;
if(temp==NULL)
{
cout<<"node is one only";
return;
```

```
}
}
ptr = (struct node *)malloc(sizeof(struct node));
cout<<"enter the no: ";
cin>>no;
ptr->data=no;
ptr->add=temp;
temp1->add=ptr;
}
void del1()
{
struct node *tmp;
if(start==NULL)
cout<<"linked list empty";
else
{
tmp=start;
start=start->add;
cout<<"deleted element is"<<tmp->data;
free(tmp);
}
}
void del2()
{
struct node *tmp,*ptr;
if(start==NULL)
cout<<"linked list empty";
else if(start->add==NULL)
{
tmp=start;
start=NULL;
```

```
cout<<"deleted element is"<<tmp->data;
free(tmp);
}
else
{
ptr=start;
while(ptr->add!=NULL)
{
tmp=ptr;
ptr=ptr->add;
}
cout<<"deleted element is"<<ptr->data;
tmp->add=NULL;
free(ptr);
}
}
void del3()
{
struct node *ptr,*temp;
int i,loc;
cout<<"enter the position";
cin>>loc;
if(start==NULL)
cout<<"empty list";
else
{
ptr=start;
for(i=1;i<loc;i++)
{
temp=ptr;
ptr=ptr->add;
```

```
}
cout<<"deleted element is"<<ptr->data;
temp->add=ptr->add;
free(ptr);
}
}
void display()
{
struct node *ptr;
ptr=start;
while(ptr->add!=NULL)
{
cout<<"\n"<<ptr->data;
ptr=ptr->add;
}
cout<<"\n"<<ptr->data;
}
```

- Output:

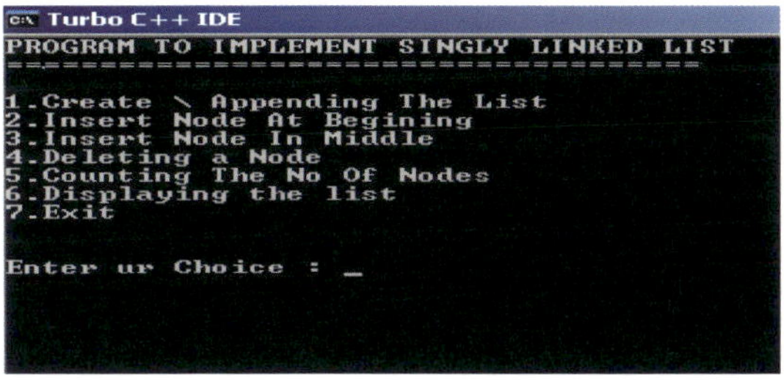

- **Viva Questions:**

1. What is singly linked list?
2. What are the advantages of singly linked list?
3. What are the applications of singly linked list?
4. What is the condition for linked list overflow and underflow?
5. How linked list is represented in memory?

EXPT. No. 7. Write a Program to Implement Bubble Sort.

- **Aim:** To implement a program of bubble sort.
- **Theory:** The algorithm gets its name from the way smaller elements

"bubble" to the top of the list. Because it only uses comparisons to operate on elements, it is a comparison sort. Although the algorithm is simple, most of the other sorting algorithms are more efficient for large lists.

Bubble sort has worst-case and average complexity both $O(n^2)$, where n is the number of items being sorted. There exist many sorting algorithms with substantially better worst-case or average complexity of O(n log n). Even other $O(n^2)$ sorting algorithms, such as insertion sort, tend to have better performance than bubble sort. Therefore, bubble sort is not a practical sorting algorithm when n is large.

The only significant advantage that bubble sort has over most other implementations, even quicksort, but not insertion sort, is that the ability to detect that the list is sorted is efficiently built into the algorithm. Performance of bubble sort over an already-sorted list (best-case) is O(n). By contrast, most other algorithms, even those with better average-case complexity, perform their entire sorting process on the set and thus are more complex. However, not only does insertion sort have this mechanism too, but it also performs better on a list that is substantially sorted (having a small number of inversions).

Bubble sort should be avoided in case of large collections. It will not be efficient in case of reverse ordered collection.

- Algorithm of Bubble Sort:

```
void bubblesort(int a[],int n)
BEGIN
for(i=0; i<n–1; i++) DO
for(j=0; j<n-i–1; j++) DO
if(a[j] > a[j+1])
BEGIN
SWAP a[j] and a[j+1]
END-IF
END-FOR
END-FOR
END
```

Ø **Program:**

```
#include<iostream.h>
```

```
#include<conio.h>
void main()
{
int a[20],i,n,temp;
clrscr();
cout<<"enter the no of element in array\n";
cin>>n;
cout<<"enter the element in array";
for(i=0;i<n;i++)
{
cin>>a[i];
}
for(i=0;i<n;i++)
{
for(int j=0;j<n–1–i; j + +)
{
if(a[j]>a[j+1])
{
temp=a[j];
a[j]=a[j+1];
a[j+1]=temp;
}
}
}
cout<<"element after sorting are";
for(i=0;i<n;i++)
{
cout<<"\n"<<a[i];
}
getch();
}
```

- Output:

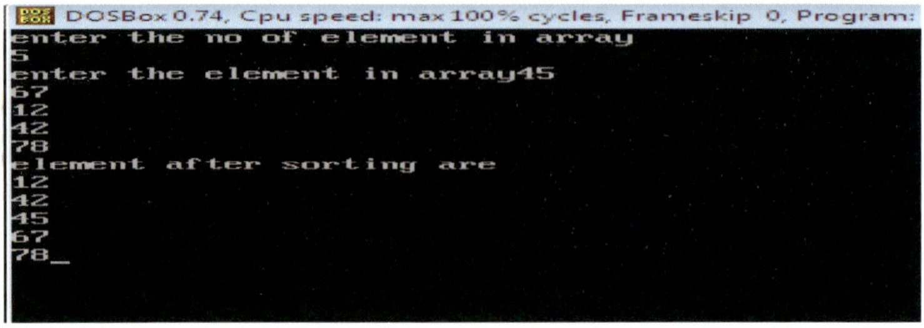

- Viva Questions:

1. What is the running time of bubble sort is best case
2. What is the running time of bubble sort in worst case?
3. What is the running time of bubble sort in average case?

EXPT. No. 8. Write a Program to Implement Insertion Sort.

- **Aim:** To implement a program of insertion sort.
- **Theory:** Insertion sort is an example of an incremental algorithm; it builds the sorted sequence one number at a time. This is perhaps the simplest example of the incremental insertion technique, where we build up a complicated structure on n items by first building it on n – 1 items and then making the necessary changes to fix things in adding the last item. The given sequences are typically stored in arrays. We also refer the numbers as keys. Along with each key may be additional information, known as satellite data. [Note that "satellite data" does not necessarily come from satellite!]. Since multiple keys with the same value are placed in the sorted array in the same order that they appear in the input array, Insertion sort is stable. This algorithm does not require extra memory.
  - For Insertion sort we say the worst-case running time is $\theta(n^2)$, and the best-case running time is $\theta(n)$.
  - Insertion sort use no extra memory it sort in place.
  - The time of Insertion sort is depends on the original order of an input. It takes a time in $\Omega(n^2)$ in the worst-case, despite the fact that a time in order of n is sufficient to solve large instances in which the items are already sorted.
  - **Algorithm of Insertion Sort:**

INSERTION_SORT (*A*)

FOR j ← 2 **TO** length[*A*]

DO key ← *A*[*j*]

{Put *A*[*j*] into the sorted sequence *A*[1. *j* – 1]}

i ← *j* – 1

WHILE *i* > 0 and *A*[*i*] > key

DO *A*[*i* +1] ← *A*[*i*]

i ← *i* – 1

A[*i* + 1] ← key

Program:

```
#include<iostream.h>
#include<conio.h>
void main()
{
int a[20],i,n,temp,j;
clrscr();
cout<<"enter the no of element in array\n";
cin>>n;
cout<<"enter the element in array";
for(i=0;i<n;i++)
{
cin>>a[i];
}
for(i=0;i<n;i++)
{
temp=a[i];
j = i – 1;
while((j>=0)&&(a[j]>temp))
{
a[j+1]=a[j];
j = j – 1;
}
```

```
a[j+1]=temp;
}
cout<<“element after sorting are”;
for(i=0;i<n;i++)
{
cout<<“\n”<<a[i];
}
getch();
}
```

- Output:

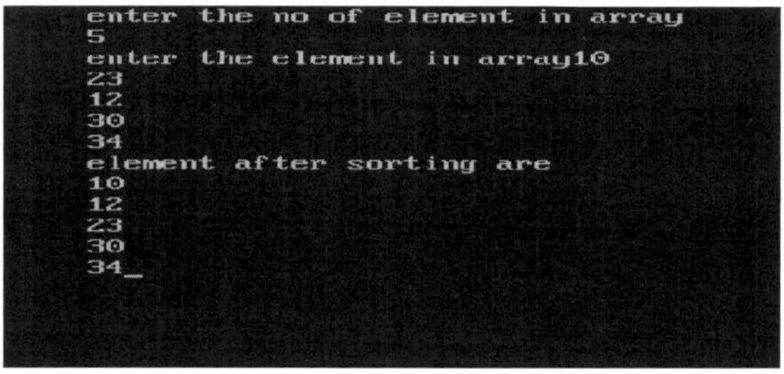

- Viva Questions:

1. What is the running time of insertion sort is best case?
2. What is the running time of Insertion sort in worst case?
3. What is the running time of Insertion sort in average case?

EXPT. No. 9. Write a Program to Implement Selection Sort.

- **Aim:** To implement a program of selection sort.
- **Theory:** Selection sort is not difficult to analyze compared to other sorting algorithms since none of the loops depend on the data in the array. Selecting the lowest element requires scanning all n elements (this takes $n - 1$ comparisons) and then swapping it into the first position. Finding the next lowest element requires scanning the remaining $n - 1$ elements and so on, for $(n - 1) + (n - 2) + \ldots + 2 + 1 = n(n - 1) / 2 \in \Theta(n^2)$ comparisons (see arithmetic progression). Each of these scans requires one swap for $n - 1$ elements (the final element is already in place).
- **Algorithm of Selection Sort:**

```
void selectionsort(int a[],int n)
BEGIN
```

```
int i,j,large,ind;
for(i=n–1;i>0;i– –)
DO
large = a[0];
ind = 0;
for(j=1; j<=i; j++)
DO
if(a[j]>large)
BEGIN
large = a[j];
ind = j;
END IF
END-FOR
a[ind] = a[i];
a[i] = large;
END-FOR
End
```

- Program:

```
#include<iostream.h>
#include<conio.h>
void main()
{
int a[20],i,n,temp,loc,min;
clrscr();
cout<<"enter the no of element in array\n";
cin>>n;
cout<<"enter the element in array";
for(i=0;i<n;i++)
{
cin>>a[i];
}
for(i=0;i<n;i++)
{
min=a[i];
loc=i;
```

```
for(int j=i+1;j<n;j++)
{
if(a[j]<min)
{
min=a[j];
loc=j;
}
}
if(loc!=i)
{
temp=a[i];
a[i]=a[loc];
a[loc]=temp;
}
}
cout<<"element after sorting are";
for(i=0;i<n;i++)
{
cout<<"\n"<<a[i];
}
getch();
}
```

- Output:

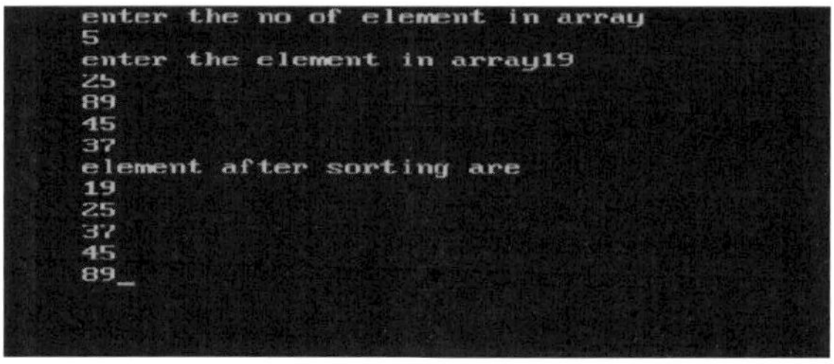

- Viva Questions:

1. What is the running time of selection sort is best case?
2. What is the running time of selection sort in worst case?

3. What is the running time of selection sort in average case?

EXPT. No. 10. Write a Program to Implement Linear Search.

- **Aim:** To implement a program of linear search.
- **Theory:** Linear search is a very simple search algorithm. In this type of search, a sequential search is made over all items one by one. Every item is checked and if a match is found then that particular item is returned, otherwise the search continues till the end of the data collection.
- **Algorithm of Linear Search:** Linear search (Array A, Value x)
- **Step 1:** Set i to 1
- **Step 2:** If i > n then go to step 7
- **Step 3:** If A[i] = x then go to step 6
- **Step 4:** Set i to i + 1
- **Step 5:** Go to Step 2
- **Step 6:** Print Element x Found at index i and go to step 8
- **Step 7:** Print element not found
- **Step 8:** Exit
- **Program:**

```
#include<iostream.h>
#include<conio.h>
void main()
{
clrscr();
int a[20],i,no,n,flag=0,pos;
cout<<"\n enter how many no u want to enter in array";
cin>>n;
cout<<"\n enter element in array";
for(i=1;i<=n;i++)
cin>>a[i];
cout<<"\n element in array are";
for(i=1;i<=n;i++)
cout<<a[i]<<" ";
cout<<"\n enter no to be searched";
cin>>no;
for(i=1;i<=n;i++)
```

```
{
if(a[i]==no)
{
flag=1;
pos=i;
break;
}
}
if(flag==1)
cout<<"\n search sucessful no found at position"<<pos;
else
cout<<"\n search unsucessful";
getch();
}
```

- Output:

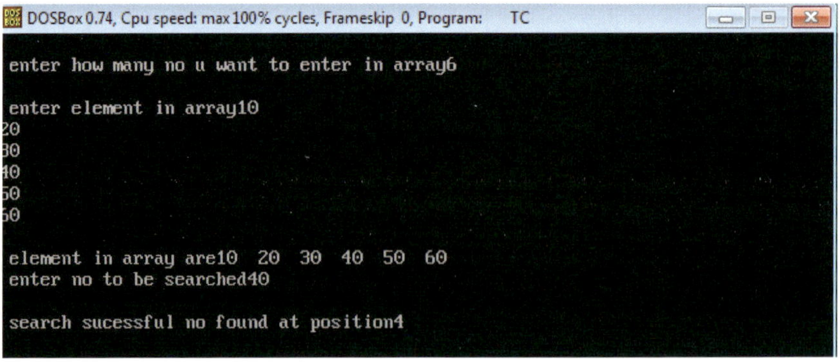

- **Viva Questions:**

1. What is the running time of linear search algorithm?
2. What are the advantages of linear search?
3. What are the disadvantages of linear search?

EXPT. No. 11. Write a Program to Implement Binary Search.

- **Aim:** To implement a program of binary search.
- **Theory:** Techniques for searching an ordered list in which we first check the middle item and – based on that comparison –

"discard" half the data. The same procedure is then applied to the remaining half until a match is found or there are no more items left.

A binary search halves the number of items to check with each iteration, so locating an item (or determining its absence) takes logarithmic time. A binary search is a dichotomic divide and conquer search algorithm.

- Algorithm of Binary Search:

```
int binary_search(int A[], int key, int imin, int imax)
{
// test if array is empty
if (imax < imin)
// set is empty, so return value showing not found
return KEY_NOT_FOUND;
else
{
// calculate midpoint to cut set in half
int imid = midpoint(imin, imax);
// three-way comparison
if (A[imid] > key)
// key is in lower subset
return binary_search(A, key, imin, imid–1);
else if (A[imid] < key)
// key is in upper subset
return binary_search(A, key, imid+1, imax);
else
// key has been found
return imid;
}
}
```

- Program:

```
#include<iostream.h>
#include<conio.h>
```

```
void main()
{
int a[20],i,n,temp,no,loc,beg,end,mid,flag;
clrscr();
cout<<"enter the no of element in array\n";
cin>>n;
cout<<"enter the element in array";
for(i=0;i<n;i++)
{
cin>>a[i];
}
for(i=0;i<n;i++)
{
for(int j = 0; j < n – 1 – i; j+ +)
{
if(a[j]>a[j+1])
{
temp=a[j];
a[j]=a[j+1];
a[j+1]=temp;
}
}
}
cout<<"enter the element to be searched";
cin>>no;
loc=0;
beg=0;
end=n – 1;
while((beg<=end)&&(no!=a[mid]))
{
mid=((beg+end)/2);
```

```
if(no==a[mid])
{
cout<<“\nsearch is successful”;
loc=mid;
cout<<“\nposition of number”<<loc;
flag=flag+1;
}
if(no<a[mid])
end=mid–1;
else
beg=mid+1;
}
if(flag==0)
cout<<“search is not sucessful”;
getch();
}
```

- Output:

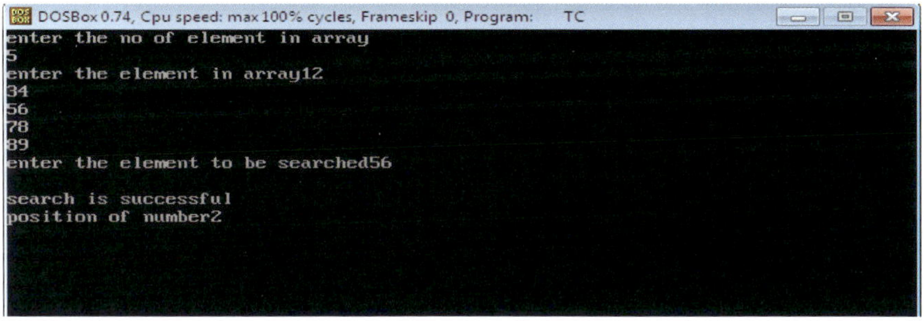

- Viva Questions:
- What is the running time of binary search algorithm?
- What is divide and conquer approach?

CHAPTER 8

VIVA QUESTIONS

1. What is a data structure?
2. What is linear data structure?
3. What are the ways of representing linear structure?
4. What is a non-linear data structure?
5. What are various operations performed on linear structure? What is a square matrix?
6. What is a sparse matrix?
7. What is a triangular matrix?
8. What is a tridiagonal matrix?
9. What is row major ordering?
10. What is column major ordering?
11. What is a linked list?
12. What is a null pointer?
13. What is a free pool or free storage list or list of available space?
14. What is garbage collection?
15. What is overflow?
16. What is underflow? What is a header node?
17. What is a header linked list?
18. What is a header node?

19. What is a grounded linked list?
20. What is circular header list?
21. What is a queue?
22. What is infix notation?
23. What is polish notation?
24. What is reverse polish notation?
25. What is recursive function?
26. What is a priority queue?
27. Define a deque.
28. Define Tree, Binary tree, Binary search tree.
29. What are various ways of tree traversal?
30. What is an AVL tree?
31. What are similar trees, and when the trees are called copies of each other?
32. What is searching?
33. Why binary search cannot be applied on a linked list?
34. What is a connected graph?
35. What is depth-first traversal?
36. What is breadth-first traversal?
37. Why is the algorithm for finding shortest distances called greedy?
38. What are advantages of selection sort over other algorithms?
39. What are disadvantages of insertion sort?
40. Define the term divide and conquer.
41. What is a pivot?

BIBLIOGRAPHY

1. Three beautiful quicksorts. J. L. Bentley. Google Tech Talks, August 9, 2007. Three implementations of quicksort along with historic context.
2. Optimal stable merging by A. Symvonis. The Computer Journal, Vol. 38, No. 8 (1995). *In-place and stable mergesort.*
3. Quicksort by C. A. R. Hoare. The Computer Journal, Vol. 5, No. 1, pp. 10-16. *Quicksort algorithm.*
4. Practical fast searching in strings by R. N. Horspool. Software: Practice and Experience, VOl. 10, pp. 501-506. *Simpler variant of Boyer-Moore.*
5. Efficient randomized pattern-matching algorithms by R. M. Karp and M. O. Rabin. IBM Journal of Research and Development, Vol. 31, No. 2, pp. 249-260 .
6. Computational investigations of maximum flow algorithms by Ravindra K. Ahuja, Murali Kodialam, Ajay K. Mishra, and James B. Orlin. European Journal of Operations Research, Vol. 97, pp. 509-542. *Comparison of several maximum flow algorithms in practice.*
7. Robert Lafore, *Data Structures & Algorithms in Java*, Second Edition, Sams Publishing, 2003.
8. Data Structures and Algorithms in Java" by Lafore
9. "Data Structure and Algorithm in C++" by Adam Drozdek

INDEX

P

Q

R

S

T

U

W